The New South's New Frontier

New Perspectives on the History of the South

Florida A&M University, Tallahassee
Florida Atlantic University, Boca Raton
Florida Gulf Coast University, Ft. Myers
Florida International University, Miami
Florida State University, Tallahassee
University of Central Florida, Orlando
University of Florida, Gainesville
University of North Florida, Jacksonville
University of South Florida, Tampa
University of West Florida, Pensacola

New Perspectives on the History of the South
Edited by John David Smith

"In the Country of the Enemy": The Civil War Reports of a Massachusetts Corporal, edited by William C. Harris (1999)

The Wild East: A Biography of the Great Smoky Mountains, by Margaret L. Brown (2000); first paperback edition, 2001

Crime, Sexual Violence, and Clemency: Florida's Pardon Board and Penal System in the Progressive Era, by Vivien M. L. Miller (2000)

The New South's New Frontier: A Social History of Economic Development in Southwestern North Carolina, by Stephen Wallace Taylor (2001)

The New South's New Frontier

A Social History of Economic Development in Southwestern North Carolina

Stephen Wallace Taylor

Foreword by John David Smith, Series Editor

University Press of Florida
Gainesville · Tallahassee · Tampa · Boca Raton
Pensacola · Orlando · Miami · Jacksonville · Ft. Myers

06 05 04 03 02 01 6 5 4 3 2 1

Library of Congress Cataloging-in-Publication Data
The new south's new frontier : a social history of economic development in southwestern North Carolina / Stephen Wallace Taylor ; foreword by John David Smith.
p. cm. — (New perspectives on the history of the South)
Includes bibliographical references and index.
ISBN 0-8130-2116-2 (cloth : alk. paper)
1. North Carolina—Economic conditions. I. Taylor, Stephen Wallace, 1965– . II. Series.

HC107.N8 N49 2001
338.9756'9—dc21 2001034783

The University Press of Florida is the scholarly publishing agency for the State University System of Florida, comprising Florida A&M University, Florida Atlantic University, Florida Gulf Coast University, Florida International University, Florida State University, University of Central Florida, University of Florida, University of North Florida, University of South Florida, and University of West Florida.

University Press of Florida
15 Northwest 15th Street
Gainesville, FL 32611–2079
http://www.upf.com

For Maggy, of course.

Contents

Figures

Tables

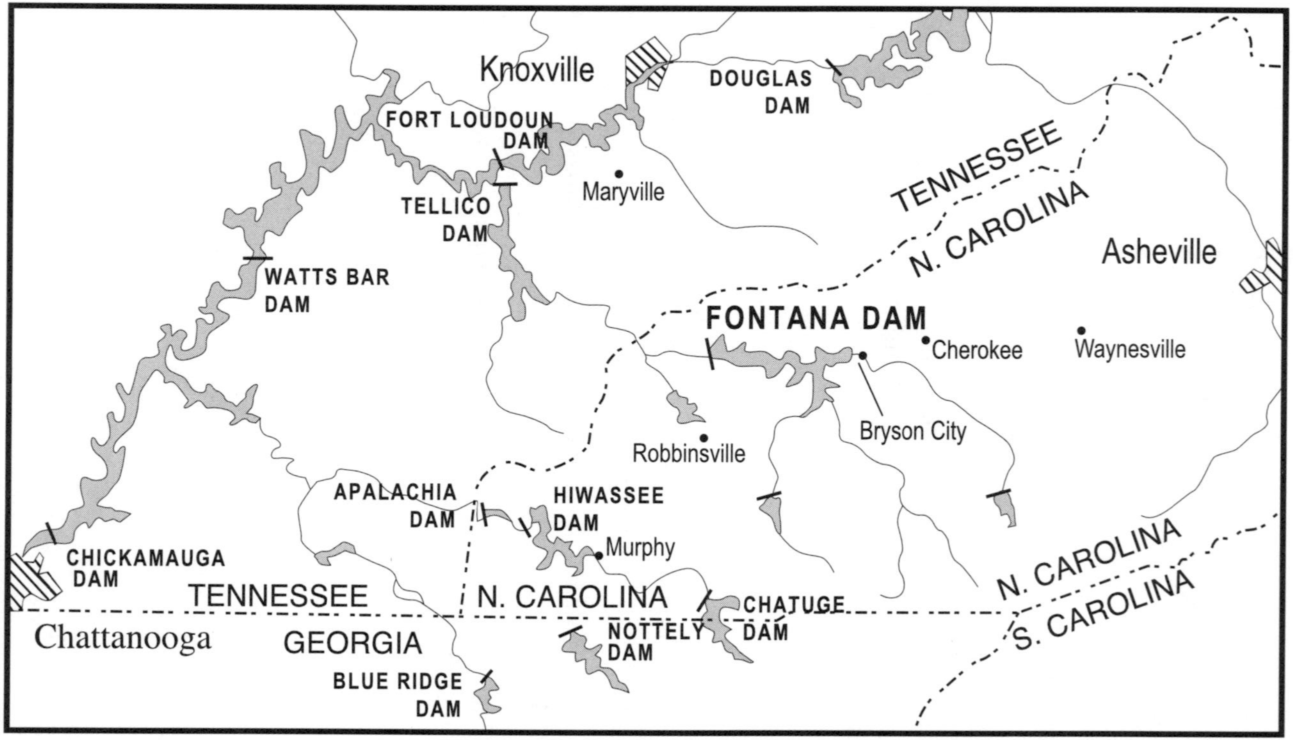

Figure 1. The upper Little Tennessee Valley of southwestern North Carolina. Map adapted from Tennessee Valley Authority.

Foreword

Myths about the history and culture of the American South die hard. "The idea of the South," George B. Tindall explains, "or more appropriately, the ideas of the South, belong in large part to the order of social myth." Through much of southern historical consciousness F. Garvin Davenport Jr. observes, "the light of simple myth defies the shadows of complex reality." The power of mythology is as strong, if not stronger, in our understanding of the South's Appalachian region as it is with its former plantation belts, its various piedmonts, and its towns and cities.

In his contribution to New Perspectives on the History of the South, Stephen Wallace Taylor examines one corner of southern Appalachia long shrouded in myth: the upper Little Tennessee Valley. Taylor's *The New South's New Frontier* revises long-standing misconceptions about the people, economy, and culture of southwestern Appalachia. About 150 miles long, the Little Tennessee River rises near the north Georgia boundary and moves north through Macon County in southwestern North Carolina, and then flows north and west across the Tennessee border and into the Tennessee River in Loudon County in east Tennessee. In 1945 the Tennessee Valley Authority (TVA) constructed the 480-foot-high Fontana Dam along the course of the Little Tennessee in Graham and Swain Counties, North Carolina, at the south end of the Great Smoky Mountains National Park. Taylor's well-researched, broadly conceived, and gracefully written narrative charts the economic transformation of the upper Little Tennessee River Valley over the course of several industries: lumber, mining, hydroelectric power, and tourism. In doing so he challenges long-standing assertions that North Carolina's mountain region differed significantly from other parts of the South in terms of economic development. Taylor trains his analytical guns squarely on "the intoxicating wordsmith" Horace Kephart, who in *Our Southern Highlanders* (1913) characterized the southern Appalachian region as isolated and romantic, backward and semicivilized, a static and solitary place he labeled "The Back of Beyond." By examining "modernization" over more than a century in this section of southern Appalachia, Taylor identifies surprising patterns of economic and social diversity and more similarities than differences between southern Appalachia and the rest of the South. Land speculation, sharecropping, industrialization, transient wage labor, markets, company towns, boosterism, the spirit of enterprise, and the receptivity to outside ideas have been as much a part of the political economy of the upper Little Tennessee Valley as they have elsewhere in the region. As early as the 1920s tourism held the key to the region's economic future. The building of Fontana Dam, in fact, "accentuated and amplified tendencies already evident before the arrival of TVA." And by the end of the twentieth century, Taylor concludes, "a combination of local boosters, outside economic forces, and government agencies . . . transformed this corner of the bustling New South into a 'New Wilderness.'"

In tracing the economic development of the upper Little Tennessee, Taylor pays careful attention to complex and oftentimes conflicting social, cultural, and political interests. Area preservationists and conservationists, for example, had different visions for the national park that came to pass in the region. TVA and the Aluminum Company of America (Alcoa), equally determined to harness the narrow, deep valley of the Little Tennessee for water storage and hydroelectric power, disagreed over national economic planning versus private property rights. While constructing Fontana Dam, TVA officials perpetuated many stereotypes, including Kephart's anachronistic sentimentalism and the condescension typical of "outsiders." Both inaccurate stereotypes, Taylor argues, ignored "the subtleties of the region's social and economic life." TVA educational and social programs raised serious questions about the merits of top- down reform and the possible deleterious effects of "progress" on residents of the upper Little Tennessee River Valley. In the end, Taylor argues, neither TVA nor the National Park Service provided the systematic economic direction that local boosters had envisaged. Today the area suffers from stagnation and hard times.

Looking to the past to explain the present, contemporary boosters have revived Kephart's romanticized image and promoted the Little Tennessee Valley as a nature museum designed to attract tourists. Ironically and sadly, Kephart's fictive "Back of Beyond" image has become more or less reality. While Taylor's book has much to teach us about Appalachian economic development, it also reminds us of the power of myth in southern history.

John David Smith
Series Editor

Preface

This book originated when, as a young and naive graduate student, I accepted a three-month summer internship with the Tennessee Valley Authority's Cultural Resources Program in 1990. The job at hand was indexing the agency's photograph collections and entering the results into a computer database. The internship became a two-year part-time job when it became apparent that the collection contained not the 8,000 photos originally estimated but instead something over 20,000.

In the process of identifying and indexing these photos, most of which had been taken by TVA photographers, I uncovered more than a few stories worth telling. Among the countless publicity shots of visiting dignitaries, construction progress shots, and the like were quite a few photos of "ordinary" individuals, some pictures apparently staged and others relatively candid. The most vivid, at least to me, were those of the thousands of workers who built Fontana Dam during World War II. Fascinated by these images, I sought out the agency's *Technical Report Number 12,* which purports to tell the whole story of the Fontana Project. The agency, I assumed, had found it necessary to build roads, railroads, and even telephone lines because of the area's "remoteness." From the report's perspective, I came to believe that the area surrounding Fontana Dam had been utterly undeveloped before TVA came in. And so I had unwittingly fallen into the same trap, the "isolation argument," that had captured generations of outsiders who tried to study the mountains of western North Carolina—from Horace Kephart and Mary Noailles Murfree to Jack Weller and Harry Caudill and many TVA operatives.

Others, most notably Ronald Eller, have long recognized the fallacy inherent in the isolation model, but they have proposed an almost equally flawed "outside exploitation" model to replace it. The outside exploitation model presumes that things were going reasonably well until outside capitalists unfairly seized the resources of the area, cutting all the timber, taking much of the land, and leaving the residents with nothing. In its purest form this model assumes that there is no shared context between the exploiters and the exploited, no shared values or expectations. It assumes that the people who lived in the mountains never aspired to capitalism and consumerism. In other words, while it discounts the notion of economic isolation, it still requires an assumption of some sort of cultural isolation from the larger currents of American society.

The difficulty that these and other very able scholars have faced points out the truth in Jack Temple Kirby's admonition in *Rural Worlds Lost* that "writing about the Appalachian . . . highlands is fraught with danger."[1] I have become convinced, through the learning process that resulted in my own book, that the truth is far more complicated than even Eller's widely cited treatment allows. It is true that lumber companies had cut down most of the trees during the 1910s and 1920s, but they generally obtained the rights to cut those trees from people who had intended to make a profit off the land in some way or another. Furthermore, many of those "speculators" were also local townspeople and even farmers. Indeed, those who moved into the mountain regions in the first place did so hoping to make money from the enterprise in some fashion, whether by farming or speculating in mineral rights or some other means.

Most residents of the mountain areas were what Margaret Lynn Brown calls "the valley people." They lived in small towns and villages where they were never fundamentally isolated from the currents that drew Americans into a capitalist system. They lived much as other southerners did. While slavery never dominated the area the way it did in, say, the Mississippi Delta, it was an important economic and social force in the late antebellum period, as John Inscoe has ably demonstrated. Even so-called subsistence farmers produced livestock, honey, and other specialties for sale to broader markets. The Southern Railway arrived in the upper Little Tennessee area in the 1890s, bringing not only the lumber industry but also the Sears catalogue. By the 1930s nonfarm homes accounted for about a third of all households in the area, and nonfarm households were far more likely than farm households to have electric lighting, radios, and flush toilets.

By the mid-1930s, the National Park Service had laid claim to quite a bit of the cutover land of the Great Smoky Mountains, although it had not yet obtained title to the area that came to be known as the North Shore. In order to preserve the "rustic authenticity" of the area—an authenticity almost but not quite entirely fraudulent—Park Service officials actively sought to erase most traces of previous habitation from the areas under their control, destroying any structures built after 1890. TVA, too, had bought into this myth wholesale and had even helped to market the area as a virtually untouched wilderness—an altogether remarkable claim, given that both TVA and the Park Service continued to face legal action well into the 1980s concerning the loss of mineral rights and access to previously settled areas.

So then, if the people I saw in TVA photos weren't the stereotypical mountaineers who spoke Chaucer's tongue and drank only the purest spring water or moonshine, who exactly were they? Some, certainly, were subsistence-plus farmers who lived on fertile valley land. Others were refugees from the collapsing lumber and mining industries—a "residue" in the words of one TVA observer, people who had traveled wherever those industries would employ them and who became stranded when there was no longer any money to be made cutting timber or digging copper ore. Still others were opportunists who followed TVA from project to project, gaining marketable skills and decent wages in return for their willingness to work within TVA rules. And of course some of them were town folk, people accustomed to factory work, who found the lure of a high government wage attractive enough to induce them to leave Knoxville, Maryville, and Alcoa.

As one might expect from such a diverse group, they did not speak with a single voice concerning their experience with TVA. Some, to be sure, expressed bitterness at what they viewed as government fraud by either TVA or the National Park Service in the taking of land, and these people have been extremely vocal about what they consider a terrible injustice. Their complaints have found a willing and sympathetic audience among activists who oppose big government as well as romantics who still believe in the myth of Appalachian isolation. Others, however, have expressed generally positive thoughts about the changes the area has undergone since the 1930s.

Why the difference? The answer to that question may lie with the experience of the individual—some may have been defrauded and others not, for example. But I suspect that the answer also must have something to do with the circumstances in which the person doing the remembering finds himself or herself as a result of all these changes. The formation of Citizens Against Wilderness and the remarkable success with which the town of Cherokee has marketed itself to tourists would suggest that there is profit to be made from the heritage of wilderness and wildness. There is even a billboard in Bryson City directing tourists to the "Road to Nowhere," the abortive Park Service project aimed at satisfying claims arising from the takeover of the North Shore land, which has come to serve as the area's own "lost cause" myth. Are we to presume that the descendants of squatters and land speculators are somehow above marketing their "selective recollections" to a public still infatuated with Kephart's "Back of Beyond"? This is a public that still flocks to the heavily fictionalized outdoor dramas *Christy, Horn in the West,* and *Unto These Hills* and watches reruns of *The Waltons* and even *The Beverly Hillbillies.* This is also a public that flocked to see the 1998 cinematic rerelease of *Gone with the Wind.* One look at the phenomenal sales of the early *Foxfire* books should dispel any notion that Appalachian heritage is not a marketable commodity. More than one professional historian writing in the last few years has fallen prey to the tendency to treat oral history as though it has no present-tense context.

The present narrative, then, has taken on quite a daunting task. It seeks to present the evolving relationship between a small corner of North Carolina—the upper Little Tennessee Valley—and the rest of American society. There have been many works on the origins of the Great Smoky Mountains National Park, most of which either gloss over the problems the park created or ignore the role the residents themselves played in those problems. Dan Pierce's recent dissertation at the University of Tennessee ably demonstrates the extent to which the park was the result of political coalition building among groups with widely diverging reasons for wanting it established, yet his study does too little with the context in which ordinary citizens either supported or opposed the park. One fine recent work, a doctoral dissertation by Margaret Lynn Brown, examines the environmental history of the region and the political dimensions of that environmental history, from the lumber boom through the construction of Fontana Dam, but fails to address sufficiently the economic transformations accompanying the environmental ones. Moreover, Brown's use of oral history materials fails to place those materials in the postwar political and economic context in which they were created; most of her interviews were conducted during the 1980s, many of them for a television program called *The Heartland Series,* at a time when area residents were engaged in a massive public relations battle over the area's "mountain heritage."

By taking a broader chronological view that addresses the postwar context, I hope to avoid such difficulties. My study places the evolution of this so-called wilderness area in the context of the emergence of the New South. While others have argued that the North Carolina mountains are so different from the rest of the South that they do not fit within the New South paradigm, I intend to demonstrate otherwise by examining the evolution of the region's economic structure and the political dimensions of that evolution.

This book ends with a few pages in which I attempt to capture the spirit of the area as it existed in the year 2000. The central irony becomes apparent here, as the rustic image of a "strange people in a peculiar place"—a romanticized and frequently negative image popularized largely by outsiders—has finally become an asset to the region. This image is one of the few money-making resources those outsiders have allowed the region's inhabitants to keep. It has also been one of the most sustainable and renewable; as recent news reports concerning the flight of fugitive Eric Rudolph demonstrate, the media still seem willing to believe that this once-bustling countryside is really a primeval wilderness. Given their gift for hyperbole and the public's apparent taste for it, one might well expect television networks to announce that the FBI, in seeking Rudolph, have inadvertently found Adam and Eve, D. B. Cooper, Jimmy Hoffa, or Sasquatch.

A major theme is the role of Bryson City's handful of self-appointed boosters. Boosters heralded the arrival of each new industry—lumber, mining, hydroelectric power, tourism—as the key to unlocking perpetual prosperity for the region. In the process those boosters turned a blind eye toward the negatives associated with those industries until the damage had been done. Moreover, as the people most likely to have developed contacts outside the region, these local merchants, politicians, and professionals bridged the often-exaggerated gap between the rural life of the upper Little Tennessee and the larger currents of economic, social, and political life in the rest of the state and the rest of the nation.

The critical role of this small-town group—I avoid calling them a "class"—might tempt some social scientists to call upon world-system theory to explain the history of the upper Little Tennessee. While the area might fit that model, I am not convinced that there exists sufficient evidence of suppressed dissent from the booster ideology to prove "booster hegemony." I will happily leave to someone else the task of constructing a theoretical edifice for the experience of the residents of the upper Little Tennessee and the task of testing other regions for conformity to it; my purpose is merely to describe how a combination of local boosters, outside economic forces, and government agencies whose constituents were spread all over the United States transformed this corner of the bustling New South into a "New Wilderness."

Acknowledgments

It is customary to thank as many as possible of the people who have influenced or assisted in the creation of a book of this size. I am afraid that such an attempt will invariably cause me to miss someone, as no book is entirely the product of one author working in isolation. Nonetheless, I would like to thank all of the people who have helped me to understand the process of modernization as it applies to western North Carolina, with all of the assumptions it implies.

Chief among these are Jim Cobb, John Gaventa, Mike McDonald, and Margaret Stair. Jim Cobb, who directed my doctoral dissertation on which this work is loosely based, helped me to understand the booster mentality at work in the New South and suggested to me that it was not confined to the Piedmont and similar areas. John Gaventa inspired me to examine the concept of hydroelectric power as a nationalizing strategy and taught me a lot about development theory. At a point in my graduate career when I had learned to "play the game," he helped me to move beyond the graduate school routine and become a more effective thinker. Mike McDonald served as a magnificent sounding board during the early stages of this project, despite his serious health problems. He never pulled any punches, for which I am immensely grateful. Margaret Stair was my colleague and office mate; we both studied western North Carolina and shared many ideas concerning the area's history.

I would like to thank Dan Pierce and Bren Martin, graduate school colleagues of mine, whose work has influenced my own greatly and whose contribution cannot be narrowed to any specific description. I would also like to thank Anne Mitchell and Margaret Brown, with whom I served on a panel at the Appalachian Studies Association years ago; while my work differs from theirs in several important ways, the experience of sharing ideas with them helped to shape who I am as a historian. David Carlton of Vanderbilt University also deserves a note of appreciation for the relentlessly challenging discussions we have shared concerning southern capitalism and industrialization. David's encouragement and his unwillingness to accept facile answers have been invaluable as I have worked to transform a doctoral dissertation into the volume you see here. As much as these fine colleagues have shaped my perspective, any errors of fact or interpretation that remain in the book are my sole responsibility.

Meredith Morris-Babb has been been unflagging in her support for my work, and I am deeply appreciative. The staff members of the North Carolina State Library and Archives deserve thanks, as do their counterparts at the National Archives Southeast Region, the Great Smoky Mountains National Park Archives, the Tennessee State Library and Archives, and Knoxville's McClung Collection. George Frizzell at Western Carolina University's Special Collections Library deserves mention for his selfless and relentlessly helpful approach to my entirely unreasonable demands, as does Ben Lea, formerly of the North Carolina Political Broadcast Archives at Pfeiffer College, for the same reasons. I am convinced that these people genuinely enjoy being allowed to help, especially when the request is for something incredibly arcane, and I owe them a tremendous debt for all their assistance.

But the greatest debts I owe from this lengthy process are to my family: my parents and grandparents, who taught me wisely and let me grow up, and my wife, Maggy Shannon, who not only understood when I was busy and tense and held my hand through the difficult times but also broke into a salvage yard and crawled into a badly wrecked, gasoline-soaked minivan in order to retrieve the only printed copy of the manuscript while I was hospitalized following a 1995 accident. That kind of commitment and support is more important than anything else in the world.

1

A Southern People in a Mountain Region

Western North Carolina is a mountainous region. The Blue Ridge Mountains, with which sociologist Howard Odum identified the entire region, are one of many subchains of the Appalachian Mountains that dominate the western quarter of the state and may well be the oldest mountain chain on earth. Most of the area's natural vegetation is birch, maple, and hemlock forest, and chestnut trees flourished until an early twentieth-century blight killed off most of them. Mountain laurel thrives near even the smallest streams. Muskrats, squirrels, and raccoons feed on the blueberries, blackberries, and nuts growing around them. The highest peaks harbor plants otherwise known only much farther north.[1]

The rock that forms the mountains is varied. Deposits of copper, iron, and lead are interspersed with occasional pockets of precious stones, especially rubies and sapphires. Acid-producing rock strata such as the Anakeesta and Nantahala formations occasionally leach heavy metal ions into the area's streams. Unlike much of the Appalachian region, there is no coal. Many of the area's rock formations are unstable, and slides are common in times of heavy precipitation.[2]

Heavy precipitation itself is common, too. The area receives more rainfall than any other location in the southeastern United States. The rain provides needed moisture for the lush vegetation of the area, but also contributes to the erosion of topsoil.[3] That topsoil generally ends up deposited in the narrow river valleys below the peaks. Small rivers such as the French Broad, the Pigeon, the Little Tennessee, and the Hiwassee drain the slopes of the mountains.

The Little Tennessee rises near the town of Franklin in Macon County, near the Georgia border. A few miles north, it is joined by the Nantahala River near Almond. The river continues generally north, then makes a sharp westward bend at its confluence with the Tuckaseigee.[4] Thus redirected, it continues west to the Tennessee state line, then turns west-northwest before joining the Tennessee River near Lenoir City, Tennessee.

Figure 2. The narrow valley of the upper Little Tennessee River between Franklin and Bryson City, North Carolina. Photo: Stephen Wallace Taylor.

The valley of the upper portion of the Little Tennessee is particularly narrow. Good bottomland in the flood plain was a precious commodity for those who intended to farm it. The bottomland of the Nantahala and Tuckaseigee Rivers was among the first settled by Cherokees, who built the "Overhill Towns" and the "Valley Towns" in the narrow floodplains. The Cherokees held the bottomland of the Nantahala, the Tuckaseigee, and the Little Tennessee until 1819, when they lost control of the Nantahala to whites by treaty. The Tuckaseigee and Little Tennessee remained in Cherokee hands until the treaty of New Echota in 1835, which added 1,112 square miles to the state's control. During the next two years, the land was surveyed and graded with respect to quality. Minimum prices were set between twenty cents and four dollars per acre, depending upon the quality rating. Many whites, unwilling to wait for the land to be sold, took physical possession from departing Cherokees and sorted out the legal niceties later.[5]

The state disposed of the land acquired through the New Echota treaty at a massive sale in Franklin in 1838. Many buyers paid on the installment plan, with one-eighth down, one-eighth at the end of the first year, and one-fourth per year thereafter until the balance was paid off. One local historian has noted that fifty-three buyers spent in excess of $1,500 each to purchase land in the newly opened region, with one buyer spending over $16,000 in a day when "a good farmhand could earn about eight dollars and board per month." Among the largest purchasers was merchant and self-taught lawyer William Holland Thomas, operator of a trading post at Quallatown, who bought over $8,000 worth of land in 220 separate tracts mostly of the lowest (fifth-grade) quality. Beginning in 1831, Thomas also served as a legal advocate on behalf of the Cherokees who remained in the area, and the land he purchased would later form the nucleus of the Qualla Boundary reservation.[6]

Predictably, the same bottomland that had served the Cherokees' needs for so long was the first to be claimed by white settlers in the 1838 sale, with most paying cash. Cash-poor buyers tended to gravitate toward the cheaper hilly land, but much of the lowest-quality hilly land was bought by speculators or remained unsold. According to land transfer rolls, much of the bottomland remained in the hands of the same families for generations, while the hilly tracts tended to change hands frequently.[7]

The Cherokees who remained in western North Carolina, collectively known as the Eastern Band, existed in an anomalous legal status, neither citizens nor full dependents of the federal government. Following the removal, the Eastern Band increasingly encountered pressures for acculturation and assimilation into white society, and some Cherokee leaders actively encouraged this trend. Though the practices of plantation agriculture and slave labor became common among the Cherokees of northern Georgia as early as the late 1700s, this mode of production was impractical in the narrow valley of the upper Little Tennessee, and most members of the Eastern Band remained small farmers operating on tracts best described as "subsistence-plus," with livestock and a diverse selection of other agricultural products going in small quantities to markets in more agriculturally specialized South Carolina, eastern North Carolina, and other cash-crop regions.[8]

Like their Cherokee precursors and neighbors, the white settlers who arrived in western North Carolina did so expecting that they would be able to make a decent living or at least recover their expenses quickly enough to avoid foreclosure. Some, especially in the counties of Buncombe, McDowell, Burke, Caldwell, and Henderson, built large farms on which slaves were used. This model was followed as well by several of the families who settled in the upper Little Tennessee, including the Brysons for whom the postbellum town of Bryson City would later be named. But far more built smaller farms of 50 to 200 acres, comparable in size and scope to those built by their Cherokee neighbors. In most parts of the valley, the bottomland was too scarce and too widely scattered to provide for all the needs of an agricultural enterprise, so these farmers tended to reserve it for the most profitable food crops, such as corn and wheat. The hilly land above the rivers frequently rose at such an angle that large-scale planting was impractical, but some food crops could be grown there for local use nevertheless. The higher lands were also useful for grazing cattle and sometimes sheep. Hogs could forage for themselves in the woodlands above the fields, woodlands which also provided firewood and occasionally lumber or logs for constructing a home.[9]

As the state organized county governments in territory taken from the Cherokees, county seats were formed, often by decree. The towns of Franklin, Sylva, and Waynesville began as courthouse towns but quickly became local market centers as well. While the towns were often as violent as frontier towns in the West, a relatively "civilized" business class gradually emerged. Members of that group took great pains to differentiate themselves from the rougher people of the countryside, deploring the latter's rude manners, lack of education, and predilection for violent resolution of disputes.[10]

Small-scale farming could not provide the growing population of the region with enough income to keep up with the market-economy changes that swept most of the nation in the first two-thirds of the nineteenth century.[11] Little surplus production was available to provide cash for the purchase of manufactured goods or other items that could not be made, grown, or done without. The market ties that held town merchants and larger mountain farmers in close relationships with each other and with the rest of the South often had less influence over the operators of smaller farms. With fewer contacts and fewer interests in common with their larger counterparts, many small white farmers in the upper Little Tennessee, like their counterparts across the Smoky Mountains in Tennessee, sided with the federal government during the Civil War. Others sided with their downstate yeoman counterparts, creating a conflict within western North Carolina that mirrored the national tragedy.[12] Durwood Dunn has noted, in particular, the divisive nature of this conflict in adjacent sections of eastern Tennessee, arguing that the conflict produced lasting resentments that actually encouraged Unionist mountain communities to isolate themselves further from the surrounding areas. Although historian John

Inscoe argues that more western North Carolinians supported the Confederacy than the Union, he also concedes that the region was by no means unanimous in supporting the Confederate cause.[13]

Partially as a result of the persuasive abilities of longtime advocate William Holland Thomas, many members of the Eastern Band fought in support of the Confederacy, though the Cherokees were no more unanimous in their sentiments than their white neighbors were. The support that Cherokee leaders gave to the Confederate cause resulted in the acknowledgment by the North Carolina legislature of a "permanent right to residence" for the Eastern Band in 1866.[14]

In the aftermath of the Civil War, with most of the South prostrate from the collapse of the slave economy, white western North Carolinians as a group found themselves for the first time identified—ironically, like the Cherokees whom they had partially displaced—as a separate sort of people. While the lives of those who lived in the mountain towns had not been radically different from those of their Piedmont counterparts, the war experience helped to set the mountain residents apart. The ambiguous position of many mountain regions with regard to the Civil War and slavery marked their residents as atypical among southerners; similarly, their language, culture, and economic activities differentiated them from "Yankees." As the rest of Americans struggled to understand these people who did not fit into the neat categories of "southern" and "not southern," the concept of "Appalachian otherness" came into currency. Appalachians, some observers contended, were pure, unspoiled frontiersmen, remnants of colonial life preserved intact by the supposed isolation of the mountain coves in which they dwelt. Moreover, these outside observers failed to note the crucial social distinctions between the isolated, cove-dwelling, bear-hunting, moonshining mountaineers and the small-town merchants, lawyers, farmers, and preachers who had always looked down upon those mountaineers. David Hsiung argues that the stereotypes associated with Appalachia as a whole originated with small-town Appalachians themselves, who looked with disfavor upon neighbors who chose isolation voluntarily:

> By communicating to [outsiders] such distinctions between old and new, the townspeople in effect told the entire nation about the characteristics that distinguished them from their mountain neighbors. Yet the [outside observers] treated Appalachia as a single entity, devoid of the finer distinctions wrought by geographic, economic, and

> social factors. The town residents . . . did not realize that despite their real and perceived differences with the mountaineers, the local color writers would paint both groups with the same brush.[15]

Henry D. Shapiro has traced the popularization of these stereotypes to the postbellum local color movement, a literary style that focused on description rather than analysis, tended toward short essays rather than lengthy pieces, and developed in order to appeal to a mass-market middle-class audience including readers of such magazines as *Harper's, Lippincott's, Scribner's,* and the *Atlantic Monthly.* Heirs to pre–Civil War romanticism, local colorists emphasized the picturesque, emotional, and "interesting" rather than the scientific or clinical. The style was, in Shapiro's words, "intended to entertain, to give pleasure through its artful reportage of the experiences of a particular person. Not the object of observation, nor the naked act of observation, but 'sensibility,' that nexus between observer and observed, was what made such material interesting." According to Shapiro, the first published local color piece associated with Appalachia was Will Harney's "A Strange People and a Peculiar Place," published in *Lippincott's* in 1873. Harney's title aptly and concisely introduces the reader to a view of Appalachian "otherness" that dominated outside expectations of Appalachia and Appalachians for the next century. Travel sketches and short stories alike reinforced this view by presenting the experiences of the narrator as "typical scenes."[16]

One of the most popular early local colorists of Appalachia was Mary Noailles Murfree, whose work combined a meticulously descriptive treatment of the mountain scenery of eastern Tennessee with a rather melancholy treatment of the region's people. They were, in Murfree's writings, alien, star-crossed, and tragic figures engaged in "unrequited love, tragic misunderstanding, and fatal accident." While Murfree's tales were set in a pre–Civil War Appalachia, many of her contemporary readers took her work as representative of an unchanging society in the early 1880s. Ironically, Murfree's own experience with the region was limited largely to summers spent at a Tennessee resort for wealthy tourists.[17]

The importance of the local color movement for historians of Appalachia is, in Shapiro's words, that "the vision of reality thus offered . . . became the basis for private or public action." The works of James Lane Allen and especially the very popular John Fox Jr., both focusing on Kentucky, continued the process of popularizing the idea of Appalachian otherness, bringing with them an implicit justification for future attempts to change the region's distinctive characteristics.[18]

After abolition, and particularly after Reconstruction, reformers sought common ground upon which a new American culture could be built. While some bemoaned Appalachia's deviation from the supposed norm, other reform-minded evangelists and secular progressives saw the supposedly isolated mountaineers as worthy ancestors whom the rest of the nation had passed by. Studying these remnants of the pioneer past would help the nation return to its roots. Furthermore, the benefits of modern technology could be applied to the older culture, permitting the establishment of the transcontinental cultural unity the reformers sought while simultaneously forging a synthesis of the best of the old order and the new.[19]

Throughout the last two decades of the nineteenth century, missionaries from various Protestant denominations with national organizations took the lead in "civilizing" Appalachians, bringing with them some of the same preconceptions generated by the local colorists. Indeed, Murfree's *In the Tennessee Mountains* served as an introductory textbook on the area for new missionaries. By 1890, the churches and many secular reformers had come to describe Appalachia quite explicitly as "a problem to be solved" because of its deviation from the supposed American norm. As Shapiro observed, "Appalachia appeared no longer as the exception which proved but as the exception which challenged the rule of progress and of national unity and homogeneity." Moreover, Appalachia's apparent refusal to be modernized challenged the validity of the values that informed the missionary efforts.[20]

The romanticized local colorist vision of the upper Little Tennessee would find its staunchest supporter in a refugee from the "new order" of urban life. Horace Kephart left a cozy librarian's job in St. Louis in 1900, going in search of a mythical pioneer lifestyle. Kephart believed he had found it in the woods of Swain County, North Carolina, in a solitary place he lovingly called "the Back of Beyond" in the headwaters of the Little Tennessee River. Kephart's meticulous description of the physical environment harkens back to the naturalist descriptions of Lewis and Clark, providing academic students of the region with excellent descriptions, maps, and sketches of the flora and fauna of the area. His notebooks present a fascinating and detailed natural survey of the region. Some of his best-known works are treatises on backcountry camping and a guide to sporting firearms, and he later became extremely important in popularizing the idea of the Great Smoky Mountains National Park. His objective descriptions of the physical world of western North Carolina aside, however, the romantic individualism and rugged lifestyle of which Kephart wrote in his signature work, *Our Southern Highlanders,* is a popular but misleading stereotype of the region. Just as Margaret Mitchell's romance of the plantation South and Thomas Dixon's violent white supremacist novels—and their highly memorable interpretations on film—helped shape popular views of the allegedly typical "southern experience," Kephart's backwoods adventures helped mislead readers into seeing the upper Little Tennessee as isolated and romantic. Though he was frequently identified with the preservationist mentality of the early twentieth century, and though he insisted he was merely passing on what he had been told rather than writing fiction, Kephart's style and influence place him among the ranks of Murfree and the other local colorists of the southern mountains.[21]

Had they been so inclined, the reformers who sought to "fix" Appalachia could have found plentiful targets among those who developed the resources of the upper Little Tennessee after 1890. Mining and timbering companies from other parts of the nation would extract the wealth of the region rapidly, providing a temporary source of income for residents while damaging the landscape. Yet many, perhaps most, residents welcomed the arrival of the companies that paid in actual cash, every week, unlike their struggling farms, providing the material comforts and necessities to which they, like the rest of America, were increasingly becoming accustomed.

Paradoxically, the romanticized focus on alleged Appalachian otherness and isolation popularized by Kephart and others reached its zenith after the region had already settled on a definite type of extractive relationship with the "outside world."[22] In some ways this relationship resembles that described by James C. Cobb in *The Most Southern Place on Earth.* Cobb was writing about the Mississippi Delta, a region whose poverty, racial relations, language, literature, and music have come to exemplify the South in the minds of reformers and academics alike. And as Cobb points out in the epilogue to that work, the Mississippi Delta is both uniquely southern and typically American:

> The Delta's capacity to provide a . . . window on American society at large should come as no surprise. Despite its image as an isolated, self-sustaining, ultra-southern anachronism, many of the . . . Delta's primary identifying qualities . . . are less a reflection of its Old South beginnings than a postbellum experience characterized by more than a century of consistent and close interaction with the pervasive influences of the modern American economic and political system.[23]

Cobb's words would serve more than adequately to describe the mountains of southwestern North Carolina, despite the obvious physical and social differences between that region and the Delta.

In *The Promise of the New South*, Edward Ayers contends that one of the most important developments in southern life in the thirty years after Reconstruction was the rapid growth of very small towns, villages of less than 2,500 inhabitants. These towns served as marketplaces for local goods and as points where local culture, economy, and politics intersected with the larger currents of the nation as a whole. Railroads and, after 1900, usable highways provided the mechanism for this intersection in most southern areas. The fortunes of entire communities frequently rose and fell with their role as marketplaces, and thus rose and fell based upon their relationship to the "outside world."[24]

In the upper Little Tennessee, the town of Charleston, soon renamed Bryson City, sprouted in the 1880s as just such a market center. The town, which served as the seat of Swain County, provided a jumping-off point for the timber industry's entry into the economy of southwestern North Carolina. It also published the area's only weekly newspaper for a time. As new inventions enticed Americans toward a machine-age popular culture, Bryson City provided the only automobile dealers and service facilities, the only photography studios, and the only movie theaters within a twenty-mile radius.

Other villages would arise with more modest missions. Some twenty miles downstream from Bryson City, in the Forney Creek township of Swain County, lay Bushnell. Initially, the site of Bushnell offered few advantages beyond its easy access to the Little Tennessee and Tuckaseigee Rivers. Neither of the rivers was commercially navigable, but logs could be floated to a sawmill in even these fairly shallow streams. Bushnell's population swelled to nearly 1,000 after the arrival of a railroad spur built in the late 1880s by the Western North Carolina Railroad, which was absorbed into the Southern Railway in 1894. The rise of the town was thus inextricably linked to the activities of J. P. Morgan, whose consolidation of the assets of the defunct Richmond and West Point Terminal Company and several small railroads into the Southern Railway system formed an essential link in what C. Vann Woodward called "an economy . . . of branch plants, branch banks, captive mines, and chain stores."[25] Although the town never saw the establishment of any such branch plants, banks, or chain stores, and the nearest productive mine was twenty miles downstream at Fontana, Bushnell did become a center for transferring goods between the railroad's main line and the Fontana spur, where they would reach backcountry dwellers. The town was incorporated by an act of the North Carolina legislature in 1901, and its boundaries were enlarged by another legislative act in 1915.

From its inception, the Fontana rail spur was a two-way route. Copper mines on Hazel Creek and Eagle Creek provided quality copper ore for shipment across the mountains to Copperhill, Tennessee, and excellent timber grew in the area as well. The community of Fontana thus grew rapidly on both sides of the Little Tennessee, straddling the line between Graham and Swain Counties about twenty miles west of Bushnell. Founded by the Montvale Lumber Company in 1902, Fontana originated as a makeshift logging camp. By 1907 it had moved to a more level site and encompassed a school, a community recreation center, a modest hotel, a church, and a company store. While the mines, the center of the village, and most of the timber were located in Swain County, many of the miners lived across the river in Graham County. Both counties maintained schools in the Fontana area. A pedestrian bridge and later a cable-operated ferry made travel between the two Fontanas feasible.[26] The copper mines attracted miners with the skill to identify and dig out the commercially valuable ore. As the mining operations grew, they provided cash income for residents, turning Fontana into a modest but active market for manufactured goods.

Between Bushnell and Fontana, the timber industry built the town of Proctor. Situated a few miles up Hazel Creek from the Little Tennessee in Swain County, Proctor existed primarily to provide the Ritter Lumber Company of Columbus, Ohio, with as much old-growth timber as the company could sell. Incorporated as a town in 1911, Proctor grew rapidly enough that at its peak during World War I it rivaled Bryson City in population and amenities. As a by-product of its logging operations, the Ritter Company even established a passenger railroad to connect Proctor to the Fontana spur, giving residents easy access to the rest of the South by way of the Southern's main line connection at Bushnell. Proctor also harbored a few miners who worked the Hazel Creek copper mine.[27]

South of Proctor and Bushnell, in Graham County, lay the mountain township of Stecoah. Unlike Proctor, Bushnell, or Fontana, the name Stecoah denoted not so much a village as a region containing several small communities, including Brock, Tuskeegee, and Japan. These communities differed from those of Swain County in that they lacked railroad connections to local market centers. In particular, members of the fifteen or so families of Japan traded more readily with merchants in Bushnell and Almond, across the river in Swain County, than with those in their own county seat of Robbinsville, across the Unaka Mountains.[28]

Robbinsville was founded in 1872 so that the newly created Graham County would have a seat of government. The site seems to have been chosen arbitrarily, and one widely circulated legend claims that the courthouse was built next to a moonshine still where the surveying party had stopped for refreshment. The town served as a market center for that portion of the county not already accustomed to trading across the river in Swain County, but grew much more slowly than Bryson City. Robbinsville's future growth depended upon the timbering and mining activities in Yellow Creek township, in the northern part of the county, and repeated corporate bankruptcies hampered the development of those resources. The town's greatest population growth would not come until the 1920s, coinciding with the construction of new highways through the county, the opening of the Graham County Railroad, which connected with the Southern at Topton, and the establishment of the Bemis Lumber Company's sawmill. Robbinsville never served as a major tourist destination, but it succeeded modestly as a wayside rest stop while developing its extractable natural resources mostly with local capital. For many years the Bemis Lumber Company would serve as the county's largest and frequently only industrial employer, and it would operate Graham County's only rail line.[29]

The twin farming communities of Almond and Judson, in southern Swain County's Nantahala township, contrasted sharply with the extractive settlements at Proctor and Fontana or the slow and undirected growth of Robbinsville. Two miles apart on the banks of the Little Tennessee a few miles south of Bushnell, the two villages bore a much closer relationship to Bryson City than their downstream counterparts. Here, fertile bottomland made agriculture possible and occasionally profitable. The presence of economically feasible agriculture gave these communities a sense of permanence not shared by Fontana or Proctor. A few farmers, storekeepers, and other entrepreneurs prospered in Almond and Judson. Almond was incorporated in 1905, but ceased to operate as a municipality after the Aluminum Company of America (Alcoa) began purchasing land in the area. The village's population, which peaked at 148 in the 1920 census, dwindled rapidly thereafter. Judson was never incorporated, but did manage briefly to diversify its economic base during the World War I timber boom.

The Cherokee territory known as the Qualla Boundary was formed in Swain and Jackson Counties from lands acquired piecemeal by the Eastern Band during the 1840s and 1850s, largely through the efforts of William Holland Thomas. The community of Yellow Hill gradually became the most important of several small settlements within the Qualla Boundary, largely because of its status as the administrative center for the various federal agents commissioned on behalf of the Eastern Band. By 1900,

Qualla Boundary was home to 795 of the 875 Cherokees living in Swain County; an additional 340 Cherokees lived in the Jackson County portion of the Qualla Boundary. Smaller settlements, such as Big Cove, Wolf Town, and Paint Town, composed mostly of traditionalists preferring less contact with whites, had waned in size by the 1880s, as the principal "town of Cherokee" composed of the villages of Quallatown, Yellow Hill, and Bird Town, emerged as a center for administration, education, and acculturation. Several small communities, notably the Snowbird (also known as Cheoah) community in Graham County, remained virtually isolated and unacculturated, speaking only the Cherokee language; other Cherokee families scattered throughout western North Carolina assimilated almost completely into white society and spoke only English. Nonetheless, Cherokee was the primary point of contact between the Qualla Boundary and the white-dominated world, and the town became the center of an identifiable Cherokee community life by 1900. While Cherokee was undoubtedly more difficult to reach than, say, Bryson City, it was the nearest point in the Qualla Boundary to the Southern rail line, which passed some five and a half miles to the south at Whittier. Moreover, like the white settlements of the upper Little Tennessee, it grew rapidly during the 1880s and 1890s because of an influx of outside institutions, in this case including a federal Indian agency and a Quaker boarding school.[30]

With the new communities came new inhabitants who developed a different sort of connection to the area. The arrival of these transient families points out a peculiar dichotomy between the popular image of Appalachia—as exemplified by Kephart's static mountain settlements in the "back of beyond"—and the reality of a turbulent and vital economy. With that turbulence one would expect social change, and it is a culture's ability to respond to such changes that will mark it as either living or dead. Writing of a different group of southerners in *Black Culture and Black Consciousness,* Lawrence Levine stated, "Culture is not a fixed condition but a process: the product of interaction between the past and the present. Its toughness and resiliency are determined not by a culture's ability to withstand change, which indeed may be a sign of stagnation not life, but by its ability to react creatively and responsively to the realities of a new situation."[31] Residents of the upper Little Tennessee Valley communities exhibited these characteristics of a living, creative, adaptive culture throughout the period covered by this study. Many residents of the upper Little Tennessee Valley, far from stuck in time and space, moved about so frequently that their connections to a particular family dwelling or "ancestral homeplace" lasted no more than a generation.[32] Furthermore, entire communities came and went as industry and employment did.

What most people in this region did was to "get by," whatever that might require at the moment. Getting by might require taking employment in local industries, such as mining and timbering, or working for the Southern Railway. It might also require growing vegetables or cutting pulpwood. It might even require leaving one's family behind and working elsewhere temporarily. The initial appeal of a regular wage-paying job in Gastonia or Kannapolis textile mills frequently wore off as the dingy, crowded conditions and the regimentation of the company whistle grew tiresome. So when it was possible to do so, some longtime residents of southwestern North Carolina seem to have preferred to live at home and get by even in hard times.[33]

The region offered limited opportunities for them to do so. Small businesses such as stores and sawmills provided both farming and nonfarming families with needed goods, as well as occasional supplementary employment. Successful stores sprang up at Deals Gap, Fontana, Proctor, Bushnell, Japan, and Stecoah. Store owners sometimes owned more than one such enterprise, and their enterprises were often scattered among the small communities of western North Carolina, eastern Tennessee, and northern Georgia. Stores changed ownership frequently and sometimes simply vanished when the owners became frustrated with the economic or political climate of a site, perhaps because their limited inventory could be so readily disposed of or consolidated with that of another store.

These patterns of population change and economic activity—of getting by or moving on—suggest strongly that the unchanging Elizabethan culture described in *Our Southern Highlanders* and similar works is misleading. The region boasted no coal mines, no cotton mills, no paper mills, no steel mills, no cigarette factories, and no Henry Grady to trumpet its coming renaissance, although Kelly Bennett would play a very public booster role. But the upper Little Tennessee Valley was no stagnant backwater bypassed by the development of the New South; indeed, it participated actively in the formation of that New South. As Ayers points out:

> Although railroads, stores, and towns came into sudden prominence throughout the South, each place had its own local chronology. Any given year would find some places in a buoyant mood as a railroad approached or a new mill opened, while others, bypassed by the machinery of the new order, fell into decline. The arrival of a rail-

> road could trigger many consequences: rapid population growth or population decline, a more diversified economy or greater specialization, the growth of a city or the death of small towns.[34]

While historians Jack Temple Kirby and Ronald Eller, among others, have argued that the relationship between the "outside world" and the southern mountains was essentially predatory, that view discounts evidence suggesting that many people within the region actively sought these relationships with outside industry.

Aside from small stores and the occasional sawmill, illicit tavern or boarding house, most small businesses took root in the area's towns, Bryson City and Robbinsville. Bryson City, at least, included a substantial business class among its leaders, some of whom could trace their families' residence in the area to the 1838 land sale at Franklin. As members of the Whitaker, Cabe, Cable, DeHart, Wiggins, Leatherwood, Welch, Colvard, Sherrill, and Bryson families remained important links between the area's past and its present, they also diversified, becoming merchants, attorneys, and skilled craftsmen in Bryson City. Meanwhile, relative newcomer families such as those of A. M. Bennett and Stanley Black found opportunity in Bryson City as well.

A. M. Bennett, along with his son Kelly, epitomized the successful small business owner. Those who would seek to romanticize the lifestyle of the small-town "self-made man" would find much to admire here. A. M. Bennett was born in Cataloochee, Haywood County, in 1861, the grandson of an early settler there. He obtained a medical degree from Louisville Medical College in 1885 and became a licensed pharmacist in 1888. He moved to Bryson City in 1893 and established the Bryson City Drug Co. in 1905. Kelly Bennett, who earned a pharmacy degree from the University of North Carolina, inherited the drugstore and became a fixture in the town's business and political life, serving as mayor, head of the chamber of commerce, and state senator during the course of a seventy-year career.[35]

Stanley Black was no less typical of the Bryson City burgher than A. M. and Kelly Bennett, although his experiences were much different. Black was born in Illinois, and his sister married into Swain County's wealthiest and best-known family. In the 1890s Black studied law under his brother-in-law, Thad Bryson, and he later cofounded the firm of Black and Whitaker, which served as local counsel for Union Development Company and Alcoa. Black served Alcoa as its legal representative when the company began buying up land for its hydroelectric projects, and while he was occasionally called upon to defend the company and its subsidiaries in personal injury cases and other such claims, real estate issues consumed the bulk of his practice. In 1906 he also helped orchestrate the birth of the Bryson City Bank, which invested heavily in speculative real estate ventures in the area with Black's apparent encouragement. In 1929 he became the bank's president, just in time for it to fail during the Great Depression. In part because of his connections to Alcoa, Black became one of the area's leading opponents of the Tennessee Valley Authority.[36]

Both A. M. Bennett and Stanley Black entered Bryson City when it was a young, turbulent town. Both provided professional services that were in demand in the area—Bennett provided medical care and pharmaceuticals to a population rapidly becoming aware of advances in medicine, while Black provided legal services to a region rife with land disputes and messy inheritance struggles. Both established firms that remained highly visible and important after the retirement of their founders. Black became a leading figure in Republican politics; Kelly Bennett chaired the Swain County Democratic Party for a number of years. The Bennetts and Black presided over a community in transition from unsettled outpost to small-town stability. They and their counterparts among the merchants of Bryson City would play an important role in determining the course of the region's development.

As we shall see, the Little Tennessee Valley in the late nineteenth and early twentieth centuries participated as fully as other rural southern regions in the attempt to recruit outside industry, capital, and attention and quickly became as dependent on these outside factors as did the rest of the New South. The arrival of the railroad spur in Bushnell in the 1880s promised an influx of jobs to the region, as did the arrival of the Ritter Lumber Company in Proctor, the various mining interests along Hazel Creek and Eagle Creek half a generation later, and Alcoa a few years after that.[37]

2

Railroads, Good Roads, and Sawmill Villages

Those who created a New South often focused their attention first upon the tangible evidence of industrial progress. The number of miles of railroad track, the spindle count in cotton mills, and the total dollar amount invested in a particular area could serve as evidence of the area's "progress" toward the goal of economic modernization. North Carolina, one of the poorest southern states in 1860, led the charge toward modernity with a series of what political scientist V. O. Key called "progressive plutocrats" providing the necessary if one-sided political leadership necessary to turn the state into a showcase of New South development. As noted social historian Dwight Billings has demonstrated, North Carolina planters, weaker as a class than their Deep South counterparts, seized upon industrialization as a means to protect and even enhance their personal status. Planters, working together with what could be called a "modernizing elite" among the townspeople and also working frequently with northern investors, created the New South's North Carolina incarnation.[1] In the upper Little Tennessee, only the balance of power among these interests differentiates the area from the rest of the state. In particular, while it is a misnomer to identify most of the large landowners of the upper Little Tennessee as planters, we shall see that the area was developed by outside capitalists with the aid and support of local and regional elites who clearly resemble David Carlton's town-builders of South Carolina. The dominant, but not sole, motivation was economic growth coupled with social stability.[2]

Let us begin with the railroad, the most visible evidence of "modernity" in American life and, by extension, the most visible evidence of the New South's accommodation to that American system. Built in the 1850s with state funds, the North Carolina Railroad (NCRR) was a horseshoe-shaped trunk line through the Piedmont region, connecting Goldsboro to Greensboro, Salisbury, and Charlotte. In 1854 the state authorized the construction of two extensions by private companies with state financial assistance. These were the Atlantic and North Carolina (A&NCRR),

which would connect Goldsboro with Beaufort on the coast, and the Western North Carolina Railroad, which would connect Salisbury with Asheville. At Asheville, the line would split into a northern branch reaching across the Blue Ridge Mountains to connect with the East Tennessee and Western North Carolina Railroad (ET&WNC) near Paint Rock and a 120-mile southern branch pointing west-southwest across the mountains and through part of the upper Little Tennessee Valley to Murphy, North Carolina, and Ducktown, Tennessee. The northern branch of the WNCRR was intended to tie the NCRR to the upper Mississippi and Ohio Valley markets, while the southern branch was aimed squarely at both the markets of the Tennessee Valley and the lower Mississippi, and the rich copper mines of Ducktown. When completed, the expanded rail lines would provide the state with a valuable link to the rest of the nation. In the flat coastal plains of eastern North Carolina, construction proceeded rapidly, but the Civil War interrupted construction before the western line could be built beyond Morganton on the western edge of the Piedmont.[3]

After the war, the Richmond and Danville Railroad (R&D) expanded rapidly, connecting to the NCRR at Greensboro. This provided unwelcome competition for the A&NCRR. Additionally, in 1871 the R&D acquired a thirty-year lease allowing it to operate the NCRR. Meanwhile, construction costs consumed all of the available funding for the WNCRR, and the state purchased it outright after it fell into bankruptcy in 1872. It soon proved too expensive to be politically tenable, and the state legislature voted in a special session to sell the railroad to a consortium of investors led by William J. Best, a New York financier. Best's offer included both a legally binding agreement to complete the route and a nonbinding statement of intent to further develop the state's railroad system. The state bill included a provision requiring the completion of the northern branch before title could be conveyed, although the southern branch needed only to be extended about twenty miles to the Pigeon River near Canton. It also required the buyers to pay off all of the WNCRR's outstanding debts. Among the supporters of the deal was the very influential two-term governor and then senator Zebulon Baird Vance.[4]

Best's backers declined to pay off the WNCRR's floating debt, effectively abrogating the deal he had brokered on their behalf. Best nonetheless insisted upon his intention to purchase the railroad. At the behest of Governor Thomas Jarvis, who was involved in a rather heated contest for his party's nomination,[5] Vance was dispatched to find some way to assist Best in his plans. Vance in turn sought the assistance of A. B. Andrews, superintendent and vice president of the R&DRR, to locate appropriate investors for the Best scheme. This placed Vance and Jarvis in a difficult position, since many North Carolina residents had expressed dissatisfaction with the R&DRR's management of the NCRR. As it turns out, the perception that the R&D might someday exercise monopoly power over North Carolina commerce was not entirely unfounded; while Andrews and Best were negotiating financing for the WNCRR, New York capitalist William P. Clyde, owner of a steamship line and a coastal railroad in Virginia, had already begun negotiating for control of the R&D itself, with the intention of transforming it into a feeder system for the Upper South. While Best's planned trunk system echoed an earlier tradition of "natural territory" in railroad development, Clyde's plans coincided with a general transformation in the character of railroad expansion in the South, emphasizing through traffic rather than local traffic, a transformation which would result in the consolidation of dozens of southern rail systems into a handful of supersystems.[6]

Best did reach an agreement with the R&D for a $50,000 loan, which if left unpaid after ninety days would result in Best's forfeiture of one-twelfth of the railroad's stock. Until the loan was repaid, the R&D held almost all of the assets of the WNCRR as collateral. The details of the deal were kept out of the public eye to protect the financial interests of Andrews and Clyde and the political stature of Jarvis and Vance. An article in the *New York Times,* reprinted in the *Raleigh Observer,* brought the matter to public attention only after Jarvis had won renomination. The article claimed that the northern branch of the route was to be completed immediately, but made no mention of the southern line. Meanwhile, Best failed to secure the necessary funds to repay the loan, and the R&D claimed control of all but 7,500 shares of WNCRR stock on July 31, 1880. Vance was displeased by the takeover, but felt strongly that the road should be built, even if it would be done by the hated Virginia company.[7]

The general assembly met in January 1881 and promptly mounted a bipartisan inquiry into Jarvis's role in the railroad matter. Jarvis responded to the initial inquiry by providing a surfeit of specifications concerning the construction program for the railroad but almost no information concerning its ownership. The state senate's Committee on Internal Improvements took up the matter in mid-February 1881, when one senator introduced a bill permitting the R&D to assume greater control over the WNCRR and several other railroads. Best and Andrews testified before the committee, as did R&D president A. S. Buford, leaving no doubt that the R&D already controlled the WNCRR completely. The fate of the southern line was ambiguous; only the Paint Rock connection was essential to the success of the R&D master plan, and the southern line would siphon off valuable funds from the larger expansion plan, but the original sale agreement between Best and the state remained in force. That agreement required the completion of the entire length of the Ducktown line by January 1, 1885. Moreover, it also required that the whole Paint Rock line and the first twenty miles of the Ducktown line be completed by July 1, 1881, some four months away. As construction had barely reached Asheville by that time, completion by the deadline was virtually impossible. Without the completion of that line, the entire WNCRR would revert to state ownership after a ninety-day grace period, upon a vote of two of the three state commissioners overseeing the project. Considering that the commissioners were Jarvis, Vance, and State Treasurer John M. Worth, it seemed possible, even likely, that the state would regain control over the railroad. The commissioners also had the power to grant an extension, however. Andrews, predictably, sought the extension of the deadline, promising completion of the Paint Rock line within four months after the original deadline and, Jarvis believed, indicating his intention to complete the Ducktown line as well.[8]

The commissioners agreed to the extension provided that the R&D's principal financiers each agreed to several amendments to the agreement, including a commitment to maintain 300 laborers on the Ducktown line at all times. By the time all the necessary signatures were obtained, Vance had departed for Washington and Worth had gone back home to Asheboro. Jarvis pledged to present the matter to the commissioners at their next meeting; Andrews could thus claim that the delay prevented the R&D from transporting workers to the Ducktown line in a timely manner.[9]

Meanwhile, Best presented Vance with an alternate reorganization plan for the WNCRR that would refocus on the original goal of uniting the state by rail. Vance, a resident of Charlotte, where protests against R&D rate policies constituted an important political issue, was never a fan of the R&D in the first place. He quickly became convinced that Best's new plan was sound and withdrew his consent to the extension of the R&D contract. Vance wrote Jarvis and Worth with his intentions; Jarvis quickly informed Andrews, who rushed to the governor's office and threatened to stop all construction on the WNCRR immediately if he did not get the extension. Worth was placed between the two most powerful politicians in the state when Jarvis wrote him, seeking his support for the extension. The letter from Jarvis arrived first; Worth consented to the extension even when informed of Vance's opposition.[10]

Vance responded with tremendous anger, arguing that Worth's consent had been obtained by unlawful means. Best traveled to Raleigh to present his "Boston syndicate" to the commissioners as an alternative to the R&D plan. The syndicate offered to lease the A&NCRR and build a new trunk line (the Midland line) connecting Goldsboro and Salisbury, cutting off the R&D-controlled NCRR and effectively linking the A&NCRR with the WNCRR to form the statewide trunk system first proposed in the 1850s. The plan hinged upon successfully wresting control of the WNCRR from the R&D. Probably not by coincidence, the proposed Midland line would go right through Worth's hometown of Asheboro. Convincing Worth of the wisdom of the plan was easy. Vance, too, offered his support, while also asking the commissioners to declare the R&D extension void. In what R&D executives would view as a remarkable about-face, Jarvis enthusiastically agreed to assist the Boston group in regaining control of the WNCRR while insisting that this position did not conflict with his previous support for the R&D. Indeed, Jarvis sought to cover his bases by working with both groups to guarantee that one or the other would get the western railroad done.[11]

The two groups thus competed for the chance to control the WNCRR. The R&D continued its expansion plans throughout the Upper South, while Best's group leased the A&NCRR and began work on the Midland line. On June 23, 1881, the commissioners temporarily suspended the extension of the R&D contract on the grounds that the R&D had placed fewer than the requisite 300 workers on the Ducktown line and had not made sufficient progress on either branch. Thus, the commission failed to ratify the unorthodox manner in which the extension had been obtained, but also failed to repudiate it. Andrews continued construction, assuming that the extension was still valid and that his "new" deadline would be difficult enough to meet.[12]

On August 1, 1881, the commissioners released to the R&D a copy of the secret agreement they had made with the Boston syndicate. Jarvis attempted to broker a peaceable settlement in which the R&D would voluntarily relinquish control of the WNCRR in exchange for the money offered by Best's new backers. On August 25, the commissioners "officially" notified the governor (one of their own, of course) that the R&D had failed to live up to its agreement. Jarvis also sent a copy of the notification to President Buford of the R&D. Vance then used his newspaper connections to publicize what he viewed as the R&D's malfeasance, including a smorgasbord of charges of rate discrimination along with the delay in constructing the WNCRR. Andrews responded with claims that the R&D

now had 700 workers on the Ducktown line, and he denied any discriminatory pricing. His trump card was the release of his copy of the agreement between Best and the commissioners, in which the commissioners had promised to "use all the means in their power" to wrest control of the WNCRR from the R&D. The *New York Times* even weighed in, accusing the R&D investors of intentionally undermining Best's original efforts.[13]

These conflicts made it abundantly clear that the R&D would not give up the WNCRR without a fight. R&D officials even intimated that Governor Jarvis would not have been nominated by his party if they had not rescued the WNCRR plan. Meanwhile, using electric lighting to lengthen the working day, the R&D crews quickly added mileage to the western lines, convincing Jarvis of their ability to complete the job. Meeting in November 1881, the commissioners acknowledged that the R&D was guilty of some of the charges of rate discrimination, but they declined to use this to force forfeiture of the contract, since the incidents in question did not occur on the WNCRR. Vance pressed the issue of timely construction, but Worth sided with Jarvis in granting a formal four-month extension.[14]

Sectional politics, frequently a force in North Carolina, dictated that Vance would lose support from voters in the western part of the state for "trying to confiscate the WNCRR from the very enterprise which was finally building the road." Meanwhile, voters in the eastern part of the state, long subjected to what they viewed as the R&D's discriminatory tactics, would take issue with Jarvis and Worth for their unwillingness to force the issue and take control of the WNCRR. Many easterners also expressed disappointment at the slow progress Best's group was making on the Midland line, which would liberate them from dependence on the R&D.[15]

Ultimately, the R&D retained control of the WNCRR, completing the northern branch before Jarvis left the governor's office in 1885. The southern line finally reached Ducktown in 1891, passing through territory that R&D executives considered peripheral to their company's needs but central to the realities of doing business in politically charged North Carolina. Three years later, the R&D was bankrupt, and J. Pierpont Morgan assumed control of the company's assets, integrating them into his new Southern Railway. Thus, by aligning themselves with outside capital interests from New York, western North Carolinians seeking economic development got their long-sought railroad and, with it, better access to Deep South and Ohio Valley markets.[16]

The southern line to Ducktown passed through the upper Little Tennessee Valley, with stops at Waynesville, Bryson City, Bushnell, Murphy, and countless smaller places. The railroad may not have transformed every aspect of the region's life, but it did bring sweeping changes. It brought rural free delivery in 1896, with the Sears catalog only one of many new arrivals. It brought lumber companies. It brought a renewed interest in mining. It brought a renewed interest, too, in land speculation. It brought the prospect of a regular paycheck. It also brought tourists, who found the mountain scenery irresistible.[17]

What the railroad began, the Good Roads Movement was supposed to complete. Although begun by New England bicyclists, the Good Roads Movement quickly became a farmers' campaign in many parts of the South. Many farmers recognized in the construction of better roads a viable economic alternative to the high freight charges assessed by railroads. Better roads would also reduce the strain on draft animals, allowing fewer animals to pull a greater load at greater speed and ultimately improving access to markets.

Initially, farmers in western North Carolina were reluctant to support the Good Roads Movement because they feared tax hikes. Most farmers were content with the old "labor tax" system used throughout most of the nineteenth century, in which able-bodied males periodically came out and worked together to maintain the individual roads that were most important to their own community. The labor tax was a community ritual providing both an occasion for contact with their neighbors and a means of maintaining their meager roads. Their outlook on the world was dominated by local and county-level concerns; they could see no reason to invest their modest cash reserves in road construction that would benefit other areas, presumably at their own expense. Those who could see beyond their own personal economic issues were similarly worried about the prospect of county and state governments going into tremendous debt to finance such road schemes.[18]

North Carolina's movement for better roads began instead with Mecklenburg County, already home to the state's most rapidly growing city, Charlotte. In 1885 Mecklenburg County's state representative for many years, S. B. Alexander, sought and received state authorization for a special county tax levy for building and maintaining roads, applicable only in his home county. During the following ten years, Mecklenburg County's roads built largely with convict labor were cited as an example by transportation advocates and business progressives throughout the state.[19]

Asheville, which had blossomed from a tiny town of 2,000 to a bustling resort area of 20,000 during the 1880s with the coming of the Western

North Carolina Railroad, also founded the state's first voluntary Good Roads organization in 1899. Asheville's business community, especially those members whose attention was focused on tourism, quickly saw the utility of improving the area's roads, and they had a ready example in the lush estate of George Vanderbilt just south of town. Delegates from the Good Roads Association of Asheville and Buncombe County even went to neighboring counties in North Carolina and Tennessee to help promote the economic advantages of road development. Thus, in North Carolina good roads were an extension of the same urban boosterism that characterized much of the rest of the New South. Despite the antirailroad rhetoric some Good Roads advocates employed, even Southern Railway president Samuel Spencer helped promote the movement through his Good Roads Trains, a successful promotional campaign.[20]

Despite the statewide promotion of the Good Roads Movement, most participants still viewed roadbuilding and maintenance as a fundamentally local issue. They generally limited their efforts to promoting the creation of more local advocacy associations rather than attempting to formulate a development strategy at the state level. This localized strategy would place the movement in an advantageous position for claiming and mobilizing grassroots support when the state finally did take action on the issue. Furthermore, that strategy would help to defuse criticism that the state was taking undue authority unto itself.[21]

One popular movement for road improvements consisted of the "Good Roads Days," two legal holidays set aside in November for the purpose of bringing out members of each community to work on the roadways. The brainchild of Governor Locke Craig, who would later gain the appellation "the Good Roads Governor," this movement attempted to resurrect the best features of the old labor tax—community spirit and free labor—while creating a festival atmosphere that he believed would translate into more support for improved transportation. While the Good Roads Days succeeded in attracting attention to the cause, at least one commentator who remembered traveling on roads built using the labor tax system complained that having "everybody, inexperienced and otherwise, fooling with the roads" was not necessarily the best way to guarantee the quality of the road work, regardless of how much community spirit it might help raise in the short term. Despite the criticism, the event sparked widespread participation. Schools were closed so that children could help out, and even Governor Craig, himself an Asheville resident, traded his customary business suit for a pair of overalls and spent a day on the road crew.[22]

Good roads quickly became the most popular type of pork-barrel spending available as reelection insurance. Counties issued forty-year bonds for road construction, hoping to show a large increase in mileage each year. The sand-clay roads they built had an undeserved reputation for simplicity of construction, with the result that few were properly constructed. Furthermore, since there was little glamour in road maintenance, the money raised through bond issues generally went for new construction rather than for taking care of what was already built. One commentator complained that counties were, in effect, borrowing money for forty years to build roads that would disintegrate in two years. This neglect of maintenance, coupled with the tendency of counties not to cooperate in constructing longer routes, helped convince some road advocates that county governments could not be counted upon to use road funds efficiently for the benefit of all. This became a more critical issue as the widespread availability of the automobile made traveling times shorter and increased the distance farmers would be willing to travel for market contacts.[23]

Like their counterparts in the rest of the state, residents of the Little Tennessee Valley fought to attract state and county highway dollars as soon as the utility of such action became apparent to them. Leading the crusade in Swain County were Kelly Bennett, the young pharmacist who as a twenty-seven-year-old state legislator introduced the first Good Roads Bill to come from Swain County, and Reverend Thomas Joshua "Uncle Josh" Calhoun, pastor of the Bone Valley Baptist Church near Proctor. The lure of Rural Free Delivery, coupled with the very real threat to withdraw that service if local governments did not act to improve the roads, provided one early motivation. The Federal Aid Law of 1916, promising matching funds for any state willing to raise money for roads, provided another, as North Carolina's government passed the obligation for raising the matching funds on to individual counties. Initially, like most Good Roads figures, Little Tennessee road advocates considered their job a local one, and some feared that "through roads" would adversely affect local merchants. Indeed, in many counties the roads built with Good Roads support ended a few hundred yards from the county line. During the debate over what became the state road law of 1919, one state representative from Macon County reflected the concerns of many that Asheville and the urbanized counties of the Piedmont would get the lion's share of the benefits from any road appropriations. He asked an influential colleague from Ashe County, an equally remote county in the northwestern part of the state, whether the legislative conference committee on road improvements was willing to "take care of the little counties" and guarantee that they would receive enough funds to take care of their needs. Assured that the senior colleague would make certain of it, the Macon County delegate reportedly resumed his nap.[24] The 1919 bill created a new highway commission, substantially enlarged in both personnel and authority, and divided the state into nine districts. All of southwestern North Carolina would be represented initially by James G. Stikeleather, an Asheville real estate speculator and developer.[25]

Even among the members of the larger Good Roads associations, conflicts arose during the 1910s over the best way to create a network of roads that would serve the entire state's economy. Harriet Berry, secretary and de facto head of the North Carolina Good Roads Association, favored local control and a state network connecting all 100 county seats. Charlotte's Colonel T. L. Kirkpatrick, founder of a rival association called the Citizens' Highway Association, advocated a single state-of-the-art trunk route connecting Wilmington on the coast with Charlotte in the Piedmont and Asheville in the mountains. Kirkpatrick later modified his position to include multiple trunk lines and feeders, but his initial plan so aroused suspicion in counties not connected by it that he became ineffective in his advocacy role.[26]

Some Good Roads boosters sought improvements for moral reasons. Better roads would help young people leave the farm occasionally, so that they would not burn with curiosity about the outside world. Thus, roads would help preserve the way of life of the family farm by removing the mystery and attraction of urban life from the realm of temptations faced by rural youth. In an editorial piece published in the *Jackson County Journal*, "Charity and Children" even argued that good roads were a religious issue. Good roads would make it easier for families to get to churches more often, and would also enhance the ability of circuit-riding ministers to serve their flocks more regularly.[27]

As Howard Lawrence Preston has pointed out, however, most of the successes attributable to the Good Roads Movement came from its appeal to those seeking economic improvements, often at the expense of neighboring towns and counties. Competition among counties for good roads was the rule. The *Jackson County Journal* put it succinctly: "As roads are built you will see this county go forward by leaps and bounds."[28]

Swain County lagged behind the rest of the state in road construction. The *Jackson County Journal* noted, "For some time the roads of Swain County have been a standing Joke; but the proposed Atlanta-to-Asheville highway and the prospect of its not touching Swain have brought the people of that county to the realization . . . that in improving the farms, in opening the mines, in working up the timber, in exploiting the potential wealth of a county you must first improve the highways."[29] Clearly, Swain County needed good roads in order to attract and keep industry. Residents of Bushnell, Fontana, and Proctor began agitating for a better road to Bryson City by 1913. Optimism and fear often worked together to produce strong public sentiment, as the *Jackson County Journal* pointed out in 1919: "The time has come when we must have better roads or we will be practically left off the map." The introduction of the affordable automobile, Henry Ford's Model T, also provided a useful impetus for road improvements, as did the Federal Aid Road Act of 1916.[30] In the early 1920s, a twisting, gravel-surfaced road would be built parallel to the Little Tennessee from Bryson City through Bushnell and Fontana to Deals Gap, where it would connect with U.S. 129 at Tapoco, and in 1927, Swain County would finally get its first paved section of highway, a few miles of U.S. 19 connecting Bryson City with Wesser, thus tying it to Dillsboro, Franklin, and ultimately Atlanta.

The new roads and railroads were among the most obvious changes to the landscape of the region. Change was afoot in other dimensions of the life of the upper Little Tennessee as well. While agricultural families whose ancestors had participated in the Franklin land sale of 1838 still controlled much of the bottomland along the river banks, smaller holdings along the tributaries had been consolidated through the efforts of speculators eager to cash in on the sale of timber rights. While the "owner-farmers" of the nineteenth century persisted in their endeavors, sometimes successfully, they no longer held the greatest wealth in the area. The North Carolina Exploration Company and various timber companies owned much of the land that had been adjudged worthless seventy years earlier. Absentee owners continued to hold many of the upland tracts, while groups of heirs living in the area contested claims over much of the rest. In 1910, with the help of Bryson City attorney Stanley Black, the Aluminum Company of America (Alcoa) began buying up bottomland in the area in anticipation of building a dam at Fontana, further altering the balance of power in the region to the detriment of the older farm families. Many residents stayed on and lived as tenants on their former land, paying rent to Alcoa until such time as the aluminum company might decide to begin building the dam.

Because of the question of land ownership, it is very difficult to trace patterns of short-distance migration. More than half of the farming families listed in any given census said they owned their own land, but such ownership did not necessarily imply legal title to that tract. Many "owned" the land in the common-law sense of having occupied it for several years, having made improvements, having harvested produce or timber from it, and having paid no rent. They considered the land theirs, although the legal title might belong to some individual, group of individuals, family, or corporation whose claim was not clearly defined in the minds of those who actually occupied that particular tract.

Lacking the necessary cash for starting their own businesses, and hampered by the difficulty of obtaining good productive farmland, many families in the upper Little Tennessee found that their best chance for survival was to work for wages. Most employment opportunities involved working for the large companies developing the region's natural resources: minerals, timber, hydroelectric power, and scenic beauty.

Mining provided employment for a number of residents in Graham County and western Swain County. Copper, in particular, provided a potential source of wealth for the region. The ore was of higher grade than that found in Tennessee's famed Copper Basin, but because it was situated in deeper rock strata and in more difficult terrain, mining companies operated in the region only when the demand for copper was high. The Adams-Westfeldt mine on Hazel Creek operated intermittently from 1899 to 1943, as worldwide copper demand warranted and as the legal situation permitted.[31] But while the profitability of mining was uncertain, the optimism of the area's boosters was not. The *Bryson City Times* asserted that the opening of the new Fontana mine at Eagle Creek in 1923 "goes to prove that when the forests of Swain County have been denuded of their luxuriant growth of timber, valuable deposits of mineral will be found under the surface . . . that will add materially to the wealth of our county. The development of this new industry will be watched with deep interest and hailed with delight."[32]

Timbering was a more reliable source of employment than mining, but it was nonetheless seasonal and irregular even in the best of times. Timbering and mining created a small number of jobs in subsidiary industries, especially railroading. Ritter Lumber Company built the Smoky Mountain Railroad, which ran branch lines from the Southern up all the major tributaries of Hazel Creek, carrying goods and mail to the inhabitants of the logging camps and of course also carrying timber down to the sawmill at Proctor. The lumber companies brought with them a new local market for the goods raised by local farmers—pork, apples, corn, beef, and whiskey. The railroads owned by the logging companies also made it easier for those who raised livestock to get more animals to market, creating an incentive for overgrazing that compounded the environmental damage done by logging itself. Still, the growth associated with the lumber boom brought additional income even to those who did not work in the lumber camps, and most residents willingly participated. As Margaret Lynn Brown noted, "What mountain people and Cherokees felt about the devastation of their environment was complicated by their economic role in it."[33]

Historian Robert S. Lambert has divided the history of logging in the Great Smoky Mountains into two distinct phases. The first phase, roughly from 1880 through 1900, involved selective cutting along river valleys and in other easily accessible areas, with black walnut, cherry, ash, yellow poplar, and oak being the most prized woods. Investors included W. E. Heyser of Michigan and the Buffalo firm of Taylor and Crate, both operating on the Little Tennessee, and the Scottish Carolina Timber and Land Company on the Pigeon River. Typical methods of transporting logs relied on natural stream flow, resulting in closure during dry seasons and disastrous flooding losses in times of heavy rainfall. The use of splash dams or booms to catch logs was cheap but inefficient; a log that spent too much time in the water was worthless as lumber. Workers tended to be local farmers who earned sixty to seventy-five cents a day to augment their farm income. Customers typically were small furniture makers and home builders. The most important result of the early phase of logging was the increased information available concerning the content of the forests of the area.[34]

Demand for lumber began to increase as the nation recovered from the disastrous depression of 1893–97. Producers already familiar with the area began buying up large tracts of land covered in apparently virgin timber. This second phase, which continued through about 1930, involved large-scale clear-cutting using steam-powered machinery. Although a few companies had set up small sawmills earlier at Waynesville, North Carolina, and Newport, Tennessee, only during this second phase did most logging companies install substantial manufacturing and processing facilities. This move toward larger operations was completed with the installation of a new pulp mill by the Champion Fibre Company at Canton, North Carolina, which would purchase the by-products of the lumbering industry and make large-scale cutting more profitable. Local entrepreneurs and large companies alike built tanneries to make use of the bark delivered to them by local farmers during their downtime.[35]

During the first decade of the twentieth century, land speculators gambling on the value of timber rights purchased large tracts of land. John C. Arbogast and a consortium of investors from West Virginia bought 33,000 acres from the Eastern Band for $245,000 in 1906, reselling it for

$630,000 three years later to a Philadelphia firm. Charles J. Harris and W. H. Woodbury bought up thousands of acres on Forney Creek, Deep Creek, and the Oconaluftee River, all tributaries of the Little Tennessee; the partners actually did some logging before selling the land again at a profit. Although its primary holdings were in Virginia and West Virginia, the W. M. Ritter Lumber Company of Columbus, Ohio, purchased thousands of acres along the Hazel Creek watershed. The R. E. Wood Lumber Company of Baltimore did the same with the Eagle Creek area, forming the Montvale Lumber Company to exploit its holdings and building a sawmill at Fontana that started production in 1907. Norwood Lumber Company bought 17,000 acres further upstream, on Forney Creek, and commenced production in 1910. Overlapping land grants and haphazard marking of trees by earlier owners to signify tract boundaries contributed to a 1915 dispute between the Ritter and Montvale firms over timber rights in the Bone Valley Creek area between Hazel Creek and Eagle Creek. The dispute involved thousands of acres of mostly unoccupied land claimed variously by the Wikle, Cable, Sherrell, Love, Sawyer, Buchanan, and Bryson families among others.[36]

Companies intending to cut large amounts of timber found themselves constructing short-distance railroads for easier transportation of logs to mills. Eventually they also constructed mills of their own near the logging sites. Such mills, located far from major towns, incorporated offices, services, and worker housing as well. Such a mill formed the nucleus of the town of Proctor, on Hazel Creek.[37]

Those who moved to the area seeking employment in the lumber industry tended to look to their employers for more than just a paycheck. Clarence O. Vance, who grew up in Proctor, remembered W. M. Ritter as a benevolent employer who genuinely cared about the people who worked for him. "We felt like a family," he told an interviewer. Ritter provided the school and church buildings, as well as a community building. Ritter hired a company doctor to deliver babies, assist the sick, and tend to injured workers; single men paid one dollar a month for his services, and families paid just fifty cents more. Each Ritter-owned home at Proctor had a fenced garden, and the company provided land for residents to range cattle and hogs. Board sidewalks built by Ritter lined the unlit streets of Proctor. Mail came on a Ritter-owned Smoky Mountain Railroad train each afternoon around five o'clock, and residents gathered at the Ritter commissary to collect it, picking up a few groceries on credit at elevated company store prices while they were there. Ritter brought temporary houses for families up to the outlying camps on log cars.

Ritter's paternalism extended beyond the necessities of life; the company provided entertainment as well as sustenance. At Proctor, residents from all over western Swain County converged to watch silent movies shown with a projector owned by Ritter, run by electricity provided by Ritter. Each Christmas, Vance's father drove a Shay steam engine pulling a train up the Smoky Mountain Railroad line to each lumber camp, carrying toys and candy provided by Ritter to the children of the area. Electric lights shone in Proctor homes for a few hours each evening, courtesy of Ritter, and Ritter even provided notice that it was bedtime by flashing those lights fifteen minutes before the power was turned off. The entire settlement was reminiscent of any other southern mill town, except that the mill in this town was a sawmill instead of a cotton mill. All in all, within the boundaries of company town life as Vance described it, "We lived pretty good." A cynical reader might justly note that living pretty good required submitting to a company routine that might be uncomfortable, harsh, and even dangerous, but Vance exhibited no regrets.[38]

Of course, Ritter's paternalism was self-serving to an extent. The more cordial the relations were between employer and employee, and the more the employer provided for the employee, the less likely the employee was to file a lawsuit if injured on the job. Ritter faced numerous lawsuits from workers over personal injuries during its twenty or so years in the upper Little Tennessee. Charles F. Patton was injured while loading cross-ties, because the sawmill was producing them faster than he could load them and the mill could not be stopped. N. A. Green sued the lumber company when he lost a hand to a defective planing machine at the company sawmill. E. G. Tolley was disabled when his clothing was caught in the gears of a moving locomotive while he was attempting to obey an order to open a cooling valve. Tolley was dragged twenty feet underneath the locomotive, which was traveling at four miles per hour. All these cases resulted in judgments against Ritter. Other lumber companies, including Bemis, Suncrest, Norwood, Kitchen, and Montvale, also faced numerous personal injury and wrongful death claims arising from company negligence, as did the Fontana Mining Corporation and the North Carolina Exploration Company. Not all of the injuries sustained on the job were the result of company negligence, however, as when one locomotive engineer admitted repeatedly that he would not have been hit in the head with a fourteen-foot piece of green oak if he had not been drinking whisky underneath the loading dock, in direct violation of orders.[39]

Growing up in a company town, as Clarence Vance did, one cannot help but absorb some of the corporate ethos. Ritter promoted a mind-set focused on production and company loyalty above all else. In its corporate magazine, *The Hardwood Bark,* Ritter actively sought information about new records for volume production, publishing monthly updates by type of wood, type of equipment, and conditions. Far from producing a simple newsletter intended for management, the editors of the *Hardwood Bark* aimed their glossy monthly publication squarely at the rank and file who lived and worked in the company towns. The magazine explicitly aimed to form a community from the disparate interests that made up the Ritter workforce. Along with features on key figures from the head office in Ohio, community news of the same sort which appeared in local newspapers dominated the pages of the *Bark,* including marriages, deaths, and recent arrivals in town. Occasionally, correspondents from the towns would complain in print about not having been visited lately by management, and a few months later some obliging executive would pose for a photo with some workers in front of a record day's production, amid the sort of pomp and circumstance that would have accompanied a visit from, if not the president of the United States, perhaps a local congressman. This sort of corporate culture helped to encourage worker loyalty in an industry where the local average wage was twelve cents an hour in 1912, but as one historian has noted, "residents . . . who went to work for the big lumber companies probably didn't realize the wages were low."[40]

World War I dramatically increased the demand for lumber in 1914, and the lumber companies obliged by cutting more aggressively and updating their equipment to improve efficiency and speed. Steam-powered ground skidders and eventually overhead cableway skidders brought logs to a central location, where they were loaded onto logging trains for transportation to the sawmills. Shay and Mallet locomotives pulled logging trains up and down the steep valleys of the tributaries of the Little Tennessee, just as they did in other valleys of western North Carolina; incline railways or water flumes were used for the steepest portions.[41]

Mechanical logging made it impossible to be selective in cutting trees. Lumbermen took anything big enough to sell—typically, this would mean anything a foot in diameter at a height of four feet from the ground. Alongside the popular hardwoods, they cut hemlock and spruce, which could be used for lumber or pulpwood.[42]

As the demand for lumber continued to increase, more people came to the area looking for the good wages the industry promised. Experienced loggers were hired and told to go hire a crew. The crew chief would provide draft animals to assist in moving the logs, and he would be paid based on the number of board-feet delivered. In turn, he would pay his crew members an agreed-upon sum. While many loggers were experienced in different facets of the job, the best positions, such as railroad engineer, skidder operator, and mill supervisor demanded a level of training previously unnecessary for the small-scale logging operations of the 1880s. Sometimes residents reacted negatively to the behavior of the lumber companies, as when the Norwood Lumber Company of Forney Creek was nearly blown up in 1915 by "persons unknown" who planted dynamite under the lumber camp clubhouse and under the house of the head salesman.[43]

The efficiency of clear-cutting came with a price. Poorly maintained machines in close contact with piles of brush left over from the cutting process frequently caused fires that destroyed plant life and private property and delayed logging operations.[44] Moreover, such indiscriminate cutting did not allow adequate time or leave sufficient resources for regrowth. By the mid-1920s, much of the quality timber had been cut along the right bank of the Little Tennessee, and logging companies had already begun to disappear from the economic picture. Ritter ceased large-scale operations at Proctor in 1924, and Norwood did so the following year.[45] Bemis Lumber Company, a latecomer to the Yellow Creek area along the south shore of the Little Tennessee, was recruited during this period through the efforts of R. Bruce Slaughter, a lifelong Republican who had served Robbinsville as mayor, register of deeds, county accountant and treasurer, and general community booster. Although it did operate its own railroad, the Graham County Railroad, Bemis generally ran on a smaller scale than the earlier operations, and would continue to function into the 1980s, frequently as the county's only industrial employer.[46] Throughout the twentieth century, residents also continued to cut pulpwood on private tracts and sell it for whatever cash it would bring in Bryson City as a supplement to their other income.

Southern Railway and its subsidiary, the Tallulah Falls Railroad, provided employment for a number of residents, as well as transportation for themselves and their products. Railroading played a significant part in the economy, and Southern was particularly vulnerable to charges of rate gouging, inefficient scheduling, and promoting the region's population decline. Southern fought back with traveling exhibits focusing on the railroad's promotion of scientific agriculture and by lauding the region's pure Anglo-Saxon labor stock. The railroad was eventually forced to expand service and stop offering "colonist rates," one-way special rates for people leaving the South. The relationship between community leaders and the Southern remained tense for years.[47]

The development of manufacturing in western North Carolina would have several obstacles to overcome. While railroad connections were finally available and good roads were forthcoming, access to electric power was still uneven at best. The area's many swift streams would serve as the focus for developers seeking to remedy this deficiency. Early attempts to develop western North Carolina's vast hydroelectric potential focused on small-scale projects. The Toxaway Power Company and Nantahala Power and Light Company each built small dams to serve residential and small business customers. Local newspapers urged the development of these resources on a larger scale. On January 29, 1915, the *Jackson County Journal* concluded: "We of this section have very naturally fallen into the habit of developing [scenic resources] to the partial exclusion of others that are equally, if not more, important. . . . It is in harnessing the never failing and everabounding supply of power that flows ceaselessly down the mountainsides and through the valleys, and turning with it the busy wheels of industry . . . that our towns are to become industrial centers."

The *Jackson County Journal* foresaw problems with hydroelectric power as a strategy for economic development. On June 29, 1923, the editor objected to a proposed dam on the French Broad River, saying that other streams had greater potential for developing hydropower, and this dam would flood the best farmland in western North Carolina. Similarly, on November 2, 1923, the *Journal* expressed reservations regarding a proposed hydroelectric development on the Hiwassee River, this time arguing that the electric power would be used to benefit Tennesseeans, while North Carolinians would bear the cost by sacrificing their best farmland.

More difficult to overcome than the technical obstacles would be the localism exemplified by this position. Just as they had competed for road funds and had jealously guarded local trade against any attempt to connect to larger markets, some community boosters would resist any attempt to integrate resources they considered uniquely theirs into any sort of larger regional system. As the irremediable damage wrought by the lumber companies became more apparent, some became even more protective of local privilege. But industrial growth of a more permanent nature would depend upon attracting the attention of a large corporate entity willing to invest in long-term development of the entire region. To many local observers, Alcoa appeared to be just such a company.

The cost of electricity is a major factor in the cost of manufacturing aluminum. Locating an aluminum plant near a major metropolitan area would raise the cost of that area's electric power substantially. So in the absence of a statutory rate ceiling, large-scale aluminum production must take place where there is little competition for the available electric power. In the minds of Alcoa founder Charles Martin Hall and his compatriots, the natural answer to the problem was to locate new facilities near sources of undeveloped hydroelectric power and control the development of that power. Beginning in 1910, the company bought up large tracts of land along the Little Tennessee from Maryville upstream as far as Bryson City. The Bryson City law firm of Black and Whitaker served the company on retainer, representing its interests in six western counties and in many instances persuading area residents to sell their land to the company for the good of the region. Alcoa management viewed the Little Tennessee as a superlative site for the development of hydroelectric power, which the company would then use to produce its aluminum.

By 1928 the company had completed Cheoah and Santeetlah dams in Graham County. But the real prize site would be upstream at Fontana, where the company had made plans for massive hydroelectric development. A system of two smaller dams was initially planned, and it was this system that Bryson City Good Roads advocates apparently considered in proposing the construction of State Highway 288. But a 400-foot-high dam that would flood the upper Little Tennessee almost to the Bryson City limits would provide more power potential at a time when the demand for aluminum products was growing rapidly. Such a dam would wipe out entire communities at Bushnell, Almond, and Judson, but would also facilitate expansion, which in turn would provide jobs for many hundreds of workers at Alcoa's new plant near Maryville, Tennessee.[48]

Despite the hopes of many area residents that Alcoa would bring large-scale industry to the area, the *Jackson County Journal*'s warnings about the development of the Hiwassee River were equally applicable to the lower Little Tennessee. The number of North Carolinians Alcoa employed in the upper Little Tennessee was negligible after the construction phase of these projects, as most of the long-term jobs created were located at Alcoa's plants at Calderwood and Maryville, Tennessee, far enough away to make daily commuting difficult. While Alcoa publicized tentative plans for a smelter at Andrews, North Carolina, during the 1930s, the proposed plant never materialized.

Whether they lived in communities or in isolated coves, residents of the Little Tennessee area looked to outside interests such as Alcoa or Ritter for employment whenever practical, because they were sufficiently acquainted with hard times to expect them at any time. Additional cash could purchase improvements for the farms of Almond and Judson, or roofing materials or a radio for the nonfarm households of Bushnell or Proctor, or a squirrel rifle for the cove-dwellers of Noland Creek. When outside employment was in short supply, they simply got by on the products of the garden, with a few eggs and perhaps a foraging hog or two providing the winter's "savings account."

In this environment, the Great Depression, which forced much of the rest of the nation into economic hardship, represented nothing more than another set of hard times. In the words of one commentator, for most of the South "things just sagged a little more than usual" during the Depression.[49] Nonetheless, the period from 1926 to 1940 marks a turning point for the upper Little Tennessee, because it replaced an economic structure based upon the extraction of minerals and lumber was replaced with another that depended on different sources of income. The timber and mining companies had tied wage earners to the national market for raw materials and ultimately to the manufacturing sector of the national economy. That sector's near collapse in the Great Depression helped hurry a transformation already in the making. If anything, the Little Tennessee's residents were probably more hopeful than much of the rest of the nation, as the creation of the Great Smoky Mountains National Park encouraged hopes for a new savior, tourism, whose arrival was imminent. But the transition would be far from painless.

3

A Second Niagara Falls

By the early 1920s it was obvious to most observers that the logging boom could not go on forever. Mining, while potentially more lucrative, would require sustained market demand for copper in an uncertain manufacturing sector. Railroading depended upon the two extractive industries for its profitability; passenger service was a very small source of side revenue. In the absence of timber, mining, and railroading, what other options remained for the economic aspirations of the area's residents? Their salvation would require a steady source of cash from outside the region. Some pinned all their hopes on the sale of the region as a tourist attraction, while others placed more emphasis on attracting industries that would stay than on weekend visitors who would drop a few dollars. The quest for tourist dollars would eventually shape the region's development by severely limiting industrial development. Furthermore, the method boosters chose for attracting tourists—the formation of a national park—would set a precedent for dependence on the federal government that would hamstring the region's quest for economic self-determination after World War II.

Tourism first gained a substantial role in western North Carolina with the arrival of the railroad in Asheville in 1881. Asheville's population increased tenfold between 1880 and 1890. The area around Asheville drew wealthy tourists attracted to its mineral springs, its healthy and cool (by southern standards) climate, and its beautiful scenery. Some of these were industrialists who saw opportunity in the area's natural resources—its forests, its streams, and its mines—and returned to take advantage of them.

The arrival of the affordable automobile and the Good Roads Movement brought a broader base of potential tourists who would seek out a wider variety of attractions. Many of these came seeking a week of refuge from the urban environments in which they lived and worked. Harnessing the broadly distributed wealth of these new tourists would prove to be an important goal for local boosters in scenery-rich western North Carolina.

The attempt to create a national park in the Smoky Mountains would come from an alliance between two distinct groups. The first consisted mostly of local boosters who saw a mixture of economic opportunity and regional pride in the establishment of a national park—or a national forest, for that matter. This group included various Asheville and Knoxville associations and several local chambers of commerce, and for the most part these people continued to see tourism as part of a broader plan for developing the region's economy. The second group consisted of mostly nonlocal preservation advocates who saw the area as one of the last vestiges of unspoiled countryside and intended to keep it that way. These included members of the Wilderness Society, the Isaak Walton League, and various hiking and fishing clubs. Advocates in the first category tended to see industrialists as potential allies; those in the second tended to see those who would cut the trees, exploit the mineral resources, and build dams as dangerous enemies of the land itself. Both groups saw something special in the glorious scenery throughout the Smoky Mountains, but they had difficulty agreeing upon how best to use the resource it represented. The uneasy alliance between the two disparate sets of advocates would determine not only whether a park would exist but also what sort of park it would be.

Horace Kephart, the intoxicating wordsmith and often intoxicated mythmaker who became a local celebrity, would serve as a bridge between the two until his death in 1930.[1] Kephart's writings served to energize the preservationists across the nation in support of the park movement, while his fundraising activities and his political maneuvers served to strengthen the role of the local boosters. His ability to describe the natural world meticulously appealed to the wilderness advocates, while his tendency to downplay the effects of recent economic changes on the area's population allowed boosters to sell the park movement as a regional improvement project. The twin blows of the arrival of the Great Depression and the loss of Kephart as an advocate would force the park movement into greater dependence on outside assistance, especially from the federal government and the Rockefeller Foundation. That dependence, in turn, would sharply curtail the park's responsiveness to local concerns.

The boosters, on the other hand, were concerned almost exclusively with local matters, to the exclusion of any sense of regional or national issues. The booster mentality that had pervaded the upper Little Tennessee when logging and mining were at their peak viewed economic development as an end in itself. That mind-set was largely independent of the specific industry being sought by boosters in any given community. If one particular enterprise did not satisfy the needs of the business community, another would be swiftly recruited to augment or replace it.[2] While logging remained an important economic force in the upper Little Tennessee throughout most of the 1920s, boosters were on the lookout for continued opportunities for development. Civic leaders were already seeking the next economic boom before the present one had run its course.[3] The already established tourist economy, suitably broadened by the combination of good roads, inexpensive automobiles, and careful local promotion, would provide a welcome influx of outside cash. It would also draw the attention of outsiders to the other resources available in the area, especially the hydroelectric potential of the Little Tennessee River. As road construction made the area more accessible to tourists, local boosters began to seek a way to capitalize on the remarkable mountain scenery before logging destroyed it completely. Yet they also did not wish to alienate the extractive industries, which had brought cash into the area.

The idea of a national park somewhere in the southern Appalachian Mountains received its first recorded expression in an obscure 1885 presentation before the American Academy of Medicine. Dr. Henry O. Marcy of Boston argued that the area's "pure air, water and climate hold out . . . a hopeful helpfulness to invalids from every land. The wise legislator, seeking far-reaching results, would do well to consider the advisability of securing, under state control, a large reservation of the higher ranges as a park. . . . Like the peaks and glaciers of Switzerland, its sanitary advantages would be of value incalculable to millions yet unborn."[4] Marcy's plea came to a fledgling organization eager to explore the potential of environment as a factor in disease but not yet equipped to lobby Congress for such an esoteric proposal.

A few years after Marcy's admonition to "wise legislators," the North Carolina General Assembly passed a resolution calling upon the state's representatives in Congress to use their influence to secure the creation of a national park somewhere in western North Carolina. Again, scientific considerations—interest in the potential of the area's clear water, cool climate, and diverse plant life—helped to stimulate discussion of the issue. While a resolution was introduced into the U.S. House of Representatives in 1893 calling for such a park, nothing came of it.[5]

Private investors were quicker to recognize the profit available from scenic views. One developer by the name of Kelsey founded the resort town of Highlands, in Macon County near the source of the Little Tennessee; the same man was responsible for opening the privately owned Yonahlossee Road between Blowing Rock and Linville. Other investors poured money into the western North Carolina communities of Waynesville, Hendersonville, and Asheville, the latter with spectacular results. George Vanderbilt, grandson of Commodore Cornelius Vanderbilt, was impressed by what he saw in the area around Asheville and purchased 228 square miles of it—an area approximately one-fifth the size of the state of Rhode Island. Vanderbilt then hired Frederick Law Olmsted, the nation's premier landscape architect, to "make a park of it." Olmsted instead built a forest preserve, and Vanderbilt's close friend Richard Morris Hunt constructed the Biltmore Estate, the closest thing to a true medieval manor that late nineteenth-century America could boast.[6]

As much as Vanderbilt may have wanted to "make a park" from his holdings, the Biltmore Estate was fundamentally a private enterprise intended for his own enjoyment and not that of the public. The first concerted effort to promote the founding of a national park came from three Asheville residents: Dr. Chase Ambler, recently arrived from Ohio, Judge William R. Day, and magazine publisher A. H. McQuilkin. The three persuaded the Asheville Board of Trade to form a committee to promote the idea of such a park. The committee's first rally, in November 1899, featured a number of notables, including Senator Marion Butler, Congressman W. T. Crawford, Locke Craig, who later became the "Good Roads Governor," industrialist Moses Cone, and railroad agent M. V. Richards of the Southern Railway. The press, too, was well represented, as editors Josephus Daniels of Raleigh, Charles A. Webb of Asheville, Narciso Gonzales of Columbia, South Carolina, and Pleasant Stovall of Savannah, Georgia, appeared at the gathering.[7]

Clearly, judging from the guest list, the matter was of regional, rather than purely local, importance. Indeed, many of the speeches reflected concern that the South had been short-changed when the federal government had established national parks. Craig expressed the sentiment that the establishment of such a park would go a long way in the symbolic healing of lingering sectional divisions. As Paul Gaston noted in *The New South Creed,* "The announcement of the death of sectionalism in the South was present in virtually every discussion of the New South movement," and Craig's endorsement of the creation of a national park in the western part of the state is clearly no different.[8]

As a result of the meeting, sufficient interest was raised to support the creation of a separate permanent organization, the Appalachian National Park Association. George Powell, a retired Asheville businessman, became president, and Ambler was designated as secretary-treasurer. The ANPA immediately drafted a request that Congress consider establishing a park in the area, for reasons ranging from health to political entitlement; the memorial also suggested that the land could be easily acquired. Reflecting the group's commercial orientation as well as a fundamental misunderstanding of the difference between a national park and a national forest, the memorial suggested that substantial profits could be earned from maintaining the land as a forest preserve. This position was heavily backed by Asheville lawyer George "Bat" Smathers and by U.S. Chief Forester Gifford Pinchot, whose influence had helped to shape the Biltmore Estate as well. Other supporters of the notion of a forest preserve included Senators Jeter Pritchard and Marion Butler, as well as state forestry and geology officials.[9]

Although this early movement succeeded in placing several bills before Congress, no bill passed both houses as a result of the group's efforts. While the 1899 meeting had been well attended, raising funds to publicize the cause was a problem. Furthermore, the group's focus on raising these funds locally seems to have alienated those whose interests were broader in geographic scope. But the biggest obstacle to the group's success was the struggle between preservationists and conservationists, a struggle that mirrored a national battle taking place at the same time. Preservationists sought to maintain the area in a purely natural condition, as free as possible from any human influence. Conservation advocates, on the other hand, wanted to provide an opportunity for limited human use of the area's resources; their plans included recreation as well as carefully policed logging and mining activities.[10]

In the ANPA, the conservationists and their allies, the big lumber companies, won out. The group changed its name in 1901 to reflect its interest in creating what it termed a "forest reserve" from which resources could be harvested rather than a national park preserve from which they could not be harvested. By 1905, the renamed Appalachian Forest Reserve Association's leaders voted to disband, citing exhaustion and a lack of public support. The group then merged its membership rolls with those of the Appalachian Forestry Association, another pro-conservation group.[11]

Asheville's business community had provided much of the earliest impetus for the creation of a national park in the Smoky Mountains. The next step in promoting the idea would come from the Tennessee side of the mountains. Between 1910 and 1913, a movement in the Knoxville business community resulted in three expositions focusing their attention on conservation and intelligent use of the area's vast natural resources. These expositions, intended in part to demonstrate Knoxville's credentials as a "New South" city, also showcased the city's relatively conservative brand of progressive leadership in urban affairs, industry, and politics. By the end of the third and most aggressively promoted of these, the ambitiously named "National Conservation Exposition," thousands of residents of Knoxville and other urban centers of the Appalachian South had been exposed to the idea of a national park in the southern mountains, although the national audience that business leaders sought remained largely aloof.[12]

While Asheville and Knoxville boosters had cast their vote decidedly on the side of the utilitarian conservationists and appeared to give up on the idea of a national park, scenic preservation advocates across the United States continued their drive for national parks. After their disastrous 1912 loss of the Hetch Hetchy Valley in Yosemite National Park for the construction of a dam and reservoir to feed San Francisco, preservationists found it necessary to come up with new ways to plead their case at the national level. Utilitarian conservationists, of course, could always plead economic benefit; the preservationists needed an equally compelling reason to sway public opinion. Stephen Mather, a wealthy Chicago industrialist, complained loudly enough to the Department of the Interior to find himself designated assistant secretary in charge of national parks.[13]

Mather immediately pressed Congress to set up a separate bureau within the Department of the Interior whose job would be maintaining the national parks. Mather, by all accounts an energetic advocate, engaged New York journalist Robert Sterling Yard to promote the parks at every turn. Yard obliged as publicity director, placing articles on the beauty of the national parks in *National Geographic* and the *Saturday Evening Post,* among other widely read publications, to gain the interest and support of what he and Mather perceived as an elite market, though it would soon become less so. Yard's *National Parks Portfolio,* full of impressive photographs, was funded by railroad interests. It was distributed free of charge to each member of Congress and over a quarter million other interested citizens, many of whose appetites for adventure had been whetted by the local color writers of a generation earlier.[14]

The massive publicity drive paid off for preservationists with the creation in 1916 of the National Park Service, over the objections of the Department of Agriculture and its conservation-oriented Forest Service. The National Park Service's contribution to both publicizing and managing the national parks would play a large role in nearly quadrupling the number of visitors to national parks between 1916 and 1922. Motivated by a desire for both the public eye and the public dollar, local boosters and politicians throughout the nation found the idea of having a national park nearby a useful and highly attractive means of promoting their home region's distinctiveness, its potential, and its economic momentum.[15]

Southern politicians, never averse to promoting their region's fiscal interests, found the idea of a national park somewhere in the South very interesting. As the South elected the same leaders to national office again and again, the region gained important political clout within the congressional seniority system. Traditional southern suspicions concerning the federal government and the taking of private property for public use proved substantial obstacles to the park movement at the national level, but a rising tide of what George Brown Tindall labeled "business progressivism" and the potential economic benefits associated with tourism came to dominate the political agenda quickly in the South, as elsewhere in the nation.[16]

The political climate in North Carolina was especially receptive to the idea of what Governor Angus McLean called "administration characterized by efficiency, economy, and rational progress." McLean succeeded Cameron Morrison, whose advocacy of state spending for internal improvements had resulted in the creation of the state highway system in 1921, and while McLean's approach was somewhat more cautious than Morrison's, both fit well alongside Locke Craig within what Key called the "progressive plutocracy" of North Carolina politics. Tennessee, too, had its business progressives, notably its three-term governor, Austin Peay. Under the rule of the business progressives, both states dramatically increased spending for internal improvements; taxes rose dramatically as well. Business leaders, especially in medium and large towns, became accustomed to viewing a larger, more active state government as an integral part of the quest for economic growth and material progress.[17]

The focus on creating a national park in the Smoky Mountains gained urgency because of two related factors. Preservation advocates saw the damage wrought by the lumber companies as evidence that they would have to work quickly to save the last bit of virgin forest in the Smokies, while business progressives saw the creation of a park as a way of protecting the region against economic collapse when it became unprofitable to extract the remaining timber from the land. While preservationists and boosters both realized the need for quick action to create a national park, they would inevitably clash over how that park was to be developed and managed.

The preservationists depended from the start on mobilizing a national constituency through the efforts of the National Park Service. Yard, in particular, warned against the use of the National Park Service as a "pork barrel" to provide political favors, complaining that a flood of proposals for national parks had diluted the "standards" necessary for preserving "the noblest examples, painstakingly chosen." Yard was particularly concerned that political pressure for parks east of the Mississippi would result in the enshrinement of mediocre sites in the South.[18]

Mather responded to southern legislative pressure and Yard's criticism by forming a committee of observers from outside the southern states to evaluate proposed southern park sites. The panel included Congressman Henry Temple of Pennsylvania; Colonel Glenn Smith, a geological engineer; Major W. A. Welch; industrialist William C. Gregg; and Harlan P. Kelsey, a Massachusetts resident and a former president of the Appalachian Mountain Club whose father had founded the resort town of Highlands, just a few miles from the source of the Little Tennessee River. Both Temple and Kelsey were long-standing advocates of scenic preservation. Smith had been invited to join the group because of his knowledge of the area's topography, while Welch was chosen for his experience managing state parks. Welch also had extensive contacts with New York philanthropists, which Secretary of the Interior Hubert Work suspected might be useful. Gregg was a longtime supporter of the national park movement, but he had little specific experience to offer. The committee, christened the Southern Appalachian National Park Committee, immediately set to work developing a set of criteria for evaluating potential sites: altitude, natural boundaries, special topographic features, biological diversity, extent of economic development, and public support. At the committee's first meeting, Kelsey distributed copies of Kephart's *Our Southern Highlanders* to the other members, claiming that it contained "the truest description of this area available," thus helping to promote an anachronistic view of the area's population that would skew the site selection process in favor of the Great Smokies.[19]

Meanwhile, residents of various scenic locales throughout the southern Appalachians were busily promoting their areas to Mather and the committee. Residents of Knoxville again began to agitate for something to be done with the Smokies. W. P. Davis, who served on the board of directors of both the chamber of commerce and the local automobile club, pushed hard, forming the Smoky Mountain Conservation Association in 1924. While the chamber of commerce, led by Davis and local businessman David Chapman, worked to convince local businesspeople of the economic benefits of the park, Davis and Wiley Brownlee, a Gatlinburg real estate developer, embarked on a campaign to convince the National Park

Service of the scenic superiority of their chosen site. There was no disguising the fact that lumber companies had cut over much of the Smokies, so the campaign carefully publicized the scenic value of the areas that had not been logged.[20]

Davis, Brownlee, and Chapman led a trip into the Smokies in May 1924, partly to inspect it for themselves and partly to "build a liaison with like minded individuals in Bryson City." The group met with a delegation from Bryson City led by Kephart, Kelly Bennett, who was then Bryson City's mayor, and S. E. Varner, chairman of the Swain County Commission. Kephart's high profile as a nationally recognized author—and his overly dramatic description of a region penetrated by "only a few herdsmen, hunters, lumbermen and surveyors"—helped gain the attention of the *New York Times,* which quoted *Our Southern Highlanders* in a July 1924 editorial favoring the Smokies as a national park site.[21]

Despite the favorable publicity, park advocates—both boosters and preservationists—still faced substantial opposition. In particular, though they had extracted a tremendous number of board-feet, the lumber companies were not yet finished with the area in 1925. Seeking to maintain a permanent role for logging in the region, the Western North Carolina Lumber and Timber Association went on record in July 1925 with a resolution opposing what it termed the "agitation" to create a national park in the Smoky Mountains. The group's opposition focused on the importance of the timber lands to the economy of the region and, of course, to the continued operations of member companies. The most vocal opponent was Champion Fibre Company, the area's largest landowner, which had engaged in some long-term reforestation experiments on its western North Carolina holdings. Employees of the U.S. Forest Service also apparently began spreading rumors among residents that the National Park Service would condemn their homes and would not pay enough to cover their relocation costs.[22]

Such complaints, coupled with lukewarm public support in North Carolina, spurred threats from the Southern Appalachian National Park Commission to redraw the boundaries so that the proposed park would lie entirely or mostly within the state of Tennessee, which had demonstrated greater public enthusiasm. The commission complained that "the holdings of two or three of the largest timber corporations are difficult to acquire as virgin areas" and that if they "are not secured until after the timber is cut off they will not be fit for a national park for recreational use." The threat of losing the national park altogether spurred Asheville journalist Charles Webb to action. Webb, copublisher of the *Asheville*

Citizen, formally endorsed the Smokies park and complained publicly that area residents would find themselves out in the cold if they did not begin to work actively for the park. Webb also pledged that his paper would buy 100 acres of land for the park. Other journalists recruited Kephart to write a series of articles on the Smokies as a national park, and the articles were widely reprinted. Most crucially of all, the area attracted national figures with influence. Arno Cammerer, the assistant director of the National Park Service, visited the proposed site and gave it a very public endorsement, as did Robert Sterling Yard, who had earlier criticized the site as chosen for political rather than scenic reasons. W. P. Davis's plan for selectively showcasing the Smokies had worked; after climbing remote Mount LeConte and Gregory Bald and touring the farming community of Cades Cove, Cammerer told Park Service director Stephen Mather that "most of the area is absolute virgin wilderness."[23]

In the search for sufficient funds to organize a national park, boosters found it very difficult to attract donors outside their own region. A booklet written by Kephart with photographs by his friend George Masa proved to be a useful tool, as did a similar book put out by Tennessee's Great Smoky Mountains Conservation Association. The Knoxville Chamber of Commerce had promised to lobby the city government to pay for up to one-third of the cost of acquiring the Little River Lumber Company's land in Blount County, but the city proved reluctant. Chambers of commerce in Asheville and Knoxville organized motorcades for publicity, with the Knoxville group touring small towns throughout the area and promising great dividends if the park became a reality. Logging companies fought back with arguments questioning whether tourism was a sound basis on which to build an economy, but they were trumped by the *Asheville Citizen*'s publication of before-and-after pictures of logged areas. The *Citizen* also alleged that the aggressive logging had resulted in half a million cords of cut pulpwood unsold and rotting in Swain County lumberyards. Most devastating was the claim by the *Knoxville Journal* that further logging would result in massive erosion and flooding that would destroy the region's hydroelectric potential, a particularly stinging charge in light of one park advocate's boast that protecting the Smokies as a national park would help preserve those sites and turn the area into an American Ruhr.[24]

Unlike national parks created from public lands in the West, the eastern parks would be culled from lands already in private hands. There was no federal money available for purchasing such large blocks of land, so park advocates had to raise funds for land acquisition from private sources.

Local fundraising campaigns were never more successful than in diminutive Bryson City. In the first day of the campaign alone, Bryson City's boosters raised over $25,000 from over 200 citizens—in a town with a population of less than 1,600 inhabitants. It would later raise another $22,500. Asheville, with twenty-five times the population, could raise only five times as much money in three weeks. Knoxville banks contributed $12,000 of the total $215,000 the city raised in the first phase of its campaign; boosters even urged school children to dip into their piggy banks. Asheville newspapers kept the campaign very well publicized, with an *Asheville Citizen* editorial promising that a national park would "operate as splendidly and as incredibly as a modern combination of Aladdin's Wonderful Lamp, the touch of Midas, the Magic Urn and the weaving of straw into gold by Rumpelstiltskin."[25]

Haywood County boosters found themselves in a very difficult spot when attempting to kick off their fund drive. Lumber company employees packed the meeting hall and transformed the rally into a fiasco. The chief forester for the Champion Fibre Company fiercely denounced the park movement. A company lawyer for Suncrest Lumber then took on the pro-tourism argument, presenting the rather unorthodox view that Adam and Eve were doomed by too much access to entertainment: "This mad age of pleasure and recreation is carrying us to hell as fast as possible." Damnation evidently slowed the fundraising effort momentarily; Haywood County park advocates reached their $30,000 goal a few weeks behind schedule.[26]

In part through Kephart's florid prose and in part through the area's genuine natural beauty, boosters had succeeded in attracting the attention of preservationists. But the boosters were inherently more concerned than the preservationists with economic matters. Logging companies had clear-cut large areas in Graham, Swain, Jackson, and Haywood Counties, as well as in the adjacent counties of Blount, Sevier, and Cocke in Tennessee, leaving little of value behind in the most accessible and most populated areas. The pace at which Ritter and other lumber companies had worked to supply the demand during World War I meant that there simply was not much good timber left.[27] A few small sawmills would continue to operate in the area, but these could provide small incomes for their owner-operators and little for anyone else. Those living on wooded land would still cut pines for pulpwood, much as they might gather mushrooms or berries for sale, but there was not much hardwood left for lumber.

In this atmosphere, with the pull of the tourist dollar and the push of the coming economic uncertainty both at work, a competition evolved quickly between the Smokies and the Grandfather Mountain/Linville Gorge area. Unlike the Smokies, Linville Gorge was more convenient to the central and eastern part of the state, and the powerful Senator Furnifold M. Simmons supported it over the Smokies. Joseph Hyde Pratt, a geologist and the president of a booster group called Western Carolina, Inc., also supported the Linville Gorge site, as did the *Asheville Citizen*. Of the members of the Southern Appalachian National Park Committee, Harlan Kelsey was most familiar with western North Carolina, and he had ties to both Linville Gorge and Macon County. Kelsey scrupulously attempted to avoid any appearance of local favoritism and urged park boosters to do the same, lest the entire park idea be seen as a pork barrel project.[28]

Facing tremendous interstate competition for the attention a national park would bring, the General Assembly appointed a commission to present the state's claims to scenic greatness. The commission included a number of business progressives of stature, as well as several representatives from the area immediately around Linville. The two Ashevillians on the commission were neutral, leaving only J. H. Dillard of Murphy as a Smokies partisan. The commission proposed a 1,000-square-mile national park that would connect practically all of the proposed sites, from Grandfather Mountain and Blowing Rock in the north, through the Smokies, to the Pisgah Forest in the south.[29]

After visiting twenty sites in North Carolina and a large number in other states, the Southern Appalachian National Park Committee reported quite favorably on the scenic virtues and biodiversity of the Smokies, but concluded that the area's ruggedness and altitude would make it difficult to develop for tourists. The committee also complained that the area's excessive rainfall might limit its appeal as a recreation center. Instead, the committee decided to recommend a site in Virginia's Blue Ridge Mountains supported by the powerful Byrd machine. Recognizing that the final decision would be made in Congress, North Carolina and Tennessee congressional delegations sprang into action, applying pressure wherever possible to ensure that the Smokies would be included in any national park to be established in the South.[30]

Some politicians, notably Congressman Zebulon B. Weaver, feared that the Smokies site, while undoubtedly beautiful, would compromise the value of industrial plans already in the works for the area. In particular, Weaver was swayed by Sen. Furnifold M. Simmons's argument that the park would disrupt plans for important hydroelectric developments already planned by Alcoa. Kephart lobbied Weaver, who hailed from Asheville, encouraging him to break with the Simmons machine and support the Smokies site. Kephart approached Weaver's fears on multiple fronts: first, he claimed that "there is no water power site of any consequence in the territory under consideration," and second, he challenged Weaver to "ask the water-power people themselves" if they would prefer continued clear-cutting with its attendant erosion problems rather than a park with a stable soil base. Kephart then shifted gears to appeal to Weaver's pragmatic side, reminding him that "the climate and the scenery . . . attracted wealthy outsiders. . . . There is the great commercial asset of this country." Kephart concluded his effort by urging Weaver to consider "the rise of Asheville real estate, and its future, then turn and consider what our mountain land is worth when the timber is all cut off." Kephart's lobbying, the pressure from the North Carolina and Tennessee congressional delegations, and the last-minute addition of Kentucky's Mammoth Cave area into the proposal helped garner sufficient votes to allow the park movement to proceed. The proposal to draw boundaries for all three parks—the Great Smokies, Mammoth Cave, and the Shenandoah National Park—passed in early 1925.[31]

National Park Service associate director Arno Cammerer drew the boundaries for the Great Smoky Mountains National Park, leaning heavily on the advice of Knoxville civil engineer Frank Maloney. Horace Kephart, Kelly Bennett, and Harlan Kelsey also worked closely with Cammerer to produce what became known as the "Cammerer line," an aggressively drawn boundary that enclosed some 704,000 acres in six counties—three in North Carolina and three in Tennessee.[32]

Park boosters knew that actually acquiring the needed land would still depend upon their ability to continue to raise funds. Land speculators forced organizers to pay unexpectedly high prices for key tracts. Legal costs associated with using the power of eminent domain were higher than expected, too. Lumber companies that owned many large tracts fought condemnation at every possible opportunity, hoping that the park boosters would simply run out of resources to continue.

Further compounding the problems facing the boosters, the money pledged by individuals was not coming in. While businesspeople in the upper Little Tennessee certainly knew that logging would not sustain the region's economy permanently, the arrival of the Great Depression was not something park boosters had anticipated. They had depended upon pledged donations from both big businesses and individuals. Many donors, unemployed or otherwise financially distressed, proved unable to meet their pledges. Bank failures, too, created problems for the movement.

The election of Franklin D. Roosevelt as president helped salvage the movement, though, as his administration allocated over $1.5 million to assist the groups with land purchases already planned. Another $5 million came from the Rockefeller Fund, with the proviso that the park boundary be redrawn so that the Rockefeller family could claim that they had provided fully half the necessary funds for the purchase of land for the park. Among the lands thus removed from the park boundary were the riparian properties owned by Alcoa along the Little Tennessee, most of the Eagle Creek and Hazel Creek watersheds, and the properties of the Ritter Lumber Company and the North Carolina Exploration Company—including the towns of Proctor, Bushnell, and Fontana. In contrast to the largely uncut holdings of Champion Fibre Company in what Carlos Campbell called "the very heart of the park," the areas along the Little Tennessee—priced out of the range of the park boosters—were "expendable" because they had been cut over.[33]

Land acquisition followed a rather haphazard policy. Just as the boundaries themselves were in flux, park boosters had not developed a clear sense of what sort of park they intended to create. Many still envisioned a sort of living forest preserve in which residents would continue to live in their own homes within the park, and both boosters and National Park Service officials made promises to that effect. But residents who were initially viewed as a scenic asset and invited to lease their former lands because of their "quaint mountain ways" became a problem when they insisted on continuing to fish, hunt, and grow crops on what they still saw as their land. Soon they were joined by others, opportunists taking advantage of the lack of effective enforcement of park regulations.[34]

In 1938 the National Park Service commissioned a team of consultants to report on ways to present the National Park Service's vision of mountain culture, a vision which did not include land speculators, lumber companies, or the entrepreneurial spirit in any form. The committee disapproved of the relatively modern reality of life in the Smokies and insisted on the removal of all structures and artifacts constructed after 1890. They emphasized live demonstrations of the "pioneer lifestyle" and even recommended that former residents be invited to remain in the park area and "live as their ancestors did." According to this plan, the National Park Service would be placed in the dubious position of removing contemporary frame dwellings and replacing them with log cabins, disposing of all farm tractors, and dismantling any structures deemed "inappropriate" for the intended audience. This plan was never enacted, though a collection of "mountain heritage" artifacts was assembled by the National Park Service for a museum project which, sixty years later, had not come to fruition.[35]

Eventually, the notion of a living history museum in the park was abandoned and practically all residents were ordered to evacuate. However, a group of resort cabins located in the Elkmont area received a reprieve, and the National Park Service granted their wealthy owners lifetime leases while evicting many whose only dwelling was within the park boundary.[36]

The isolation of the mountain residents, never as pure as it was portrayed by outsiders, became a selling point for the park itself. As Dan Pierce has pointed out, "The portrait of southern Appalachian life presented by Horace Kephart in *Our Southern Highlanders* played an especially powerful role in forming the image of the mountain people among his fellow park boosters. Kephart saw the park bringing tremendous benefits to a mountain people who had previously been subject to 'a law of nature that dooms an isolated and impoverished people to deterioration.' With the coming of the park 'the highlander, at last, is to be caught up in the current of human progress.'"[37]

Caught up in the current of human progress, yes, but not in the way Kephart envisioned it, and not for the first time, either. These "highlanders," many of whom had spent far more time working in logging camps for wages than hunting bears or farming, would seize upon the opportunities offered by tourism while chafing at the changes brought by the coming of the park.

Among other families, the locally famous Walker sisters refused to move out and continued to live a "traditional lifestyle" in their home at Little Greenbrier. The National Park Service granted them a lifetime lease on their land and put up signs directing visitors to the Walker homestead, where they would see "authentic mountain culture" in action. While Louisa Walker wrote and sold poems decrying the displacement of the area's families for the preservation of the "wolf lion and the bear," her sisters peddled souvenirs to the veritable onslaught of tourists who came to see "real mountaineers." The volume of visitors was so great that in the 1950s the aging sisters asked the National Park Service to stop sending tourists their way.[38]

Other residents of the park area followed the lead of outside investors. Jim Stikeleather, the Asheville developer who had served as both highway commissioner and park booster, bought up land on Hazel Creek and built cabins, too. Young Bryson City businessman Henry Truett, who later served as clerk of court, also set up operations to serve the desires of tourists. Even John Oliver, the Cades Cove farmer who had led community resistance to land acquisition for the park, set up a few cabins on his property for tourists.[39]

Just as individuals who lived in the area used whatever resources were available to them in order to take advantage of the new tourist influx, Western North Carolina's towns competed fiercely with one another for tourist attention and revenues. The incorporated town closest to the park's boundary was Bryson City, with a population of approximately 1,600. The *Bryson City Times* trumpeted the town's claim in words that seem to echo the Manifest Destiny rhetoric of a century earlier:

> We understand that Waynesville is now calling herself the Gateway to the Great Smoky Mountains National Park. The park is certainly not wanting at all for gateways, and is beautifully blessed with such. . . . If Asheville and Waynesville are the Gateway to the Park, Bryson City is bound to be the ENTRANCE. Why the row about the GATEWAY? The park is in a fixed position, so are the towns near it. . . . We are not fighting for the Gateway to the Park. We know that what Nature bestowed upon us cannot be taken away, regardless of the wrangle. While others are calling themselves the GATEWAY, we sit back and listen for we realize that WE are the only Natural Gateway, in other words, we are the ENTRANCE.[40]

Community leaders took to the airwaves to perform the essential service of "boosting" the town's image and promoting its virtues. Kelly Bennett, Bryson City's tireless booster, proclaimed over Asheville's WWNC radio: "Bryson City is fast becoming a tourist resort. . . . There are charming drives . . . good fishing, and the primeval forest of the Smokies comes within six miles of the town. . . . [When Alcoa's 400-foot Fontana dam is built] it will be a second Niagara Falls."[41]

Larger towns such as Waynesville (population 2,940 in 1940) and Asheville (51,310) could provide more amenities for tourists but were located much farther from the park. While the major highways passed through mile after mile of dramatic and beautiful scenery, they connected the population centers to each other and not to the park area. While there was certainly much else to see in western North Carolina besides the park, the routes left Bryson City out in the cold. Bryson City's only claim to tourism was its proximity to the park's boundary, and the portion of the park most easily reached from Bryson City was still cutover land, hardly the stuff of which travel writers wax enthusiastic. Highway access to the park was poor on the North Carolina side, with Swain County having only gotten its first paved federal highway in 1927. Additionally, the highways that did exist in the park area were in danger of abandonment because they were inadequate for the projected traffic. Furthermore, Swain County suffered from a large bonded debt for the roads it had built, and the national park removed much good land from the tax rolls. With 57.7 percent of its land left nontaxable because of the park, the Cherokee reservation, and the Nantahala National Forest, the county was unable to provide the resources to develop its own infrastructure. Thus constrained, community leaders sought relief from the state and the federal government.[42]

Of course, Swain County was not the only area petitioning the federal government for help in developing the scenic resources of western North Carolina. Precious federal highway funds provided a source of conflict, just as they provided a potential for growth. One community paper chastised Asheville for its aggressive bid to become a regional hub, describing that city's attempt to manipulate the routing of U.S. 25-W as "exactly [the attitude] of a spoilt child." There was only so much highway access to go around, and Asheville was demanding more than its fair share.[43]

The more prescient community boosters recognized the destructive effect of the competition. An editorial in the Waynesville *Mountaineer* advised: "It seems that if the different cities and towns of Western North Carolina would talk less about which one of them is the gateway to the Great Smoky Mountains National Park and use that same energy in getting tourists to the park, it would benefit all concerned considerably more."[44]

The competition among towns for the title of "Gateway to the Smokies" prevented any coordinated development effort, leaving the region ill-prepared to benefit from the anticipated influx of tourist dollars. A lack of planning compounded the negative effects of competition. One small-town newspaper editor complained that his fellow residents were unable even to maintain a functioning chamber of commerce to promote the town's possibilities as a tourist center. He wrote: "Haven't we any aspirations to ever progress and become any more than a little town, gaining nothing, and aspiring to nothing? The main thing as we see it, is that the majority of the county have absolutely no foresight. They cannot seem to visualize the fact that we have right here within our midst one of the greatest opportunities ever had before [namely, the park]."[45]

Many within the towns did in fact aspire to "better things." Self-styled progressive editors in Franklin, Sylva, Waynesville, and Bryson City hailed tourism as a means of improving the region's economic position. But some saw that tourism alone would not provide the base for economic development. Hydropower was the key to industrialization. Tourism would pave the way for it by making the area more accessible and popular with those who could industrialize it.[46]

Considering the potential of the region as both an industrial site and a tourist mecca, the Great Depression was not all gloomy for western North Carolina. In certain segments of western North Carolina society, especially the more "progressive" middle class of the towns, the Great Depression was actually a time of great hope for improvement. The growing utilization of hydroelectric power, along with new roads that would draw tourists into the Great Smoky Mountains, gave many the impression that western North Carolina would soon enter its golden age.

The boosters of Bryson City expressed perpetual optimism about the park's potential. In 1932, the *Bryson City Times* celebrated the arrival of over 150,000 visitors within the park's boundary, and in November 1932 Kelly Bennett proclaimed that Bryson City was "fast becoming a tourist resort."[47]

New roads into the park were widely expected to improve the park's prospects even more, though Bennett worried in 1937 that giving the National Park Service responsibility for those roads would lead to restrictions on commercial traffic that would harm the region's economy. Bryson City also attempted to take advantage of the reluctance of the Cherokee to cooperate with the construction of the new Blue Ridge Parkway; the editor of the *Times* asked the National Park Service to reroute the parkway up Deep Creek to Bryson City, since the Cherokees apparently were not willing to work with the proposed restrictions on the road's use. The notion that the Eastern Band's reasons for refusing to cooperate might be legitimate, and that they might also apply to Bryson City, apparently was never publicly expressed by whites.[48]

Apparently the area was ill-prepared for the influx of tourists. Swain County was swamped by the Independence Day traffic in 1938. The tone of the report in the local newspaper sounds almost as though the area had repelled an invasion: "They came by the thousands but hundreds could find no place to stay. . . . Many cars with foreign state tags rolling into this section on Saturday and by Sunday night the saturation point had been passed. Many tourists could not find places to stay Sunday night. It is said that hundreds were turned away in Bryson City."[49]

Was the change the park brought welcome? Margaret Brown has argued that "although newspaper articles and even scholarly studies claimed that the mountain people happily left the Smokies for better agricultural

Table 1. Percentage of All Households Equipped with Selected Amenities, 1940

Amenities	Swain	Graham	N.C.	U.S.
Electric lighting	19.2	16.2	54.4	78.7
Running water	22.1	18.1	39.1	69.9
Indoor toilet	14.8	12.0	30.3	59.7
Private bath	14.3	11.7	24.6	56.2
Mech. refrigerator*	9.2	9.0	28.2	44.1
Radio*	38.5	41.7	61.8	82.8
Central heating*	2.3	0.6	7.8	42.0

Note: Data from North Carolina State Planning Board, *North Carolina Basic County Data* (Raleigh: State Planning Board, 1946), vols. 1 and 2. All categories, definitions, and bases are taken from these two volumes. Items denoted by an asterisk (*) are based upon the number of occupied dwellings; all others are based upon the total number of dwellings, occupied and otherwise.

lands, this was not the reality for most."[50] Yet the fact that over 200 Bryson City residents contributed an average of $125 each during the initial drive to raise funds for the park compels one to examine Brown's facile generalization more closely. Opposition to the Blue Ridge Parkway sometimes took the form of resisting initial buyout offers, refusing to talk to park officials, and continuing to engage in routine activities despite National Park Service protests. Such activities were prevalent among those living within the park boundary as well, and it seems reasonable to conclude that at least some (though not necessarily all) such activity was a sign of resistance to the idea of the park, while other such activities might be described more accurately as resistance to specific National Park Service policies such as restrictions on hunting, fishing, and commercial vehicle traffic.[51]

So while Bryson City residents had overwhelmingly supported the creation of the park, the town was not necessarily representative of the sentiments of the county as a whole. Certainly there was substantial support for the park in Bryson City, which as the nearest substantial town to the park boundary stood to benefit more from its establishment than did residents of the smaller villages within the park. But many residents of the smaller communities apparently resisted National Park Service authority.

Resistance may have appealed to those who saw the intrusion of the park as the act of outsiders. But even those who resisted had few resources with which to survive without the economic stimulus that tourists would provide. Not only were the major extractive industries in decline. The 1930s were a turbulent decade for mountain agriculture, too, as many who had left for industrial jobs in the 1920s returned to a subsistence-plus way of life during the Depression. While total farm acreage declined, the

Table 2. Percentage of Farm Households Equipped with Selected Amenities, 1940

Amenities	Swain	Graham	N.C.	U.S.
Electric lighting	5.9	7.6	23.4	31.3
Running water	8.5	9.1	6.9	17.8
Indoor toilet	3.0	5.0	4.1	11.2
Private bath	2.9	4.9	4.1	11.8
Mech. refrigerator*	1.7	4.6	11.9	14.9
Radio*	30.2	39.9	46.4	60.2
Central heating*	—	0.4	0.8	10.1

Note: Data from North Carolina State Planning Board, *North Carolina Basic County Data* (Raleigh: State Planning Board, 1946), vols. 1 and 2. All categories, definitions, and bases are taken from these two volumes. Items denoted by an asterisk (*) are based upon the number of occupied dwellings; all others are based upon the total number of dwellings, occupied and otherwise.

number of farms increased as families subdivided what land they owned in order to provide for relatives. Ron Eller noted, "As migrants to the industrial centers beyond the mountains returned with larger families, they found that the land which had sustained their ancestors could no longer support the population in a manner even marginally consistent with the demands of modern life. The returned migrants added an extra burden to an already ailing agricultural system." Jack Temple Kirby has argued that the percentage of available land under cultivation increased as well in most Appalachian areas, an effect perhaps masked in the Back of Beyond by the tremendous loss in acreage for the park. Either way, farm families remained poor and under great hardship, and the available land was unable to provide a secure living for all those seeking to live on it.[52]

Table 3. Agricultural Economy (Percentage of Total Income), 1940

Income Source	Swain	Graham	N.C.	U.S.
Livestock	5.2	6.4	2.8	22.6
Dairy products	2.4	0.9	3.6	14.3
Poultry products	2.3	1.7	3.0	7.1
Field crops	5.0	7.5	62.3	31.6
Vegetables for sale	0.2	—	1.4	2.6
Fruits and nuts	0.2	0.1	1.1	3.8
Forest products	3.9	3.0	0.9	0.5
Used by household	80.2	80.2	24.1	14.5

Note: Data from North Carolina State Planning Board, *North Carolina Basic County Data* (Raleigh: State Planning Board, 1946), vols. 1 and 2. All categories, definitions, and bases are taken from these two volumes. Items denoted by an asterisk (*) are based upon the number of occupied dwellings; all others are based upon the total number of dwellings, occupied and otherwise.

Table 4. Percentage of Rural Nonfarm Households Equipped with Selected Amenities, 1940

Amenities	Swain	Graham	N.C.	U.S.
Electric lighting	47.6	30.1	68.0	77.8
Running water	50.8	32.1	39.7	55.9
Indoor toilet	39.9	23.1	30.0	43.2
Private bath	38.2	22.4	25.8	40.8
Mech. refrigerator*	25.4	16.3	34.5	38.7
Radio*	56.2	44.7	67.6	79.0
Central heating*	6.8	1.0	5.0	27.0

Note: Data from North Carolina State Planning Board, *North Carolina Basic County Data* (Raleigh: State Planning Board, 1946), vols. 1 and 2. All categories, definitions, and bases are taken from these two volumes. Items denoted by an asterisk (*) are based upon the number of occupied dwellings; all others are based upon the total number of dwellings, occupied and otherwise.

Farming families had lost much of the local market for specialty products such as apples and honey when the lumber companies pulled out, taking many of their workers with them. Farmers thus lost much of their cash income and retreated to a near-subsistence lifestyle, growing mostly what they would consume on the farm and eschewing many of the niceties that the cash economy had made available. One 1943 study noted that 80.2 percent of the production (measured in dollars) of Swain County farms was for subsistence use within the farm household that produced it.

Nonfarm families—that is, families not solely dependent on agriculture for income—in the Little Tennessee had become even more accustomed to the availability of manufactured goods than their farming counterparts,

Table 5. Percentage of Swain County Households with Selected Amenities, 1940

Amenities	Farm	Nonfarm
Electric lighting	5.9	47.6
Running water	8.5	50.8
Indoor toilet	3.0	39.9
Private bath	2.9	38.2
Mech. refrigerator*	1.7	25.4
Radio*	30.2	56.2
Central heating*	—	6.8

Note: Data from North Carolina State Planning Board, *North Carolina Basic County Data* (Raleigh: State Planning Board, 1946), vols. 1 and 2. All categories, definitions, and bases are taken from these two volumes. Items denoted by an asterisk (*) are based upon the number of occupied dwellings; all others are based upon the total number of dwellings, occupied and otherwise.

Table 6. Percentage of Graham County Households with Selected Amenities, 1940

Amenities	Farm	Nonfarm
Electric lighting	7.6	30.1
Running water	9.1	32.1
Indoor toilet	5.0	23.1
Private bath	4.9	22.4
Mech. refrigerator*	4.6	16.3
Radio*	39.9	44.7
Central heating*	0.4	1.0

Note: Data from North Carolina State Planning Board, *North Carolina Basic County Data* (Raleigh: State Planning Board, 1946), vols. 1 and 2. All categories, definitions, and bases are taken from these two volumes. Items denoted by an asterisk (*) are based upon the number of occupied dwellings; all others are based upon the total number of dwellings, occupied and otherwise.

and they had fewer ways of satisfying that desire. Clearly the only way to keep such items accessible was to keep cash flowing into the area. They did not have to look far to see the results of the inability to attract more industry. The loss of timber and mining income, in combination with competition from trucking, caused the railroad town of Bushnell to fade from its once-prominent position. As the community withered economically, its image as a commercial center withered, too. By 1939 the WPA guide to North Carolina described the village of Bushnell as composed of about seventy-five "entirely Nordic" inhabitants, "anachronistic individualists who [forsook] all the comforts of civilization and [preferred] the wild freedom of the border," people who spoke a blend of Elizabethan, Chaucerian, and pre-Chaucerian English, the people whom Kephart had called the "Roundheads of the South."[53] Even allowing for the typical bias associated with outsiders, this is a startling picture compared with the bustling railroad town of twenty-five years earlier. Ironically, while the desolation and isolation the authors of the WPA guide described was a recent development, a product of the Depression and the exhaustion of the area's timber resources, these authors seemed to accept without question the notion that the upper Little Tennessee had been utterly static. As it was depicted in the guide, Bushnell in 1939 lacked not only economic strength and cultural vigor but also history.

The region's inhabitants fought valiantly to keep the economic depression from becoming a psychological one as well. The *Bryson City Times* complained that residents sometimes seemed immune to good news. Celebrating a momentary economic upturn, the paper editorialized on September 2, 1932: "It has become almost a habit . . . to discuss nothing but hard times. It has been customary for the majority of the people to think of anything other than hard times for such a long time that it is indeed interesting to notice that in our own town during the past two months business has increased in a number of the business places from 15 to 25 percent."

Faced with the collapse of industry and the uncertainty of the future, residents resolved to survive. One local historian recalled that in Proctor, when Ritter left, the Smoky Mountain Railroad was dismantled and the movie theater, the pool hall, and the company-sponsored holiday rituals disappeared. The telephone system Ritter had set up was allowed to decline, though local residents kept the electric plant active. Asheville developer J. G. Stikeleather bought many former Ritter buildings and set up a small wilderness resort with cabins in the upper headwaters of Hazel Creek. The Kress family, owners of a national dime-store chain, built a private club in the area for hunting on the old Hall property. Private interests kept small stores active in the area, but businesses gradually withered as people moved away or lost the ability to afford manufactured goods. Many residents followed Ritter to other jobs in areas not yet logged; others fled to the cotton mills of the Carolina Piedmont. Those who remained mostly farmed their land throughout the Depression and nourished a fading sense of community, continuing to hold church services and tent revivals. Proctor residents even initiated a new ritual, the "annual All-Day-Singing-and-Dinner-on-the-Ground," which combined the rituals of the tent revival and the covered-dish supper. Perhaps aware that the region itself was dying, they also initiated the tradition of Decoration Day, in which residents would clean up and care for all the area cemeteries.[54]

Not only would the residents of Proctor survive the Depression, but they would retain their sense of humor, especially at the expense of politicians and other "city folks" who considered Proctor a dead town. A letter from a student at Proctor High School recounts an incident in that community's life which illustrates a remarkable disdain for self-important visitors:

> September 21 was a big day for Proctor. Its people had the honor of welcoming to their bosom three important men from the metropolis of Bryson City. . . . We the people stuck away in the secluded part of Western North Carolina have hardly any opportunity to learn the things that larger places find so important to their welfare. The three gentlemen from Bryson City, namely, Messrs. John Randolph, by the

> way he desires a seat in our coming legislature; Jonah Seay, who is running for sheriff; and Walter Hughes. They attended the prayer meeting and stayed until the people had finished their services, you could tell they were getting impatient by the way they wiggled in their seats, finally their time came to say a few words. Each one talked loud and long on his own good qualities. The boys growing impatient of hearing such long speeches stepped outside the building mounted on a stump and organized a new political party.[55]

The election returns from that autumn demonstrate a willingness to persevere and a faith in the political system. Turnout was uniformly heavy. Traditional party-line affinities remained strong, as they did elsewhere in western North Carolina, but the Depression exerted a substantial influence on those preferences. Political scientists Earl and Merle Black described the political situation throughout the South as follows: "Southern whites became progovernment from sheer necessity; their options were limited and their short-term self-interest clear. Whites wanted national authorities that could understand, sympathize, and do something about the devastated economy. The New Deal meant direct financial aid for many whites without a concomitant burden of heavy taxation, since most of the recipients were too poor to pay much in taxes."[56]

In the upper Little Tennessee, the more dependent a community had been on industrial employment before the Depression, the more likely it was to support Roosevelt for president, although the valley was anything but unanimous in its support of Roosevelt. Proctor was almost evenly split between Republican and Democratic candidates in 1932, except in the race for the U.S. House of Representatives, where the Republican candidate garnered a strong majority. By contrast, Bushnell was narrowly Democratic across the board, and the more prosperous farming community of Judson was strongly Republican.[57]

Despite the Depression, then, residents of southwestern North Carolina remained involved in their own destiny. They did not passively accept economic stagnation; instead, they aggressively sought remedies for both short-term and long-term economic problems. Their search for these remedies would place them amid a debate over private property rights and national economic planning when Alcoa and TVA revealed rival visions of the economic future of the Little Tennessee.

4

Machiavelli and Monopoly in the Mountains

The Aluminum Company of America (Alcoa), which began life as the Pittsburgh Reduction Company in 1887, arose from the efforts of Charles Martin Hall to design a commercially viable process for producing pure metallic aluminum from bauxite and other ores. Hall received a patent on his process in 1886. Heavily fortified by investment from the Mellon family, Hall's company grew rapidly and established a functional monopoly on aluminum production. Prosecuted under the Sherman Anti-Trust Act in 1911, the company agreed to stop its attempts to restrict access to the critical ores but admitted no violation of the law.[1]

In addition to the ore, Hall's production process required large amounts of electric power. As early as 1899, Alcoa began focusing its attention on acquiring hydroelectric power sites because it was easier and more efficient to transport the raw materials than to transmit the electricity over long distances. The company's first purchase of hydroelectric power came from the Niagara Falls Power Company, but further expansion in New York proved problematic. The diplomatic difficulties associated with damming the St. Lawrence River at Massena, New York, encouraged the company to investigate other possible sites. The Little Tennessee River seemed ideal for Alcoa's purposes, because of its tremendous flow and its location near a cheap labor supply, and the company began acquiring land along the river in 1910.[2]

By 1930, Alcoa owned approximately 200 miles of shoreline along the Little Tennessee and its tributaries, and the tiny town of Fontana was potentially its most lucrative hydropower site. Original Alcoa plans called for two dams, but by 1930 the company had settled on a single 450-foot-high dam at Fontana. Pursuing an incremental development strategy, the company had built several smaller dams downstream, but had not yet developed the Fontana site, leaving some dissatisfied with Alcoa's intentions. The editor of the *Franklin Press and Highlands Maconian* wondered: "Who knows but that the plans of this company are to hold some of their power sites merely to maintain their throttle grip on this entire section, without any intention whatsoever of development in the next generation?" Secretary of the Interior Harold Ickes also accused the company of trying to control the nation's ability to produce aluminum by holding onto the Fontana site.[3]

Alcoa's management team may in fact have intended to hold the site indefinitely, but the reasons behind such a decision are probably more complicated than Ickes's statement reflects. The company had reached a critical point in its development. Historian George David Smith has described Alcoa in the 1930s as a strong monopoly whose survival during the Great Depression could be attributed to the fact that it had not overbuilt during the 1920s as many U.S. industries had done. While the company virtually owned the domestic aluminum industry, its attempts to stimulate consumption had met with mixed results. Its managers were already beginning to express concern about competition from plastics, stainless steel, magnesium, and other materials technologies. Caution with regard to expansion plans would be appropriate under such circumstances.[4]

Furthermore, a long string of legal challenges from private and government interests had started to wear away at the company's sense of invincibility. The Federal Trade Commission began its eight-year investigation of the company in 1922, alleging that the company had monopolized the cooking utensil business, the market for scrap aluminum, the manufacture of aluminum ingot, and the mining of bauxite, and that it had conspired to control the global hydropower and aluminum trade, among other charges. The FTC complaint would be dismissed in 1930, but a more serious threat would come in 1937, when the U.S. Department of Justice again filed suit against Alcoa under the Sherman Anti-Trust Act, claiming restraint of interstate and international trade and resurrecting many of the charges first brought in the FTC action. This time, the government's threat to "create substantial competition in the industry by rearranging the plants and properties of the Aluminum Company and its subsidiaries" could have, in effect, dissolved the entire monopoly. This threat would hang over the heads of Alcoa management for nearly a decade, and final appeals would not be decided by Judge Learned Hand until 1945.[5]

Alcoa also had public relations problems. The company's obviously profitable monopoly over aluminum production in the 1920s, together with its uncomfortably close political and financial ties to Andrew Mellon, treasury secretary in the Hoover administration, helped to fuel the perception held by many New Dealers and old-line Progressives alike that Alcoa was "a monopoly, and therefore bad; and . . . a Mellon monopoly, and therefore worse." Arthur Vining Davis, the company's chairman, was undoubtedly aware that he and the company were not portrayed in the most favorable light by the press, but he made matters worse by what contemporaries described as arrogance and by his apparent indifference to public perception. In light of the long-term financial uncertainty and the company's legal battles, Davis and other Alcoa decision makers chose to postpone their expansion plans, but the company indicated no desire to divest itself of the potential of the Fontana site.[6]

The ideological background accompanying the Alcoa approach to the Little Tennessee was simple. Corporations had long pursued the private development of vast natural resources across the United States. Railroads had built vast commercial empires around the land given to them by congressional act. Mining companies had purchased large tracts for the purpose of extracting wealth from under the ground. Lumber companies had bought up entire forests and made money by transforming them into board-feet. In keeping with these long-accepted concepts of land tenure, Alcoa's Davis claimed that since the company owned the land around the river, it owned the rights to the water and its energy. Davis argued that the company had discovered the potential of the river, it had developed it with several dams, and it sold electricity generated at those dams to private residential and business customers in western North Carolina through its wholly owned subsidiary, the Nantahala Power and Light Company (NPL). NPL was the primary supplier of electric power for much of southwestern North Carolina, and its other plants would be affected by the operation of a dam at Fontana, so it seemed logical to Davis that the company would develop the Fontana site. Moreover, Alcoa was the only industrial concern in the area large enough to use all the power that would be produced at Fontana. Thus, according to Davis, the decision when, or if, to develop that resource properly belonged only to Alcoa management, not to public opinion or to any agency of the federal government.[7]

The Tennessee Valley Authority came from an altogether different ideological tradition. If one can say, somewhat loosely, that Alcoa inherited the ideology of monopoly capitalism from its precursors in banking and railroading, then it might equally loosely be said that the Tennessee Valley Authority owed its ideological underpinnings to the often conflicting goals of Progressive Era reformers, made more urgent by the Great Depression. One important undercurrent within TVA was that strain of Progressive Era reform movements which focused on improving society by empowering individuals. George Norris, the longtime senator from Nebraska whose influence was so crucial to the creation of TVA, believed that freeing individuals from corrupting influences was the key to empowering them. According to this almost Jeffersonian view, an individual becomes corrupted when another individual or corporation controls or limits the available choices. Thus, monopolies, large landowners, and private utility companies all constrained the freedom of the individual and held coercive power. In the eyes of Norris and many other Progressive reformers, the South provided a uniquely powerful example of how coercive institutions such as United States Steel, the crop-lien system, plantation agriculture, and the one-party political system could impoverish a region rich in natural resources. As national interest in Progressive movements waned during the 1920s, Norris remained politically relevant by focusing his attention on government administration of natural resources. Norris viewed good government as the common American's tool with which to protect himself from unfair monopolistic practices, and government administration of natural resources for the public good came with that. Thus, Norris supported the creation of the Hetch Hetchy reservoir in Yosemite National Park in order to provide an inexpensive source of water for the city of San Francisco over the objections of preservationists. Norris also opposed the sale of Muscle Shoals Nitrate Plant No. 2 (built during World War I by the U.S. Army) to Henry Ford, becoming in the process the most visible advocate of national control of natural resources. This position would later lead him into authoring the act that created the Tennessee Valley Authority.[8]

Another Progressive Era undercurrent that found its way into the TVA modus operandi was the preference for delegating technical decisions to professionals. In creating the Tennessee Valley Authority in 1933, Congress gave the agency wide-ranging responsibility for promoting the economic development of the entire Tennessee Valley through multipurpose dams that would facilitate navigation, enhance flood control, and generate hydroelectric power. Industrial and residential customers could then purchase electric power from TVA at low cost. TVA's mandate was not only to provide economic relief and cheap electricity. As it was conceived by Franklin Roosevelt, George Norris, and Arthur Morgan, the agency was supposed to showcase the potential of government administration of natural resources and centralized planning for economic development. Roosevelt wrote that TVA

> should be charged with the broadest duty of planning for the proper use, conservation and development of the natural resources of the Tennessee River drainage basin. . . . Many hard lessons have taught

> us the human waste that results from lack of planning. . . . It is time to extend planning to a wider field, in this instance comprehending in one great project many States directly concerned with the basis of one of our greatest rivers.
>
> This in a true sense is a return to the spirit and vision of the pioneer. If we are successful here we can march on, step by step, in a like development of other great natural territorial units within our borders.[9]

Norris's influence is clear in this last paragraph, where centralized planning is supposed to make it possible to regain the spirit of individualism that built the nation.

The legislation that created TVA provided for a three-member board of directors in which the roles of board members were not clearly defined, reflecting the frankly experimental nature of the agency in its infancy. Roosevelt chose Arthur E. Morgan, a former college president from Ohio, as chairman. Morgan admitted to having "the prophetic urge" to convert his fellow human beings to his way of thinking. A lifelong hypochondriac, he pursued moral perfection in himself and others with neurotic doggedness, and frequently complained bitterly of his own failures. One observer wrote of him that the "combination of religion and science produced a perfectionism in which scientific method was guided by moral certainties."[10]

A mostly self-taught engineer, Morgan believed in the importance of the individual will. Like many other Progressive Era thinkers, he focused on the moral perfectibility of the individual as the key to perfecting society. He believed that all right-thinking individuals would ultimately reach the same conclusion, but that not all individuals were equally prepared to make major decisions. Thus, he never shrank from the opportunity to expound upon the reasoning behind his views, but those who disagreed with him (and there were many) after he had very patiently taught them what was right were somehow not "operating in good faith." This stern belief in moral absolutes sometimes crossed the line into paranoid behavior, and Morgan demonstrated an uncanny ability to make enemies, even to invent them. One observer, noting the apparent irrationality of Morgan's kindly and seemingly naive treatment of TVA enemy Wendell Willkie and his parallel failure to cultivate a solid relationship with the very capable Lilienthal, would conclude that Morgan "judged men, not ideas." These traits did not make Morgan the ideal manager, and his former associates at Antioch College warned his new colleagues at TVA that his administrative skills desperately lacked direction. He often spouted non sequiturs, which caused those around him to question his judgment as well as his social skills. Morgan's ever-active imagination was his greatest asset as a planner and his greatest liability as an administrator.[11]

Morgan and Roosevelt together selected the other two members: H. A. Morgan (no relation) and David E. Lilienthal. H. A. Morgan had served as a professor of agriculture and entomology at Louisiana State University and then as president of the University of Tennessee. He became well known among Tennesseeans for his understanding of the relationships between water, soil, land use, and agricultural production. People and nature depended on each other, and the different parts of nature depended upon each other as well, in what he described as a "common mooring." He is generally regarded as the father of TVA's "grassroots" approach, by which term he meant consultation with the existing power structure. He organized TVA's agricultural programs around land grant universities in what some saw as an unseemly delegation of responsibility. More than the other directors, H. A. Morgan understood the subtleties of political and social relationships in the South, and he ably worked within those relationships, often drawing fire from his more liberal critics for his unwillingness to rock the boat on controversial issues. In a landmark 1950 study that TVA critics continue to cite regularly, sociologist Philip Selznick argued that this so-called grassroots approach prevented TVA from fulfilling its stated goals of systemwide reform.[12]

Lilienthal, a smooth and eager young attorney from the Midwest, had served on Wisconsin's Public Service Commission for two years and learned a number of subtle strategies for dealing with public utilities. He took charge of legal matters and the agency's power distribution program. Lilienthal's decision-making style involved confrontation between conflicting ideas—a style that grated on A. E. Morgan's paternalistic sensibilities and his craving for orderly consensus. But Lilienthal was a gifted spokesman, and he would take the lead in proclaiming the mission of TVA after A. E. Morgan's departure. Much ink has been spilled over the personal and ideological conflicts between these two men, but they shared a distrust of monopolistic corporations. Lilienthal was not the idealist A. E. Morgan was, but the two men shared a sense that their work at TVA could provide a new direction for the entire nation. Lilienthal's version of that mission incorporated much of the utopian rhetoric of A. E. Morgan's vision, in a toned-down form. Lilienthal seems to have realized both the appeal of the reform impulse and the reckless appearance A. E. Morgan gave that impulse. Lilienthal thus became the public figure most closely identified with TVA in its early years, and his book *TVA: Democracy on the March* became a milestone in the articulation of the TVA mission.[13]

Like Alcoa, by the late 1930s TVA had faced several challenges to its existence with inconclusive results. The lofty principles stated in the TVA Act came face to face with anti–New Deal sentiments in the political arena and with the dubious constitutionality of the agency itself. In this environment the agency could have benefited from a management team unified on a statement of principles.

One principle on which TVA was supposedly founded was that it should strive to be above political matters. This principle echoed not only the Progressive Era movement toward the professional manager-council form of local government but also the concurrent professionalization of such fields as medicine, law, and engineering. Moreover, it was an integral part of the moral code Arthur Morgan developed for TVA employees. Removed from the realm of politics, technical decisions would be based on technical criteria alone, and personnel decisions were supposed to be based on qualifications alone.

Arthur Morgan's high-minded expectations for TVA would face almost immediate challenge from within. Harcourt Morgan had developed a thoroughgoing network of contacts in southern land grant colleges and universities through his long service in the agricultural extension services of LSU and the University of Tennessee. He was well acquainted with the potential of those universities in furthering agricultural research, and saw in this connection a tremendous resource to further his vision of TVA as an agency promoting the understanding of the "common mooring." His insistence upon working within the existing channels of power in TVA agricultural programs may well have furthered the ideas of progressive agriculture, but it also meant that TVA reinforced the oligarchic tendencies of the institutions connected with those channels. H. A. Morgan was a consummate behind-the-scenes player, and he tended to dismiss A. E. Morgan's insistence on separation from local politics as akin to reinventing the wheel. At least one observer has suggested that H. A. Morgan's hand-in-glove relationship with the land grant universities and other conservative forces made it possible for the agency to survive, thus providing a platform for the articulation of A. E. Morgan's more radical "social engineering" ideas. Still, H. A. Morgan's system placed substantial limits on the extent to which A. E. Morgan's utopian visions would be realized.[14]

Lilienthal's challenge to A. E. Morgan's avowedly apolitical approach was more direct. Lilienthal, unlike A. E. Morgan, quickly realized that TVA's very existence was a political issue that would require political involvement. While it was desirable for TVA to appear to be apolitical and to eschew blatant political maneuvering, Lilienthal was not above using patronage discreetly to preserve the existence of the supposedly apolitical agency. A. E. Morgan deplored this willingness, viewing it as evidence enough of Lilienthal's moral unsuitability for the job.[15]

The refusal to be subject to the political process resulted in a TVA that was avowedly nonpartisan in its rhetoric if not fully depoliticized in its actions, but it also created problems of accountability. The agency may have been above politics in the sense that technical decisions were made by technical experts rather than by elected legislators, but it was also beyond the corrective reach of political action when the experts produced proposals which those affected would consider unsuitable. If TVA was not accountable to Congress, and if it was "clothed with the power of government, but possessed of the flexibility and initiative of a private enterprise,"[16] then it represented the worst of both government and private enterprise in the minds of some. For Arthur Morgan, the least democratically minded of the three directors, it was a tool for checking the power of monopolies and for uplifting southern society through guided development. For many residents of the Tennessee Valley, though, it was a government-supported monopoly made even more dangerous because it possessed the power of eminent domain.

Hydroelectric power, of course, was the centerpiece of A. E. Morgan's notion of guided development. But that development mission, shared largely by the other directors though they would differ greatly on how it was to be implemented, also encompassed erosion control, flood control, the promotion of scientific agriculture, the production of fertilizer, the use of locks to improve navigation on the Tennessee River, and even public recreation. In all these endeavors, control of the flow of the Tennessee River and its tributaries formed the basis of development.[17]

The Little Tennessee provides a larger share of the flow of the Tennessee River than any other tributary, so the manipulation of its flow would determine the amount of power that TVA's dams farther downstream could produce. A. E. Morgan saw Alcoa's existing control of the Little Tennessee's flow as a potential obstacle to TVA's (and his own) development goals. He distrusted the monopoly Alcoa still held on the nation's aluminum supply, so he naturally feared that Alcoa would try to use its control of the Little Tennessee to gain special considerations from TVA. This distrust would set the stage for a battle between TVA and Alcoa for control of the Fontana site.[18]

From A. E. Morgan's point of view, the narrow, deep valley of the Little

Tennessee could provide a great deal of water storage, which the agency could use to guarantee a steady supply of hydropower during the dry season and control the usual spring floods in the Tennessee and lower Little Tennessee Valleys, especially at Chattanooga. Furthermore, while Morgan and Lilienthal would disagree over whether the agency should focus on serving smaller businesses or larger corporations, both would agree that TVA's development plans for the dams along the Tennessee depended on being able to provide large industrial customers with a *steady* electric power supply. Alcoa's control of the Little Tennessee could impede TVA's success throughout the Tennessee Valley, because an upstream dam controls the water level and the amount of power produced at dams further downstream. Morgan wrote: "Whoever controls the Little Tennessee River to a very considerable degree will dominate the TVA as to its power policy and as to its navigation policy and as to its flood-control policy. . . . If the Little Tennessee is administered independently of the rest of the system, whoever so administers it will have a coercive power over the administration of the river system as a whole."[19] Alcoa, then, could potentially jeopardize the entire concept of the "electric valley," and if it so desired, destroy TVA in the process. The Fontana project became Morgan's pet platform from which to win a major moral and political victory over TVA's detractors, and it had the added bonus of one-upping Alcoa's highly visible monopoly. It also provided Morgan a chance to showcase his engineering talent and that of his staff, perhaps restoring some of the prestige he had lost in the boardroom through personality and ideological conflicts.

Morgan relished his role as the board's visionary. Alcoa's control over so much of the Little Tennessee stood in the way of his vision. Morgan's propensity for hyperbole made the stakes seem high: Either Alcoa's claim based on property rights must yield to Morgan's position that the river was a "great natural resource" not subject to private control, or Alcoa would press that claim so far that TVA's control of the Tennessee River itself would be in jeopardy. In his memoirs published in 1974, he stated that he feared Alcoa might claim title to the rain falling on its land, argue that the rain belonged to the company even after it became runoff, and ultimately demand a share of the agency's income from power sales all the way to the Ohio River. TVA control of the site, by contrast, could benefit both the agency and Alcoa, if TVA were allowed to operate the Alcoa dams together with its own for greatest systemwide efficiency. TVA could show off its engineering talent and provide electricity for economic development throughout the valley, and Alcoa would have access to all the electric power it could use. Morgan considered it his moral duty to oppose Alcoa's "socially unwise" claim and prevent the waters of the Little Tennessee from being "appropriated as a source of private gain."[20]

Of course, Alcoa chairman Arthur V. Davis vigorously defended the investment his company had made in the Fontana site and elsewhere along the Little Tennessee. Davis used the familiar argument that his company's monopoly would provide the most efficient means of developing the river's potential:

> We . . . engineered out 104 miles of this [Little Tennessee River]. . . . We have had for twenty-five years, from ten to seventy-five engineers, all the time working on this engineering development and we have plans which comprise developments which completely and absolutely utilize the entire flow of the stream. There is no possible conservation plan which could be devised which would be superior to ours. . . . And whatever development could be made or ever would be made on this river would be exactly the same as ours. . . . With all this money spent, with twenty-five years of record behind us, with all this engineering data, with our plans so completely laid out for the future, we submit that we are entitled to proceed with our development, which we bought with our own money.[21]

Both participants fought hard to obtain control of the Fontana site. According to Arthur Morgan, Davis even planted an Alcoa employee in the office of TVA director David E. Lilienthal for the purpose of "extract[ing] confidential information from TVA files."[22] TVA, for its part, successfully petitioned Congress for an amendment to the TVA Act that would explicitly recognize the agency's authority to coordinate "unified control" of the water resources of the Tennessee River and its tributaries to achieve maximum power production and flood control benefits.[23]

Both TVA and Alcoa also fought for public opinion. As early as 1934, Alcoa had instigated a petition drive against TVA in order to pressure the agency to back down.[24] Alcoa's supporters focused on the potential of private enterprise in their appeal. On October 18, 1934, the editor of the *Franklin Press and Highlands Maconian* wrote:

> The impression is unmistakably given [by the petition drive] that if the TVA will get out and stay out, the Mellon crowd [who support Alcoa's claim] will turn loose millions of dollars on these [hydroelectric projects proposed in western North Carolina but as yet undeveloped], put thousands of men back to work and add many millions of

> dollars to the taxable values of Macon, Swain and Graham counties, whereas the TVA, should it come into this territory, would greatly diminish tax valuations, supplying nothing in its place, and send taxes sky-high on all privately-owned property. . . . Many people of Macon, Swain and Graham counties are being hoodwinked into the idea that should TVA come into these counties it would bankrupt all of us.[25]

The impression the *Press* editor described would not die quickly. Perhaps TVA could have built the dam without the support of community leaders, but to do so would have complicated the process tremendously. Community leaders in the region's principal town, Bryson City, actively sought the construction of the dam, by whatever agency would do so. TVA actively courted these people, seeking and eventually obtaining the support of longtime mayor Kelly Bennett and the Swain County Chamber of Commerce, in part by convincing them that Alcoa would never build the dam.[26]

For all the ranting and raving over private property rights and the virtues of private enterprise, and for all the maneuvering on the part of both TVA and Alcoa, Morgan's epic battle with Alcoa was inconclusive. It would be Morgan's archenemy Lilienthal who would ultimately receive credit for wresting the site from Alcoa. Lilienthal and Morgan had struggled for years for control over the agency. Morgan repeatedly accused Lilienthal of unethical behavior and undermining Morgan's own meticulously prepared honor code for TVA employees. Lilienthal's training as a lawyer and bureaucrat placed him at odds with Morgan's idealism, contributing to a power struggle between the two men that paralyzed the agency intermittently, delaying the resolution of the Fontana negotiations by several years. Of Lilienthal, Morgan claimed, "There is a practice of evasion, intrigue and sharp strategy, with remarkable skill in alibi and the habit of avoiding direct responsibility, which makes Machiavelli seem open and candid."[27]

Such outbursts undermined President Roosevelt's initial confidence in Morgan's vision and ability, and the president began corresponding directly with the other directors in an effort to isolate the chairman. Lilienthal convened a meeting of TVA board of directors while A. E. Morgan was unavailable, and the two directors present voted to break off negotiations with Alcoa over the Fontana site in June 1936, declaring that "no further communication is to be had with Congress concerning authorization to construct the Fontana Dam." At least one observer described this as a "point of no return" in the relationship between A. E. Morgan and

Lilienthal. When President Roosevelt attempted to limit Morgan's ability to speak publicly on behalf of the agency with respect to Lilienthal's administration of the power program and to a suspicious land claim attached to the agency's dam at Norris, the chairman rebelled vociferously. Roosevelt and Norris called for Morgan's resignation, but Morgan refused, forcing Roosevelt to rely on Lilienthal's meticulously prepared attacks against the chairman in a series of public hearings. Morgan refused to answer the charges of obstructing and sabotaging TVA's management process and was fired for "contumacy" and insubordination. Because of the personal enmity between the two headstrong directors, Alcoa possessed a clear opportunity to begin development of the Fontana site with community support and without TVA interference between June 1936, when the Fontana negotiations broke up, and March 1938, when Morgan was fired. Unfortunately for both the company and the residents of the upper Little Tennessee, that window of opportunity coincided with the so-called Roosevelt Recession, in which the manufacturing sector's fortunes slumped and the demand for aluminum, predictably, remained low enough to discourage Alcoa from investing heavily in new capacity.[28]

The collapse of negotiations regarding the Fontana site did not mean that TVA would no longer negotiate with Alcoa for the sale of electric power. A. E. Morgan deplored Lilienthal's willingness to decouple power sales from the Fontana negotiations. He wrote: "We had one bargaining point, and that was that the Aluminum Company needed power. . . . [I]f we sold them power and met their other needs for power without getting control of the Fontana site, we were giving away all of our bargaining power, our power to get control of that very critical damsite."[29] Morgan believed that agreeing to sell power to Alcoa without involving Fontana meant capitulating to Alcoa's monopolistic practices. Perhaps more important to residents of the upper Little Tennessee than a sacrifice of principle was the fact that, since Alcoa's only reason for holding the site was the need for electric power, Lilienthal's willingness to sell power to the aluminum company at preferred rates made it less urgent for Alcoa to begin construction of the dam, especially given the uncertainty of the long-term demand for aluminum.[30]

The rapid rise of Nazi Germany as a visible threat to Europe sparked calls for increased defense preparedness in the United States, and late in 1939 Congress authorized the "cash and carry" weapons sales program. This was followed by the creation of the Lend-Lease program in early 1941. These defense measures created a demand for faster construction of aircraft, which in turn placed a burden on the nation's aluminum supply.

Undercapacity, rather than overcapacity, would become the company's biggest problem by 1940. This only added to Alcoa's impetus to build the dam at Fontana, as the nation's only volume producer of aluminum also became its largest consumer of electric power. The changing political climate also increased the potential rewards and lowered the potential costs, because the federal government badly needed aluminum for defense. Alcoa did not own the nation's entire productive capacity, but it did own the vast majority of the nation's bauxite reserves. It also held the patents that covered the technology required for large-scale aluminum manufacturing. In other words, while the company did not technically own all of the nation's aluminum production, it was capable of preventing other companies from gaining a foothold and thus it controlled a major portion of the nation's defense program.[31]

Accusations of malfeasance flew right and left. Officials of Reynolds Metal Corporation and Kalunite, Inc., accused Alcoa of trying to block their access to aluminum technology and government contracts. Kalunite president Frank Eichelberger alleged that Alcoa had placed a number of officials from the Office of Production Management (OPM) on its payroll in order to secure a monopoly on the nation's aluminum production for defense contracts. Senate Chief Counsel Hugh Fulton also accused Alcoa of concealing its true production capacity and dragging its feet on developing the Fontana site in an effort to force the federal government to pay for the construction of the dam. Alcoa operations chief I. W. Wilson attributed delays in expanding the company's production to a lack of available electricity, and blamed OPM for failing to allocate additional electric power to the company. Senator Harry Truman, chairing a special congressional committee investigating problems with national defense programs, was often annoyed by the technical jargon and evasive language Alcoa witnesses used. He complained: "You know, this committee is trying to find a way to get aluminum. . . . We would be willing to buy aluminum from anybody. If we could get it. I don't care whether it is the Aluminum Company of America or whether it is Reynolds or Al Capone. . . . What I am trying to get at is, how far is the Aluminum Company of America willing to go under this emergency to help this government get aluminum?"[32]

Alcoa's complaints about the shortage of electric power were directed squarely at the federal government. Under the provisions of the Federal Power Act of 1921, the Federal Power Commission (FPC) took responsibility for insuring that industries received the necessary electricity to keep people and assembly lines working. The commission required licensing prior to the construction of any dam that might affect interstate commerce. Was the Little Tennessee a "navigable" river subject to such regulation? Boats did haul grain in the lower portions of the Little Tennessee occasionally, albeit only when spring rains raised the water level. There were also small boats operating around Fontana, of which the *Vivian* was the best known. But a series of canyon rapids near the state line prevented the sort of commercial boat traffic between the two states that would qualify as "interstate commerce." Nonetheless, the FPC ruled that the river was a "navigable waterway" subject to its jurisdiction, requiring that the aluminum company seek a license before constructing the dam and thereby creating an additional obstacle to Alcoa's plans for the Fontana site.[33]

An agreement between TVA and Alcoa in October 1940 provided that Alcoa would develop the Fontana site with its own money, secure any relevant licenses from the FPC, and operate the dam within TVA guidelines for flow downstream.[34] But the licensing agreement proffered by the Federal Power Commission gave the government the power to take over the facility after fifty years of operation if it chose to do so. Alcoa balked, ostensibly not wishing to risk shareholder investments. Alcoa's reluctance to sign a contract that might require it to hand over a major asset—its largest dam to date—is understandable at face value, even given the fifty-year grace period and the uncertainties of business cycles. But the nation's more direct involvement in the war in Europe through the new Lend-Lease program placed the company under great pressure to produce aluminum on the government's terms, and the company's history of monopolistic practices contributed to an atmosphere of mutual distrust. Upon hearing Alcoa's negative reaction to the proposed licensing agreement, the commission wrote:

> Notwithstanding the public interest, Alcoa, through its subsidiary, in effect demonstrated that in its national defense effort it was unwilling to accept the reasonable limitations on unearned increment in the value of its power project provided by Congress in the Federal Power Act. . . . The refusal of Alcoa's subsidiary to construct the Fontana project, when required to obtain a license, indicates that not even the urgent demands of national defense can alter its apparent determination never willingly to submit . . . to the duly enacted requirements of federal law.[35]

An editorial in the *Franklin Press and Highlands Maconian* put it more simply: "Alcoa is being petulant and stubborn."[36] Stung by the criticism but still seeking the best possible financial arrangements, Alcoa reversed its position and agreed to seek a license, if the Reconstruction Finance Corporation or some other government agency would agree to fund the construction.[37]

This maneuver, intended to preserve Alcoa's strong financial position and avoid the potential problem of excess capacity after the war, backfired. An indignant Senator Truman concurred with H. A. Morgan and TVA power manager J. A. Krug that if the dam was to be built with government funds, it made sense that the government, specifically TVA, should build it and operate it in the public interest. These men felt that Alcoa had acted in bad faith by seeking government financing, and that by doing so the company had abrogated the agreement reached with TVA in October 1940.[38]

TVA was back in the game now. Using public opinion as leverage, Lilienthal shrewdly backed Alcoa into a corner and forced the company to sell the site to TVA in return for a guaranteed power supply that amounted to about 20 percent of the company's total electric power needs in 1941. TVA would control not only the Fontana dam but also Alcoa's dams along the Little Tennessee in order to extract maximum electric power year-round throughout TVA's power system. If Alcoa refused, the company would be seen by the public, as it already was by some members of Congress, as an exploitative monopoly obstructing the defense of the nation. The company, still facing antitrust litigation, had few options. Davis's poor handling of the politically sensitive antitrust issue, Alcoa's failed financing gambit, and the global political situation had restored to TVA the bargaining position Lilienthal had voluntarily and perhaps naively given up in 1936, and the Alcoa chairman accepted the TVA proposal with minor amendments in June 1941.[39]

Residents of the upper Little Tennessee had appreciated the hydroelectric potential of their region, and even celebrated it, for a long time. Many had welcomed Alcoa's involvement in the region's economy despite the dislocation it would produce. But they understood how fleeting prosperity could be, and in the context of the Great Depression their support for the construction of a dam at Fontana depended less on who did it than on how quickly it could be begun and on who would benefit from the money and jobs that came with it. The Swain County Chamber of Commerce asked Congressman Zeb Weaver to use his influence to guarantee that the dam would be built, asserting that the economic stimulus it would create was desperately needed in the area. Weaver replied that in his view it was "almost imperative" that it be constructed and that he would work with

Lilienthal to get the job done. Bryson City businessman I. K. Stearns, president of the Carolina Wood Turning Company, also wrote in support of the dam, though he expected little would come of Weaver's efforts to attract defense industries to the area—"It simply isn't in the cards," he wrote. Like many area residents, such as longtime Robbinsville mayor R. Bruce Slaughter, Weaver initially preferred that Alcoa construct the dam, and he had worked closely with the company in drafting their plans for a proposed manufacturing facility at Andrews. In addition to the potential for further Alcoa development in the area, Weaver, Slaughter, and Bryson City mayor Bill Elmore expressed considerable concern over the county's lingering debt problems, which they felt Alcoa construction would help alleviate and which they feared TVA construction would accentuate. Demonstrating a lack of understanding concerning the constitutional relationship between states and the federal government with regard to taxation, Slaughter noted, "Of course we understand that the TVA will pay taxes on the production of the water power when the Fontana Dam is completed. If we were to lose the taxes on the power company properties—the dams at Tapoco, Rhymers Ferry, and Santeetlah and the transmission line to near the Nantahala—the [Graham] county would be doomed."[40]

Republican attorney Stanley Black of Bryson City, who had done much of the legal work associated with Alcoa's land acquisitions in the valley, understood more clearly that TVA's acquisition of the property owned by the Nantahala Power and Light Company would automatically take that property off the county's tax rolls. As of 1941, Black estimated that the county would lose $4,383.84 per year in tax revenue from that property alone until the dam was completed, at which point the agency would assume the obligation of payments in lieu of taxes, as required by the TVA Act of 1933. Black also estimated that the loss of taxable Southern Railway property would cost the county $18,212.79 per year, and the loss of spur lines an additional $785.40 per year. Thus, the total annual loss from these corporate properties alone was estimated at $23,382.03, or approximately 23 percent of Swain County's annual tax revenue, not including the loss of any additional taxable property then in private hands. Moreover, the county had already lost nearly half its taxable land area because of the creation of the national park. Since the county's total indebtedness in 1940 was $1,560,538.75, of which nearly $400,000 was already in default, Black felt that government ownership of this property would, in effect, put the county out of business.[41]

After the company declined the FPC license offer in conjunction with the Fontana site, Congressman Weaver switched sides and began courting Lilienthal actively. While some Upper Little Tennessee residents, notably Robbinsville attorney R. L. Phillips, continued to express distrust of TVA and accused the agency of sabotaging Alcoa's efforts, Weaver generally supported the agency's plans for the Fontana project after June 1941.[42]

Weaver's constituents elsewhere in western North Carolina expressed less ambivalence concerning the plans. Asheville real estate developer James G. Stikeleather, who owned much of the land between the national park and the Little Tennessee, was among the dam's (and TVA's) strongest advocates, as was Asheville newspaper editor D. Hiden Ramsey, one of the most outspoken critics of Alcoa's plans. Murphy hotel owner C. W. Savage also spoke to Weaver, echoing the Asheville newspaper's complaints that the delays caused by debates over the controversial Douglas Dam in Tennessee were holding up the plans for Fontana, which had no such opposition in the local area.[43]

Many residents echoed Weaver's preference for Alcoa development, but most eventually accepted the notion that a TVA dam was better than none, and resolved to work with the agency rather than against it. On March 2, 1939, five years after the petition drive, the editor of the *Bryson City Times* wrote:

> We of the Times . . . realize that from the county's standpoint we would derive much more benefit from this construction [of Fontana Dam] if the Nantahala Power Company [wholly owned by Alcoa] was allowed to build the dam. Our valuation for taxation would be doubled, which in turn would solve many of our vexing problems. But . . . if we fight TVA, we not only lose our lands from taxation but TVA will not feel like promoting the various projects and helpful developments in Swain County that it is promoting in all the other communities surrounding [us].

Ironically, despite the partisan rancor exhibited by TVA and Alcoa supporters in the valley, the aluminum company and the federal agency were both fighting over the opportunity to "export" the benefits of this natural resource. Notwithstanding the faint promise of a new plant to be built near Andrews, in Cherokee County, Alcoa's main production facilities were located at Calderwood and Maryville, Tennessee, far downstream from the Fontana area.[44] The company withdrew the Andrews plant proposal "for transportation reasons" less than a week after the OPM announced that TVA would build the dam at Fontana.[45] TVA control of the site would mean that the electric power and the industrialization it was supposed to foster would go downstream into eastern and even central Tennessee, again well beyond any direct economic benefit to the Fontana area itself.

Once TVA acquired the Fontana site, a new series of hurdles would present themselves before construction could begin. TVA needed congressional funding for construction projects. Such funding would not come until after the bombing of Pearl Harbor. Faced with a sudden wartime emergency, Congress authorized the construction of Fontana Dam, along with Douglas Dam on the French Broad River east of Knoxville, on December 12, 1941, and preliminary work began immediately. Surveyors, core drillers, and reservoir clearance crews descended on the upper Little Tennessee quickly. Construction officially began on January 1, 1942, and the Little Tennessee River and its people instantly became a critical part of the nation's defense operations.

5

I'm from the Government, and I'm Here to Help

Fontana Dam required more effort than most previous TVA projects. The remote location, along with the treacherous nature of the only road near the dam site, meant the agency would have to build not only a dam but also access roads, bridges, telephone lines, and a railroad spur. Furthermore, the relatively sparse population could not provide an adequate labor supply. TVA had to bring workers in from other areas, eventually taking responsibility for transportation, housing, food, and even recreational programs for 5,000 to 7,000 workers.

The construction phase of the Fontana project required TVA to purchase more land, build more roads, provide more subsidiary services during construction, recruit more workers, and provide more housing than it ever had. Once the dam was completed, TVA also exercised more regulatory power over private property, both individual and corporate, than it had in connection with any other project. In taking on these responsibilities, TVA set itself up as a regional development agency, a role it was ill-prepared to play while providing for the nation's wartime needs.

Ironically, then, despite the departure of A. E. Morgan, the Fontana project required TVA to assume the level of responsibility for regional planning that he had had in mind for it all along, but because the agency's mission had changed, the resulting policies would diverge greatly from his original intent. The people who designed the dam, the people who managed the construction of the dam, and the people who acquired the land for the dam celebrated the national goals of victory in the war, preservation and conservation of forest resources, and promotion of TVA itself, often with little more than token concern for the long-term future of the residents themselves.

TVA employed people from different backgrounds in management positions. Their attitudes toward the local residents ranged from sympathy to contempt, but all shared a sense that the area's past proved its people's inability to take care of themselves. A look at some representative executives from the agency helps clarify the internal tug-of-war that shaped its policies toward the upper Little Tennessee and its inhabitants.

John I. Snyder was a real estate analyst who left Dun and Bradstreet to become TVA's assistant general solicitor in 1933. Concerned by corporate land acquisition projects that often saw the last holdouts receiving many times the appraised value of the property, and probably aware of the history of land speculation in the Great Smoky Mountains, Snyder implemented a nonnegotiable settlement strategy. TVA had to convince the property owner that the project was worthwhile and necessary, that "we understood [their sacrifice, and] that we were prepared to pay them the price which we felt exceeded the actual market value of the property." Once this was accomplished, Snyder felt, property owners would see the wisdom of cooperating with the agency. Landowners could accompany appraisers to make sure everything of value was accounted for. TVA would allow them to stay on their land until it was actually needed and would give them ample notice so they could clear the property of any improvements, crops, or other valuables. "Landowners who dealt voluntarily with us had considerable advantages," he noted somewhat cynically to an interviewer.[1]

Of course, many landowners, guided by previous experience with Ritter Lumber Company, Alcoa, the park movement, and other buyers, refused to sell, encouraging TVA to initiate condemnation proceedings in court. TVA appraised property for condemnation at market value, with no allowance for inconvenience and no time allowed for salvage. So fighting TVA acquisition was difficult, and many found that fighting a condemnation order ate up all the money they received for their property. Snyder would later trumpet his own success by stating that 90 percent of all the land TVA had acquired had been obtained through voluntary purchase. He sneered at the "landowner protective associations," which formed in almost all reservoir areas to extract a maximum price from TVA. "I recall that our buyers took great pride when they were able to purchase the land owned by an officer of the protective association," he remarked years later.[2]

In contrast to Snyder, Dick Niehoff came from a background that was infused with the social gospel, which encouraged him to resent privilege and despise poverty. Born in Illinois, he grew up poor. As a graduate student he studied human behavior while working for the YMCA. His immediate reaction upon entering eastern Tennessee was one of shock. "[The poverty] was all spread out in front of you to see and one would have had to have been blind not to. I had read about it [but] . . . I was not aware of areas in the United States that had so many problems." Niehoff guided many of TVA's educational programs through their formative period.[3]

John C. McAmis grew up in rural Greene County, Tennessee, and studied agriculture at the University of Tennessee under H. A. Morgan. He worked in TVA's readjustment office during the construction of Norris Dam before becoming director of agricultural relations. McAmis saw himself as a champion of the individual and frequently struggled in vain against what he saw as excessive land acquisition by the agency. His study of families displaced by the formation of the Great Smoky Mountains National Park revealed a story of tragic proportions. The culture of sharing produce, milk, and other items with neighbors had gotten them through hard times before the park, but the loss of their neighbors had cost them both materially and psychologically. In his work at Norris, and later at Fontana despite a different title and responsibilities, McAmis sought to minimize this sort of trauma by improving the quality of land under cultivation and thereby compensating residents for the lost economic cushion formerly provided by their neighbors.[4]

George Gant's background, like that of McAmis, permitted him a level of sensitivity to the region's needs, but his intellectual approach to those needs gave his work a distinctly different, less agrarian flavor. Gant grew up in Lincoln, Nebraska, where his father owned a small publishing firm. He received a Ph.D. in history from the University of Wisconsin in 1933 and became assistant to the education director of the Civilian Conservation Corps. By February 1935, he had moved to TVA's Social and Economic Division as a research assistant, a post he soon exchanged for that of assistant chief of the Training Section. From there Gant moved up to become assistant director and later director of personnel. In that role, he supervised training programs, often administering them through local school authorities as H. A. Morgan had done with agricultural programs.[5]

Gant's insight into Appalachian life was unusual, but not unique. When asked if he had been surprised by the living conditions of people in eastern Tennessee, he displayed compassion tempered with intellectual detachment: "Yes, although not as horrified as some. Now I saw some pretty slumlike places in the mountains, but I also saw some very comfortable places . . . where the people were happy and warm and well clothed and well fed, so that I did not generalize quite as much about the mountain people . . . as some others did." Gant recalled that TVA was not always welcomed by local people, and that some TVA employees worsened the negative reaction of many inhabitants through their arrogance. "Sometimes our people didn't think that the counties were quite as aggressive [as they should have been] . . . in putting on model programs, and I'm sure the counties on occasions felt that our people were somewhat meddlesome," he noted.[6]

Gant refused to accept the notion that the Fontana area was somehow particularly isolated. "The roads there were not bad, but it took awhile to drive [from Knoxville]," he remarked. But despite his understanding of the complexities of the region, Gant viewed rural life as dull and unstimulating. He used his authority to encourage recreational programs under the general heading of "personnel relations." He described the purpose of these programs as "to give a little more life and interest and excitement and enthusiasm to some of those rural communities which had had . . . bad times during the depression." He recognized that TVA's presence in the region disrupted many normal community activities. His goal was not to minimize the disruption but to make the disruption productive.[7]

In general, TVA policies toward the area lacked Gant's foresight. To maintain amiable relations between TVA and the local population and to address the population's concerns about the impact of the dam, TVA employed a Population Readjustment Division in its Department of Reservoir Properties. This division was supposed to carry the responsibility of helping residents relocate. Population readjustment, broadly defined, included scheduling relocation, helping residents find suitable new homes and land, and sometimes interceding with other TVA departments and even other governmental agencies on behalf of residents. The purpose of population readjustment was to minimize the impact of TVA's arrival on the lives of residents, not necessarily to better their circumstances as Gant would have preferred.[8]

Arnold Hyde was born in the Atoah Creek area of Graham County, the great-great-great-grandson of John Aaron Hyde, one of the area's first white settlers. Arnold Hyde's grandfather, B. N. Hyde, became one of the area's first logging contractors, and Arnold's father raised beef cattle. The Hyde family owned several tracts of land throughout Graham County, and they made a profit off the land in whatever way they could. The family had the reputation of being rather modern-minded, and one of Arnold's uncles, John Hyde, served as a teacher in the Atoah area. Arnold graduated from Robbinsville High School and attended Western Carolina Teachers' College on a Stillwell Scholarship, receiving a B.S. in education in 1938. After a stint as a teacher and basketball coach in Polk County, he returned to Graham County as a teacher before accepting employment in TVA's Population Readjustment Division.[9]

Reports generated by the Population Readjustment Division, including several authored by Arnold Hyde, serve as the primary record of TVA's actions regarding population readjustment. These reports were written by TVA officials who were in closest contact with the population, and represent the "best" information TVA decision makers received. Not surprisingly, the often flawed assumptions about the population evident in these reports, coupled with the preexisting image that TVA management had of the area, affected TVA relocation and redevelopment policies.

The population readjustment reports helped to perpetuate stereotypes of the "Appalachian way of life," stereotypes promoted by Kephart and others of his day. Ignorant of the subtleties of the region's social and economic life, outsiders from TVA tended to see the mountaineers as either the romantic, sturdy pioneers of *Our Southern Highlanders* or the benighted, isolated Elizabethan throwbacks described in the WPA guide's entry on Bushnell. Arnold Hyde, who had grown up in the area, might be expected to understand the region's people better than the outsiders did, but his own conceptions of the region's life were shaped in part by his educational experience at WCTC, an institution with an explicit mission to "uplift" the mountain people of North Carolina from within.[10] The ambiguous policies of TVA arose in part from the ambiguity of these contradictory stereotypes. The agency had struggled with the conflict between these images since its first construction project, Norris Dam, and TVA decision makers had not successfully resolved that conflict.[11]

The tangible evidence of good access, at least for the large communities, did not fundamentally alter the impression of isolation that some readjustment workers had. The isolation of which they spoke had as much to do with their perceptions of local attitudes as it did with the presence or absence of roads and trains. Arnold Hyde's description of the mountain residents indicates he did not consider himself part of the mountain culture. He wrote of "foot paths leading across the mountains into deep coves [which] serve as the only access for many families, who upon finding a cold spring, constructed a cabin with no thought given to the inconvenience of the location."[12] He criticized the residents of the remote and mountainous Stecoah area for indolence and their apparent unwillingness to work together:

> A majority of the homes are in extremely poor condition, which not only reflects something of the economic condition of the family but reflects in many instances the lack of pride as well as initiative in making necessary improvements on the farm. . . . Often the chickens

> roost in the shade trees in the yard and the pigs run loose around the house. The toilets are placed over open streams, and flies breed unmolested around the house and barnyard. All of these insanitary practices point to the reluctance of the mountaineer to make modern improvements and develop a cooperative community spirit.[13]

The message here is that the mountain lifestyle is the epitome of backwardness. For Hyde, "progress" was inevitable, and the sooner the mountaineers embraced it, the better off they would be. TVA's philosophy of grassroots bureaucracy as articulated by H. A. Morgan and popularized by David Lilienthal had guaranteed that some people from the immediate area would find suitable employment with the agency, but the demands of the population readjustment jobs were such that only the educated few could qualify, and those educated few were also those best acquainted with the values of the "outside world." Any reluctance to accede to the spirit of that outside world would mean consignment to perpetual stagnation and poverty.[14]

Hyde noted that farmers received more cash from the sale of timber products than from all other agricultural products combined. But he foresaw burley tobacco, which had recently been introduced into the region, as the cash crop of the future for the area, once timbering was no longer viable. Despite his optimism about the future of tobacco farming, however, he still considered the farming families a step behind the rest of the population. He wrote: "The standard of living varies considerably. Families living in the villages of Judson and Almond are progressive and make a fair living, but a majority of those in the more isolated regions are existing in a state of poverty. The farm homes, as a rule, are in a poor state of repair and are furnished with bare necessities." Although he often deplored the attitudes of his neighbors, Hyde understood that each community had its own structure and dynamics. He wrote approvingly that five families in the Almond-Judson area had shown the initiative to obtain electric power for themselves by building their own small hydroelectric plants. Writing about Almond and Judson, he praised local community leaders for trying to keep the community together in the face of an uncertain future, noting that during the 1920s "many families sold their property [to Alcoa] and moved out. Some sold and then rented, becoming tenants of the [Nantahala] Power Company. A few remaining land owners, who refused to sell, endeavored to keep the community spirit alive. The progress of the community has apparently been retarded by the widespread belief that Fontana Dam would eventually be constructed."[15]

While some TVA operatives assumed that poverty in the region was a constant, Hyde showed a better understanding of the region's turbulent history. Here again, though, his negative attitude toward the region's status in the 1940s is apparent in his description of a once-important community structure: "An old abandoned Methodist Church building at Judson serves as a stark reminder of the more progressive days when Methodists lived and worshipped among the native Baptists."[16]

If Hyde seems impatient with some of his neighbors and sympathetic toward the efforts of others, his colleagues in the Population Readjustment Division seem dismissive of most or all of the area's residents. Rome C. Sharp complained that TVA's readjustment work in the Proctor community was made more difficult by "the definite lack in the community of fraternal or social organization, and the clannish attitude of the natives." Sharp summed up Proctor as follows: "[This region presents] a unique picture of community decadence and disorganization."[17] Proctor, of course, was the largest community affected by the readjustment process, and it was the same town whose residents had inaugurated new community rituals such as Decoration Day during the Depression in an attempt to maintain a sense of cohesion. Blinded to any evidence of this community cohesion, Sharp recommended that the Population Readjustment Division emphasize counseling individual families, rather than addressing community organizations to gain support, as TVA had done with other projects. Sharp's recommendation cost the agency valuable support among the locals.

Sharp's report took no account of the human aspects of Proctor's history as a boomtown; indeed, while it contains important quantitative information concerning migration and the transient population, it exhibits very little evidence that Sharp had ever spoken with any of the residents, demonstrating what Michael Ann Williams called "a particular lack of effort . . . laced with stereotypical images." Readjustment operatives sometimes too easily accepted the romantic image of Kephart's lost frontiersmen in forming their impressions of the region. Still, as Sharp noted, the independence of many mountain residents was often more symbolic than real. Sharp's report on Proctor, which aside from Bryson City had been the most active prosperous community in the upper Little Tennessee only twenty years earlier, quotes Jonathan Daniels's comments on a New Deal experiment elsewhere in western North Carolina: "Maybe the experiment interrupts a process which would at last drain them to the towns where they would be closer to relief but, unskilled as they are, no nearer to independence in jobs where there are already more men than employment.

Even in a guarded dependency they may be better off on the little pieces of land so many of them love so much." Despite the condescension evident in this report, Sharp was right about at least one thing. The so-called mountaineers were dependent on the outside world. But that dependence was neither new nor limited to the federal dole. It was integral to the economic history of the region from the arrival of the first white farmers, and it was in some measure consensual.[18]

TVA workers differed on the importance of educating the residents. Sharp relied on Daniels's book *Tar Heels* for a romantic, if not very optimistic, picture of attempts to "educate" these residents: "Federal agencies had been active already, and successfully, in mitigating the illiteracy in the cabins in the coves beyond the ends of the roads in Swain. It was grand to be able to read and write, but on the edge of the preserved forest primeval—among the pioneers—for all but a sixth of the people, literacy meant only ability to sign a relief receipt."[19]

Hyde, the former teacher, strongly differentiated among residents based on their attitudes toward education, describing those with whom he agreed as "progressive." His report on Stecoah outlined the difficulties TVA and other organizations often encountered in attempting to convince residents of the advantages of education, observing that "there yet exists among the parents a lack of understanding and appreciation for the advantages offered in the field of education." Hyde then identified several of what he called "underlying causes for the indifferent attitude toward school and community progress." These causes were (1) educational "deficiencies" (his word) among the parents; (2) lack of proper medical care; (3) the long distances children would have to travel over rough terrain to get to a school bus; (4) parents' inability to afford the necessary clothes and school supplies for their children; and (5) failure of the school officials to incorporate vocational courses, which Hyde said "would attract and interest the practical minded mountaineers."[20]

Hyde assumed education and progress were one and the same. He associated education with decreases in both feuding and moonshining. He noted approvingly that with TVA's help the curriculum at Stecoah's school had been revamped to include vocational programs by 1944. TVA had also helped construct a new building for shop classes and home economics using materials salvaged from demolished buildings in the reservoir area, in hopes of attracting the attention of these same "practical minded mountaineers." Perhaps Hyde would not have approved of the fact that a school at Proctor accepted an uncertified teacher in the 1942–43 school year on the grounds that "she lived there, and it was the last year of that school anyway," but his "practical-minded mountaineers" might have.[21]

The practical-mindedness of these mountaineers provided TVA with some of its most difficult problems. Contrary to the popular perception that mountain society was static and that its people were too attached to unproductive land, Sharp recognized that the residents of the upper Little Tennessee were prone to moving about and setting up housekeeping wherever there was employment. The Sharp report described those living in Proctor in dehumanizing language which nonetheless captures the mobility of the population: "[Remaining residents are a] residue of the more prosperous periods of lumbering and mining operations carried on in this community." The report also cited population statistics to prove that the population fluctuated with the utilization and exhaustion of the natural resources of the region. Sharp's unsympathetic yet accurate understanding of the connection between population change and the availability of jobs in the area played a role in persuading the Readjustment Office to include the transient families in its mission.[22]

Both Hyde and Sharp recognized the shifts in the area's population. These shifts took two distinct forms. One was the localized movement of the so-called original families. While many of these families occupied the same community for many years, many of the dwellings in the region in 1940 were less than ten years old. This type of mobility is a recurring theme in Hyde's and Sharp's population readjustment reports. The impermanence of structures dominated the area's housing picture even before the irresistible pull of war jobs lured many from northern Georgia and eastern Tennessee to set up makeshift homes along, or even directly over, the Little Tennessee River near the construction site.[23]

The second type of population movement TVA officials saw was the influx of so-called transient households. The development of these spontaneous settlements near the construction site created problems for TVA. Project manager Clarence E. Blee initially opined that TVA should not attempt to bear responsibility for these transient households,[24] but his assessment was eventually amended, and the population readjustment reports do include these households. These new settlements nearly doubled the caseload for population readjustment workers, and the buildings often turned up on land TVA needed to control for construction purposes. Moreover, the abysmal lack of sanitation and the inadequate supply of drinking water created health hazards that could spread throughout the workforce and delay construction of the dam. TVA initiated community health education programs and voluntary typhoid immunization in an attempt to stem the spread of disease. Education was TVA's most powerful weapon against illness, just as it was against poverty. TVA policymakers saw the mountain dwellers as victims of their own ignorance, and the agency's educational programs were an opportunity for the improvement of material conditions.

The degree to which TVA officials understood the project's impact on the area's farmers depended upon their distance from those residents' experiences. Chief engineer T. B. Parker blithely assumed that "because the rugged terrain makes farming difficult and unproductive, little of the land that will be flooded is of agricultural value."[25] H. K. Menhinick, director of the Department of Regional Studies, was less callous, noting, "In most cases all cleared land on the farms affected will be inundated. The extremely rugged nature of adjacent lands makes it unlikely that families will attempt to reestablish homes on the slopes above the reservoir margin."[26] Hyde's reports on Stecoah and Almond-Judson readily and perceptively acknowledged that the loss of agriculture would destroy the way of life to which the residents had become accustomed. He elaborated further in his report on the twin communities of Almond and Judson: "The loss of the fertile bottom land, even though the acreage is small, will cause radical changes in agricultural methods. The extremely rugged nature of the adjacent lands makes it impossible for farm families to re-establish homes on the steep, unproductive land above the reservoir margin."[27]

Hyde understood that, regardless of the importance of agriculture to the economy of the region, it provided many families with a sense of security that could not be expressed in dollars and cents. He nonetheless insisted that the benefits of the project would be substantial: "The changes brought about by the program of the Authority have offered new opportunities to dissatisfied families, who realize the futility of the struggle with poverty in their present environment. The individual not only will be freed from restricted circumstances, but the community as a whole will profit by the advantages afforded by the creation of Fontana Lake."[28]

Like his colleagues, Hyde saw his job as improving the material condition of the area as a whole. In the process, he hoped to ensure that those individuals whose lives TVA changed would adopt the more prosperous lifestyle he associated with progress. His residence in the area provided him with a greater sense of the region's history, but his "progressive" sympathies helped formulate a readjustment style that focused more on national or regional goals than on the needs of the area as perceived by its residents.

The process of "freeing the individual from restricted circumstances," in the minds of Hyde and his superiors within TVA, often meant evicting families from communities with which they had maintained close ties, even if their residence there was intermittent. Similarly, in practice, "benefiting the community as a whole" meant not only attempting to convert the as yet elusive tourist dollar into an enhanced material quality of life, but also radically altering the community's structure, dispersing its population, and permanently disrupting its trading patterns. According to this view, these people who had "gotten by" on so little for so long lacked the necessary knowledge and skills to decide for themselves what was to be done in their community; their divergence from the "progressive" patterns of the so-called outside world was proof enough that they needed the assistance of the federal government in the form of employment, education, and relocation.

TVA, of course, assumed the responsibility for providing that assistance. This decision created unforeseen difficulties for the agency. In any hydroelectric project, land purchase and the removal of residents can present major problems, including disputes over ownership, the value of land and buildings, and the amount of assistance for relocation that residents expect. TVA had already relocated residents for other projects, but Fontana presented new challenges. Wartime shortages and the difficulty of synchronizing the construction schedule with the agricultural schedule augmented the already formidable difficulties associated with removal. In addition, land for relocation was scarce, and those who rented their homes received no financial help for relocation from TVA. Furthermore, landownership often changed several times between TVA's surveys and final acquisition. The widely held belief within TVA that landownership was stable contributed to the agency's inability to bring the project together as seamlessly as anticipated. John Snyder, who had been in charge of land acquisition for TVA's first project at Norris, had abolished the early practice of conducting a full title search before beginning talks with landowners, exacerbating the problem.[29]

The case of the family of Andy Chicklelee illustrates some of the difficulties valley residents encountered when attempting to abide by TVA plans. Chicklelee, a Cherokee living near the community of Japan in Graham County, had been employed by Southern Railway for nineteen years, an unusually long term of employment for anyone living in the Little Tennessee area. A TVA caseworker noted approvingly that the family spoke English well and that "the children refuse[d] to converse in the Cherokee language." White neighbors fondly remembered Chicklelee's insistence that his children obtain a college education. The family lived on land attached to the Eastern Band Cherokee Reservation, which they held by "possessory right" according to the Cherokee constitution. In addition to that tract, they owned some land and a house outside the reservation. The reservation land would be flooded by the dam, and the other tract would be cut off from road access.[30]

The caseworker described the family as "exceptionally friendly" and cooperative, noting that they often served as interpreters between TVA officials and other Cherokees. Chicklelee offered no protest when asked to move, but he did express a desire to remain in the same general area so that he could continue working for the Southern Railroad.[31]

After traveling to Waynesville in an unsuccessful attempt to secure appropriate land, he asked both TVA and the Cherokee Nation for help in relocating. Chief Jarrett Blythe of the Cherokee Nation offered him a location on the reservation, which Chicklelee refused because it was too remote. The Extension Service Office soon found Chicklelee another farm near the town of Cherokee that was within his financial means and of appropriate size, and Chicklelee intended to purchase it as soon as he received payment from the Cherokee Nation for the house he had built on reservation land.[32]

A seemingly simple process became a bureaucratic nightmare as Chicklelee's attempts to relocate were thwarted. In March 1944, the Cherokee Council offered Chicklelee and his son-in-law $2,500 for their interest in the reservation property. They declined, stating that they needed more money in order to buy a comparable farm elsewhere. Planting time came and went. Chicklelee and his son-in-law, who had intended to occupy a new farm together, split over the issue of compensation, with the son-in-law demanding that the tribe buy them a farm and Chicklelee preferring a cash settlement so he could buy a farm himself.[33]

As Chicklelee eventually found out, before compensation could be made to him for the improvements to the reservation land, Congress had to appropriate money to the Indian Land Office. The tribal council could not act. According to the TVA contract, signed by the secretary of the interior, Chicklelee had to leave the home on the reservation by September 1, 1944, but without being paid for his improvements he could not afford to buy another home.[34]

Finally, in January 1945, Chicklelee accepted the Cherokee Nation's offer of $1,200 for his improvements and rented a house on TVA property near the Almond community, itself about to be inundated. Even then, the condition of the access road leading out of his reservation home delayed the family's relocation for another eight days.[35]

Chicklelee's son-in-law, Game Walker, fared even worse. Walker refused the $1,200 offered by the Cherokee Council, arguing that he had a two-thirds interest in the property. Walker and his family moved to a rented farm near Almond, but left a stove and some chairs in the reservation home, refusing to surrender the home completely until a settlement could be reached. The TVA caseworker's terse and unsigned closing entry reads as follows: "At a later date, by some means, Mr. Walker's house and household goods caught fire and burned down. This case is closed and no follow-up is suggested."[36]

The L. W. Ammons family of Judson faced another set of obstacles. Mr. Ammons felt attached to the land; his wife felt tied down to it. The family occupied 270 acres they did not legally own, land which would be cut off by rising waters. The actual owners of the property, heirs to the McGaha family, which purchased much of the area's land in 1838, were "all scattered throughout the United States." The Ammons family did legally own an adjacent tract, but it was inaccessible by road and did not have a house on it. The caseworker's report is revealing: "Mrs. Ammons stated that she had to do all the work around the place . . . [and] expressed a desire to get out of that hole and hoped that the TVA would buy their property so Mr. Ammons would have to move. He has lived here all his life, she stated, and wishes to continue living here the rest of his life." The family cultivated 10 of their 270 acres with one ox, yielding what the TVA caseworker described as "small returns for a maximum amount of land." Probably the rest of the land was too steep for planting and was used for pulpwood or grazing.[37]

Their home was located on property owned by the McGaha family heirs. The Ammons family had lived there for ten years since Mr. Ammons purchased some sort of dubious license to occupy it from his brother. The family paid no rent, timbered the land without paying "stumpage" to the McGaha heirs, and built several structures; thus, they considered that they owned the property, despite the lack of legal title. TVA's definition of "ownership" followed the strict legal interpretation: "The contract for the purchase of tract FR-743 was closed on December 20, 1943. The McGaha heirs received the net sum of $2,398. Mr. Ammons, the only occupant of the tract, received no part of the purchase price."[38]

The Ammons family did legally own an adjoining piece of unimproved land, and the family eventually moved to that tract. Mr. Ammons followed the common local practice of purchasing several structures in the area for salvage and reusing the materials in the construction of his new home.[39]

On March 1, 1944, Mr. Ammons requested that TVA lease him several tracts of land near Judson so that he could plant a crop. He had been informed that he must vacate the land on which he lived by May 1 of that year, and he continued to negotiate for the chance to remain there until the completion of an access road, but he was unwilling to gamble on planting a crop there. TVA granted the lease on the Judson tracts, some of which the agency had already purchased from their owners for reservoir impoundment. TVA expressly denied liability for damage to any crops caused by rising water levels.[40]

In effect, Ammons gambled that the previous owners had sold out too soon and that he could harvest a crop on the land before TVA got around to flooding it. He was right. Ammons's approach to agriculture may seem unorthodox, but like the other residents of the area he was accustomed to having to work around whatever circumstances he might have to face. Ammons was no stoic, static mountaineer from the forest primeval; he might be better compared to the southerners who, sensing an opportunity for self-preservation amid the turmoil of Reconstruction, sought alliance with the Republican Party. In short, he was a survivor.

Ammons even accepted temporary employment from TVA—moving supplies for the construction of the very road that would open up access to the land he owned. This access became one of the most difficult problems for Ammons. TVA had originally told him to move from his home by December 1943. That date of possession moved to May 1944, then to November 1944. During this time TVA kept Ammons from using this land for agricultural purposes and instead leased him land for such purposes at a *lower* elevation. The agency finally canceled the leases on that land in September 1944, and Ammons moved into his new home in February 1945 upon completion of the access road.[41]

Families who had been in the area for generations often agonized over the need for relocation, but the nonfarming residents of the deep mountain coves seldom had such strong emotional ties to their land. This group, so celebrated by Kephart, often depended upon seasonal or irregular employment and had so few possessions that relocation was an easy and frequent task. Bill Fuller, one such resident, told a TVA worker that when the time came for him to move, all he would have to do was put out the fire and call the dog, and he did not have a dog. The story attributed to Fuller is a standard joke in the area; Fuller undoubtedly said this to the TVA worker, who faithfully recorded it. The TVA worker visited Fuller several times to inquire about his relocation plans and each time was told, sometimes with language that the worker described as "a tirade of oaths and . . . all sorts of vile epithets," that he had nothing to move and thus did not need to make plans. Fuller's tirade may have been a response to the caseworker's attitude toward him, exemplified by the worker's note that "his physical appearance was like that of some animal which . . . completely ignored in general the use of water for ablution purposes." Fuller's intransigence and the caseworker's patronizing attitude made his case difficult to resolve; eventually he was moved to the County Home for the Aged.[42]

Another case, that of the Missionary Baptist Church in Fairfax, illustrates some of the ways the constant turmoil characteristic of the region affected the readjustment process. The church was organized during the summer of 1943 by five men who declared themselves trustees of the church. The church building had previously been used as a saloon and "was outstanding as a place of ill repute over a period of many months" before the trustees converted it to higher purposes. Andy Reid, the operator of the saloon, received $100 plus a $25 monthly rent for the use of the building. When TVA contracted for the purchase of the land,[43] a controversy arose over ownership of the building. Andy Reid's right to the property was contested by Robert L. Cabe Sr.,[44] one of the trustees, who claimed that he had purchased the building from Reid. The court ruled that Cabe owned the building, and he began dismantling it for salvage within a few days. The church moved its operations to a grocery store building owned by Erskin Harrell on land leased from the Cable heirs sometime in November 1944, and upon the expiration of the lease in May 1945 the church apparently disbanded.

Typically, religious institutions serve as conservative forces that link the activities of the present to the traditions of past generations. The temporariness of the Missionary Baptist Church demonstrates the turbulence of the area's social structure under the stress of the wartime homefront. Indeed, the profit motive seems to be the primary element of continuity in the upper Little Tennessee. The fragile churches, schools, and other community institutions of the region's "permanent" residents were still more stable than the colonies of makeshift shelters that housed temporary or "transient" residents. TVA estimated that over half of the households in the area in 1944 contained transient workers.[45]

The homes of transient families ranged from rough-cut log houses to cheap prefabricated chipboard crates manufactured in Bryson City and sold in kit form to newcomers. These homes occupied locations chosen more for their immediate convenience than for their physical stability. A number of them occupied the flood plain in the immediate vicinity of the dam and had to be moved frequently to avoid incurring the wrath of TVA construction foremen. Others were placed on land rented out by opportunistic absentee landowners. A few were even placed on parallel logs crossing the narrow river valley, with a hole cut in the floor to serve as a makeshift privy.[46]

TVA attempted to control the growth of shantytowns for several reasons. The uncontrolled construction of dwellings made reservoir clearance difficult and complicated the process of moving materials around the dam site. Many of these shacks occupied land TVA needed immediately. Also, at least in the early stages of the project, TVA officials did not want the responsibility of relocating transient occupants after the completion of the dam. The transient nature of these households might well mean that the same families would be moved again and again, with TVA bearing the expense each time. Finally, the lack of safe water supplies and sanitation in these dwellings contributed to the spread of diseases and made it difficult to provide adequate facilities for longer-term workers.[47]

TVA's success in controlling these spontaneous settlements was limited. Simply ordering the premises vacated would solve the immediate problems of crowding and transportation but do nothing to guarantee a safe water supply or make the reservoir area easier to clear. Moreover, TVA already faced serious labor shortages. Banning all temporary dwellings would only aggravate that problem. TVA found the solution in a combination of strategies: inspection of all temporary dwellings and the demolition of those found lacking in sanitation; accelerated taking of properties needed for the construction process itself; negotiating with landowners for the construction of a private trailer camp at Proctor; and providing better access to a wider range of TVA-provided housing for workers, including larger tent camps, demountable houses, and dormitories.[48]

To build the dam as quickly as possible, TVA had to provide ways to move people, construction equipment and materials, and information to the dam site. This was particularly difficult in the case of Fontana because of the rugged terrain and the lack of major towns in the area.

Fontana Dam, conceived by A. E. Morgan as a showcase for regional planning, quickly became a rush job because of the wartime need for aluminum. Planning emphasized expediency rather than the reform goals of the A. E. Morgan era. Construction materials and equipment came from various sites. Many items, especially worker housing, were recycled from other TVA projects, notably those along the Hiwassee River. TVA constructed telephone lines so that information could be relayed quickly between Fontana and TVA headquarters in Knoxville, sixty-eight miles away over rough terrain. TVA also built temporary roads, rail lines, and bridges to make sure materials could be delivered quickly. The temporary nature of these facilities meant that they could be constructed rapidly and cheaply. It also meant that they would not provide the infrastructure necessary to enable the region to profit from the electric power generated at Fontana once the war was over.[49]

Bryson City, the region's largest town, served as a base of operations for population readjustment, reservoir clearance, and other land management tasks. It housed Fontana's largest personnel office for some time. The town also provided many support services such as housing and medical care for workers, to supplement those available at the dam site over thirty miles away. Until the construction village was completed in 1943, workers had to travel to Bryson City for movies, haircuts, laundry, a heated room, or a restaurant meal. Because of these connections, transportation between Bryson City and the dam site was very important to the timely completion of the dam.

TVA and civic leaders attempted to pressure Southern Railway into providing rail service between Bryson City and Fontana using the old Bushnell-Fontana spur, which the railroad had planned to abandon upon closure of the mine at Eagle Creek. Southern refused, saying it did not have the equipment or facilities to provide passenger service at the time, despite not only the demand from TVA but also the reopening of the old Adams mine on Hazel Creek. Eventually Smoky Mountain Stages, Inc., contracted to provide bus service to Maryville and Knoxville, Tennessee, instead. The bus ride from Knoxville to Fontana averaged approximately two and a half hours. This reduced the problem of getting workers to the dam, but TVA officials continued to press for rail service in order to use the Bryson City labor supply more fully.[50]

These transportation arrangements alone did not provide TVA with a steady enough supply of labor to maintain its construction schedule for Fontana. Many workers continued to live in tents or boxes on private land in the area, while others commuted weekly over difficult roads from as far away as Maryville, Tennessee, or Young Harris, Georgia, until tire rationing made that impossible.[51] The difficulties these workers faced, the expectations TVA had of them, and the resulting tensions will reveal much about the character of the area's residents and their response to the wartime boom economy in the next chapter.

6

Managing People and Land

The pressures of a coming war made it possible to build Fontana Dam. The pressures of a nation at war dictated the way in which it would be built, the type of workers to be hired, where those workers would live, what they would eat, how they would be entertained, and even how their children would be schooled. On the surface, that seems like a dramatic transformation. Yet in reality the war superimposed a new type of temporary employment on an economy that was already structured around temporary employment. It superimposed a paternalistic management style and a company-town organization upon a people who had experienced such paternalism before, and some of those people longed for a return to it. It brought large amounts of cash into a region filled with residents for whom cash was associated with luxury items they desperately wanted. It promised to finish the job begun by the National Park Service, that of transforming the region into a profitable tourist attraction, as soon as the dam's immediate task of providing electricity for the war effort was assured. In other words, construction of the dam accentuated and amplified tendencies already evident before the arrival of TVA. It brought more money than any previous extractive industry, but it was certainly not the first experience these people had with a cash economy. It brought more dislocation than previous industries, but it did not destroy a static civilization. It brought more government jobs, but many residents already depended on the WPA, the CCC, and the National Park Service for employment. It brought a twenty-four-hour work schedule, where earlier the workday had been from first light to last light, but it did not introduce wage labor into a carefree subsistence economy. As far as the residents of the area were concerned, only the scale was different. Fontana in the 1940s was a boomtown, just as Proctor and Bushnell had been thirty years earlier.

TVA and area residents both strove to maintain an atmosphere in which normal and even mundane activities could help cushion the stress of the wartime environment. Thus, a complete description of the lives of

Figure 3. Construction was a twenty-four-hour-a-day job at Fontana Dam, as this photo from February 1944 shows. Photo: Tennessee Valley Authority.

workers during the construction of Fontana Dam must include both the extraordinary—the round-the-clock schedule, the millions of cubic feet of concrete poured, the massive influx of workers into the area, the sheer size of the ascendant TVA bureaucracy, and the enormity of the threat posed by the Axis powers—and the ordinary—the means by which area residents dealt with their neighbors, the newspapers they read, the types of entertainment they sought, and the frustrations they faced.

TVA needed a large workforce in order to keep up with the wartime construction schedule. The estimated peak workforce of 7,000 full-time employees at Fontana exceeded the entire population of Graham County in 1940. Many of these jobs would go to trained workers whose skills were in short supply in the region. Wages at Fontana, like wartime wages elsewhere, seemed quite high after the region's retreat to a near-subsistence economy during the 1930s. Residents of the area saw the dam and the wartime economy as an opportunity to make money. They gravitated toward it as surely as their forebears had gravitated toward the lumber camps, the rail yards, the mines, and ultimately the land itself.[1]

The opportunity for wartime construction jobs lured many from the surrounding counties of western North Carolina and eastern Tennessee to apply for work at Fontana, despite the difficulty of getting to the job. The roads leading to the dam site could not handle large numbers of commuters, and their gravel surfaces quickly wore out rationed tires. TVA's attempts to arrange daily transportation for workers succeeded only near the end of the project, just as improved housing facilities at the site made transportation a less critical issue.

The initial attraction of a paying job with TVA wore off for many. Wages in wartime jobs rose rapidly, and some workers moved from job to job in search of the best paycheck. TVA had to compete with private industry throughout the nation for labor resources. TVA found it especially hard to keep workers at Fontana because of the perceived remoteness of the location and the initial absence of adequate housing. Because it was hard to maintain a large workforce, TVA had to recruit even unskilled workers from as far away as White and Habersham Counties in northern Georgia, more than three hours away over difficult roads.[2]

TVA's recruitment of workers stressed the importance of the project and the comfortable facilities available. In an eight-page recruitment pamphlet entitled "Work at Fontana Dam," TVA emphasized the cooperative atmosphere of the job site. The agency promised clean, racially segregated cafeterias, small but comfortable houses, and abundant amenities. These promises helped reassure white workers that the agency had no intention of experimenting with racially integrated living conditions. The pamphlet also implicitly reminded them that they would be expected to work as a team with, though not necessarily alongside, black and Cherokee workers. By stressing the fact that the electric power generated at Fontana would be essential to the war effort, the pamphlet maintained a careful balance between the segregationist traditions of the South and the manpower demands of the war, largely in accord with Roosevelt's overall racial policies.[3]

From its inception in 1933, TVA voluntarily instituted a racial quota system in order to ensure nonpreferential hiring practices. A. E. Morgan and his personnel director, Floyd Reeves, intended the system to be race-neutral. They based their hiring policy on the percentage of African Americans in the immediate area of each project, so that African Americans would be a large part of the workforce at Wheeler, Chickamauga, and Muscle Shoals, but not in the mountainous area surrounding the Norris, Appalachia, and Hiwassee projects. TVA resisted hiring African Americans at several projects by saying that the small numbers involved did not justify the cost of constructing separate facilities for the two races. Privately, many TVA officials expressed profound reluctance to challenge the prevailing racial climate by providing integrated housing, and feared violence if they did so. The refusal to challenge prevailing racial norms is consistent with H. A. Morgan's insistence on working within existing southern social, political, and educational institutions, and as one historian noted, TVA was fighting for its very existence throughout this formative period.[4]

After TVA refused to hire black workers at Hiwassee Dam because there were so few in the area, the NAACP and some members of the Roosevelt administration pressured the agency to guarantee that all projects would include black workers. After 1941, Executive Order 8802 required TVA and all other government agencies and contractors to "fully use all manpower regardless of race." The agency responded by increasing the percentage of black employees in its workforce. This policy affected Fontana more than other projects because Fontana already required the importation of a large workforce in order to meet urgent needs for electric power in the aluminum industry.[5]

The upper Little Tennessee had occasionally provided black families with housing and employment. A few black farmers had maintained homes on Peachtree Creek in Swain County, and the Ritter Lumber Company had recruited black workers to meet the extraordinary production demands of World War I. Alcoa, too, had brought in black workers for the construction of Cheoah Dam, itself a World War I project. But the area's black population had mostly disappeared by the 1930s. Black residents were scarce; those with the skills TVA needed were especially so. In keeping with the revised quota system, the personnel department projected it would hire ninety-six to one hundred black laborers from outside the mountain area for specific, mostly skilled jobs at Fontana. Since skilled workers were to be housed at Fontana Village in Graham County, that move would increase the black population of Graham County by 10,000 percent.[6]

Like other black TVA employees, those at Fontana actually found mostly lower-echelon jobs. Whites and Cherokees resisted black participation in the project because they saw the imported black workers as outsiders. Cherokees, in particular, had fought hard for access to jobs at Fontana and did not want competitors to be brought in.[7]

TVA's George Gant remembered whites as willing to work with members of other races. Living among those other races was another matter. "I think there was some tradition that Negroes did not spend the night in that

[Graham] county," he recalled. Indeed, rioters singled out the black workers' sleeping quarters for special treatment. A mob nearly burned down the black dormitory the first night it was occupied. After that, many black workers left. TVA dispatched additional security officers from other camps, and those officers guarded the remaining black workers for over a week while "protective" segregation measures could be instituted. As the project matured, however, some black and white workers began to interact voluntarily on a limited basis, taking the initiative to dismantle a barrier separating the movie theater. "That rope was always tripping somebody and the next thing we knew the people tore it down, and the movie house was integrated," recalled one TVA employee.[8]

Racial strife was not the only source of morale problems at Fontana. The continuing memory of the Great Depression, shortages of preferred foodstuffs, lack of adequate housing and desired services, the mix of mountain residents and urban professionals, difficulties in traveling, the unrelenting pace of construction, and serious health hazards all contributed to a sense of frustration among workers.

Federal attempts to maintain morale met with mixed results. In a letter that appeared in the *Bryson City Times* on March 5, 1942, Jo Serra expressed frustration with the seemingly endless onslaught of morale-boosting plans:

> Everybody that bobs up with a new idea or new scheme, and edges it onto Uncle Samuel's payroll, says it is for Morale. How we have got along so far without experts on morale, is hard to savvy. And Mr. George Washington, how he ever got up the courage to cross the Delaware without the help of a psychologist, or a toe-dancer, or a poet, to bolster him, is also a big question. Today you can hardly turn around without trampling on a Govt uplifter of some stripe.

Presumably without Serra's approval, the uplifting projects continued. One of the most important was education. TVA educational programs for adults emphasized practical matters such as scientific agriculture. Reading programs sought to eradicate poverty by eradicating illiteracy. The agency's apprenticeship program, an adjunct to its adult education strategy, provided accelerated training in jobs TVA needed to fill.

TVA educational policies reflected the dichotomy between the desire for reform from above and the awareness that rapid changes in social structure might not be welcome, a dichotomy which reached back to the differences between A. E. and H. A. Morgan. The agency provided additional money to existing schools in Swain and Graham Counties to offset the sudden increase in number of pupils, but otherwise exerted only limited influence over the operation of those schools. The agency sponsored the establishment of vocational programs, but did not attempt to influence the academic curriculum. One might wonder whether the agency's financial contribution to the existing schools was enough to offset the decline of small local schools during the 1930s.

The most noticeable effect of the Depression on public schools in western North Carolina had been a massive drive for consolidation, which was promoted as both an improvement in educational opportunities and a means of cutting costs. In the communities of the upper Little Tennessee, a number of petitions were circulated during the 1930s supporting the consolidation movement, but consolidation remained incomplete as of the early 1940s. The local school system inherited by TVA was thus essentially an impoverished rural system in a state of transition, with many one-room schoolhouses vanishing and students being transported farther from home, especially in the upper grades.[9]

Fontana Village was a very different environment from Proctor, Bushnell, and the other communities of the Little Tennessee. The agency built Fontana Village in order to attract and keep professionals and skilled workers who would not willingly live in the tent camps and dormitories. The professionals who lived in the village brought their families and sent their children to school there as well. Because the parents expected their children to follow in their footsteps, learning skills and pursuing a higher education, the schools that TVA built at Fontana Village employed fully certified teachers and embodied up-to-date curricula. TVA officials hoped the schools would provide a laboratory for demonstrating successful techniques that would then be copied by the existing schools. In fact, the TVA educational system was broadly similar to that suggested by progressive education advocates in North Carolina for the preceding forty years, so it would be best to characterize it as contemporary but not experimental, though it must have seemed quite radical compared with what Arnold Hyde found in Graham County before TVA.[10]

Fontana school staff members believed that in a good school, students would "face and freely discuss genuine personal and social problems." They would initiate, plan, and evaluate their own activities. Mutual help and cooperation would replace competition in academic activities. Students would seek their rewards in the value of the activities themselves, not in grades or other external measures of progress. They would criticize and revise their own curriculum to meet their evolving needs.[11]

Students at the Fontana schools ideally would be "as much concerned with learning how to get knowledge . . . as with the knowledge itself." Hands-on study of natural processes would be augmented by standardized or "scientifically developed" lessons and tests. They would learn by doing, and the things they did would emphasize marketable skills. Although most high school students at Fontana, unlike their counterparts in the schools at Proctor or Bushnell, expected to enter either the military or college, most also learned woodworking, homemaking, or other appropriate skills.[12]

The students learned good citizenship by helping out with the war effort, economizing wherever possible, and making substitutes for scarce manufactured goods. Like children across the United States, they collected scrap iron, tin cans, old tires, and paper items. Boys made menu card holders, wooden puzzles, ashtrays, and walking sticks. Girls fashioned Christmas decorations of pine cones and branches, and made washcloths and blankets. Children of all ages competed in the sale and purchase of war bonds and stamps, and the ninth-grade math class learned accounting by managing the bond drives.[13]

Budding third-grade botanists at Fontana received a hands-on education when the school principal gave the class a greenhouse. The greenhouse was located twenty-five miles away, and the students took responsibility for relocating it. Each student proposed a site for the greenhouse and wrote an essay defending the proposal. The group solicited and received the assistance of the eighth-grade class in disassembling, moving, and reassembling it, and managed to conscript quite a few of their fathers as well. The third-graders made sure the fathers knew what was expected of them, when they were expected, and so on. They also washed and polished the glass, studied gardening, and experimented with different types of seeds.[14]

The youngsters settled on lettuce, eggplant, tomatoes, cabbage, and peppers for their greenhouse produce, and many raised them at home as well. They kept the greenhouse unlocked, and visitors were welcomed. The greenhouse provided produce for sale, with the profits going for school equipment and more seeds. In addition, it provided a stimulus for a beautification project that took root in the homes of the village at the insistence of the students.[15]

Given the overcrowded conditions and frequent disease outbreaks in the area, it is no surprise that health and safety issues occupied the minds of students and teachers alike. A rigorous program of physical education emphasized variety while giving more credit for more strenuous exertion. A group of boys organized themselves into a safety patrol, while high school girls served as student teachers by watching over the younger pupils. Third-graders joined the Junior Red Cross. Students and faculty worked together to stage a benefit to help victims of infantile paralysis. Films and field trips emphasized health and hygiene. Safety on the construction site formed an interesting part of the curriculum for many students and, indirectly, for their parents as well. Even venereal diseases were openly discussed.[16]

From third grade on, students worked as library assistants, logging in new books and keeping the library neat. Promoting "reading for fun," the library emphasized reference books and current materials. One measure of the trust school administrators placed in the students is that even costly and scarce encyclopedias could be checked out.[17]

One sixth-grade glass became fascinated by ancient Greece. With a little encouragement from teachers, they researched the subject thoroughly, eventually planning a Greek banquet with authentic food, music, and athletic events to celebrate the traditions and achievements of western civilization. Parents were invited; presumably they applauded politely.[18]

Fifth-, sixth-, and seventh-grade students took naturally to capitalism, initiating the formation of a school store that would provide students with needed supplies. The students not only kept the financial records of the store; they also filled out orders for more supplies and wrote checks to suppliers, learning valuable real-world lessons in the process. They also operated a milk room where all students could purchase milk. Again, students took responsibility for ordering milk, washing and returning bottles, and keeping records.[19]

In a class on modern problems, high school students examined the electoral process in detail. The class sponsored a mock partisan election for "Mayor of Fontana High School." Eighty-seven students registered to vote. President Roosevelt likely would not have been pleased with the outcome, as the students selected a Republican for the job.[20]

High school students built a workshop, which they used to build desks, bookcases, and cabinets for the school. But the workshop provided more than furniture. Students worked off stress by fashioning gifts, toys, sleds, and rowboats. The gift of a handmade keepsake, a rabbit box, or a milking stool could ease the pain of friends leaving the area as their parents finished their jobs at Fontana.[21]

Parents seldom missed student activities, despite their own hectic schedules. School plays, skits, news broadcasts, dialogues, recitations, and interviews reached the entire construction site through the public address system installed in 1944. Fathers and mothers working on the dam could hear their children's voices and could rest assured that they were safe, happy, and healthy and that they were learning useful things. Project manager Fred Schlemmer described the broadcast of school activities over the public address system as one of the most important morale boosters at his disposal, because a worried or distracted employee was unlikely to be productive and might well be dangerous. Moreover, Schlemmer recognized the importance of providing some degree of "normal life" to employees working under such extraordinary conditions.[22]

One class project that began as a lesson on pets eventually integrated lessons in accounting, carpentry, and elementary capitalism as well. One first-grader brought a hen for show-and-tell. The hen tried to set, so the children bought eggs for her to incubate. Two cents admission to their staging of *Little Black Sambo* and *The Three Billy Goats Gruff* was each adult's contribution to the initial egg purchase.[23]

The hen hatched ten chicks, which the children fed on food scraps from home. In due time, three of the resulting fryers were sold to buy feed for the rest. With so many hens now laying, the geometry class had to design and build a henhouse. By this point, eggs could be sold for feed money. At Christmas, members of the school staff bought the chickens, providing money for more hens and some needed school equipment. Reading, writing, and arithmetic assignments pertained to the chickens, and "sex education came easily and naturally" as the students learned the basics of animal husbandry.[24]

Presumably the production of poultry was no accident. Like most other Americans during World War II, workers at Fontana experienced difficulty obtaining enough food, especially meat, to satisfy their appetites. TVA chairman David Lilienthal personally appealed to the Office of Price Administration for extra rations for those working on the Fontana project. Prentiss Brown, administrator of the OPA, declined to provide additional supplies despite the project's priority rating from the War Production Board. Brown referred the matter to the office of Archie M. Palmer, also of OPA, who had already rejected the request. Palmer passed the request on to other OPA officials, who in turn offered a partial solution in the form of an increase in general rations, but declined to give Fontana any special consideration.[25]

Even after the increase in meat supplies, rationed meats were limited to one meal per day. Administrators dining at Cafeteria Number One ate an average of two fish meals and four chicken meals per week, while the larger Cafeteria Number Two for laborers served three fish meals and five chicken meals per week. Meat or cheese sandwiches were provided in packed lunches on average three times a month. A TVA report noted that the 2.8 pounds of rationed meat provided to Fontana employees each week before the revised order compared well with the 2 to 2.25 pounds allowed for average civilians, but it went on to observe that average civilians had access to restaurant meals to supplement their rations. The new ration order increased Fontana's average to four pounds per week, considerably more than the normal civilian average. By July 1943, Fontana workers consumed nearly twice the amount of fresh fruits and vegetables OPA considered necessary for the diet of a healthy adult, and meat supplies were ample. Additionally workers averaged four eggs per person per day. A present-day dietitian might blanch at the protein, fat, and cholesterol evident in this diet, but by the standards of the summer of 1943 this was considered a healthy "working man's diet." J. Ed Campbell reported that in July 1943 workers at Fontana consumed "enough food to load 226 1½ ton trucks which would form a caravan two miles long."[26]

Food and other supplies for Fontana workers generally came from Tennessee. Mayfield Creamery in Athens provided dairy products and ice to the cafeterias. Brown Greer and Company of Knoxville took responsibility for making a variety of bakery goods available to workers. Hartman Beverage Company, also of Knoxville, carried root beer to quench workers' thirst. Businesses of comparable size in North Carolina were too far away to compete successfully, as transportation difficulties would raise costs to unacceptable heights.[27]

Difficulty in transportation also affected TVA's labor supply. Because of difficulty obtaining reliable and safe transportation to and from work, many TVA workers moved into the dam area. Some found clean, secure housing for themselves and their families in the community of Fontana Village. Others found substandard housing in the many trailer camps and shantytowns hastily assembled near the construction site. All who moved into the area found crowded conditions and a lack of privacy.

TVA had already established several small towns to serve its construction operations throughout the Tennessee Valley. The earliest of these was Norris, built in Anderson County, Tennessee, adjacent to the Norris Dam site. A. E. Morgan and his wife, Lucy, had reveled in the potential for building an ideal "planned community" in the Tennessee hills, and even lived at Norris themselves. Morgan and his staff had designed Norris to demonstrate what a small-town utopia might be like. The town had curved streets and liberally wooded public areas, and homes were designed to blend in with the surroundings. Built in a time of heady enthusi-

Figure 4. Workers at Fontana Dam each consumed about four pounds of meat per week and four eggs per day. Photo: Tennessee Valley Authority.

asm and imaginative experimentation, Norris was to be a permanent fixture and a reminder of TVA's mission.[28]

A. E. Morgan's departure, Lilienthal's ascendance, and perhaps most of all the coming of war transformed the nature of TVA's synthetic communities. Construction villages at Hiwassee, Appalachia, and especially Fontana dam sites used primarily temporary "demountable" houses, which arrived in pieces on flatbed trailers and could be assembled or disassembled in a matter of hours. Community centers, dormitories, and other buildings were similarly temporary in their construction, and their sites were chosen primarily for convenience rather than aesthetic appeal. At Fontana, the persistent shortage of housing even within the government village would mean that employees would sometimes bunk in tents or cars. The slightly more fortunate would be able to rent canvas-roofed cabins in campgrounds established by the agency. All accommodations were crowded as close together as possible because of the narrowness of the river valley. Thus, Fontana Village and the surrounding area more nearly resembled a wartime camp than a model town, with trailers and prefabricated homes dominating the landscape.

While it lacked the extensive facilities provided for the army's secret city at Oak Ridge, Fontana Village did offer a few community services and comforts, including a school, a small shopping area, a bank, and hair styling shops. In addition, from July 1942, TVA contracted with the Nantahala Regional Library Board to provide library services. TVA's Mary Utopia Rothrock recalled that the library she organized at Fontana provided a vital service. "It would expand their experience, you know? Just like a movie expands your experience." She admitted that she sometimes looked down on the mountain people as being uninterested in literature. But the residents surprised her. She recalled an encounter with a barber at Fontana Village. She had heard that he read a lot, and casually asked what sort of books he liked to read. Embarrassed, the barber shyly admitted it was a work of poetry. Expecting to find some lightweight doggerel, Rothrock was startled to see A. E. Housman's *A Shropshire Lad* on the barber's shelf. Others with humbler tastes would ask for "a book I can practice reading out of." She attributed the energy with which residents devoured the books to the constant stimulation of the construction schedule. "They came into a stimulating environment and they made use of it to expand their horizons," she explained.[29]

Despite the availability of library services, the primary information source for many was the *Knoxville News-Sentinel.* Unlike those who had lived in mountain areas most of their lives, many of the professionals and skilled workers found the area isolated and sorely lacking in cultural attractions. Because many of the professionals at Fontana came from Knoxville, TVA's headquarters, the newspaper was their primary link to their hometown. When the newspaper announced that it could not continue circulation in the area because of paper shortages and transportation costs, TVA's general manager complained loudly, appealing to the paper's sense of patriotic duty and reminding the business manager of the persistent labor shortage at Fontana. The implication was clear: Without news from the outside world, pressure from the work was so intense that workers would be unable or unwilling to stay on the job.[30]

While on the job, workers at Fontana lived in a variety of housing. Some who lived in the area already continued to live with their families, as TVA intended. Others, especially those recruited from outside regular commuting distance, lived in TVA-constructed tent camps at Bee Cove and Gold Mine Creek, or in demountable dormitories brought in from other TVA projects, or in shanties or trailers on private land near the

Figure 5. One of the camps in which Fontana Dam workers lived. Crowding and unsanitary conditions were formidable obstacles. Photo: Tennessee Valley Authority.

construction site. Many found rooms for rent in Bryson City.[31] Relatively few lived in the family-oriented housing of Fontana Village until the project was nearly competed. Regardless of the type of housing employees used, they lived in cramped conditions, perhaps a bit too close to their neighbors for total comfort. In the trailer camps and tent camps, fresh water supplies were inadequate.[32] Dormitory facilities provided somewhat better conditions, with communal bathrooms replacing makeshift privies. Even in the village area, houses were spaced as closely as possible, for the sake of efficiency, and the walls of the cheaply made cottages were thin enough that even with windows closed, one could hear one's neighbor's every activity.[33]

One could also disapprove of it. TVA employees came from many backgrounds with contrasting values. Fontana Village housing was reserved for families of those who expected to stay in the area for the duration of the project. In practice, this meant that professionals and skilled workers lived there, while unskilled laborers primarily resided in the surrounding area. The expectations of middle-class urbanites contrasted sharply with the more expressive lifestyles of rural laborers. Transient workers moving into formerly self-contained communities contributed further to a sense of dislocation among the more settled residents.

The influx of transient residents greatly expanded the market for illegal spirits, and the "disorderly houses" (where illegal liquor was sold) that sprang up to serve that market created disturbances that the agency would ultimately be forced to control. One Proctor resident, Mrs. Hattie Gunter, complained about an establishment where violence was encouraged:

> There were two men starting to fight, a third man, cousin of the two was trying to make peace[.] Mr. Messer shot the innocent victim in the ankle and he was unable to go to work for several days. Last Sunday night a similar incident happened. Some fellows were fighting and the third was trying to make peace[.] Mr. Messer jumped on him [and] beat him with a gun on the head and he lost a lot of blood. This thing has gone far enough. . . . Some terrible disaster will happen if it isn't closed.[34]

Demurring on the grounds that TVA did not yet technically control the site of the objectionable operation, reservoir property management officials referred the issue to the local sheriff's office, resulting in a few raids on the business. The problem persisted. Even after the agency purchased the land, TVA attorney Herbert Hudson advised against trying to shut the business down directly. Instead, J. Ed Campbell of the population readjustment office relied upon the removal of shantytowns in the area to deprive the proprietor of his clientele, a strategy that apparently succeeded.[35]

TVA attempted to provide recreation opportunities that would preserve order and stability and would enhance worker productivity. While the nation continued to work toward the defeat of Japan and celebrated the demise of Nazi Germany, those who lived at or near the dam site during the week of April 29, 1945, could enjoy such films as *Thunderhead, Son of Flicka, Woman in the Window, I'll Be Seeing You,* and *Song of Nevada,* shown in the TVA theater. They could attend church at either of two community churches served by guest ministers or borrow books from the TVA library. Little girls could attend meetings of the Brownie Scout Troop. Adults could take advantage of the opportunity to attend a dance at the Community Building and sway to the sounds of Coy Tucker and his orchestra. Men and women could participate in the softball league during the day and roller-skate to music in the evening.[36]

These opportunities served the entertainment needs of those living in the camps or at Fontana Village, but failed to reach many of the transient workers living in outlying areas or in the towns. For these mostly unskilled laborers there was little planned recreation, and they resorted to more traditional means of entertaining themselves, namely, drinking and carousing. Early in the project, the *Bryson City Times* blamed the lack of adequate recreation at Fontana for a dramatic increase in alcohol-related accidents, fights, and disorderly conduct. One editorial (April 1, 1943) summed up the situation nicely: "Bent up nerves must have some relaxation. . . . There are a great many young girls and some young men working for TVA who have no gardens to work, no homes to look after. These people need after-hours recreation. Our own boys and girls also need good *well-regulated* recreation" (emphasis added).

After this editorial was published, TVA and the Bryson City Lions Club worked together to provide adequate planned recreation for the Fontana employees living in Swain County. But not all local residents were willing to accept the notion that a lack of planned recreation led to drunkenness. One news report, describing a raid on a tavern at Deals Gap, near the dam, blamed the rise in alcohol consumption in the area on "racketeers of Knoxville, Maryville, and Georgia . . . who evidently are reaping big profits from the workmen at Fontana."[37]

Still, much of the liquor trade was local and rather competitive. As Game Walker, a Cherokee farmer later displaced by the reservoir, recalled,

> Everybody was needy. . . . I finally got to where I just didn't care. . . . We'd made a crop; I'd left it with the old lady. And I started making liquor. I had to have some money. I'd take it to Bryson City. . . . There were plenty of people who wanted it, but they didn't have fifty cents. Finally I got me an old car, but I never did bootleg much. . . . You'd get caught. So I sold mine all around Bryson City and up on Cowee Mountain. . . . I'd sell about ten gallons a week. I got two dollars a gallon to deliver. . . . Back then anybody fooling with liquor had a territory, and nobody better go in there. If they did, they'd carry a little shot back out! I didn't go to their territory, and they didn't come to mine.[38]

Just as it undoubtedly contributed to territorial disputes between illicit producers, alcohol also contributed to other disorderly behavior. Three

Fontana workers from Hiawassee, Georgia, were convicted of setting multiple forest fires in Graham County. One of them confessed that they had "had a beer or two at Topton," a few miles south of the reservoir area. When asked why they set the fires, another replied simply, "I wanted to see the woods burn."[39]

The Brewing Industry Council, certainly conscious of its image in a region noted in earlier times both for its support of prohibition and for its production of illegal spirits, responded with an image campaign urging people to "buy your beer only in reputable, decent places."[40] Faced with attacks on their retail outlets, breweries retaliated by describing drinking as an "American pastime" and stressing moderation. One advertisement read:

> The other day we were talking about George Washington—who besides being a great general was a surveyor, a farmer, and a wise statesman. "And he made mighty good beer too" says Grandma Hoskins. "His private recipe's in the New York Public Library." . . .
>
> Now Grandma Hoskins knows her history—and she told us how other famous men believed in beer and moderation. William Penn, for instance, who had his own brewery, and James Madison, who "urged the manufacture of beer in every State of the Union."
>
> When the dark years of Prohibition came along, they proved how right those early American statesmen were—that no law ever takes the place of moderation.
>
> They were right about a lot of things—Washington and Madison and Penn—and the others who founded America. And from where I sit they were certainly right about moderation too.[41]

So not only was it patriotic to work long hours to build a dam to support the war effort, it was also patriotic to buy and drink American beer, so long as it was done "in moderation."

Moderation of any sort was in short supply at Fontana. Whether in recreation or in labor, the Fontana area during the war was a seething cauldron of activity at all hours. The dam itself was to be the highest east of the Rocky Mountains, and the construction schedule required round-the-clock labor. Workers maintained an extraordinary pace. Turnover was high, due to overwork, family conflicts, and in some cases military duty. Asked how workers coped with the constant turnover, one employee recalled, "We hired some and in a few months we'd lose most of them. . . . We just worked harder, that's all."[42]

Predictably, the pace took its toll on the psychological well-being of workers, with drunkenness and absenteeism weakening the construction effort. Motivational posters and billboards were essential to maintaining morale and productivity in the harsh environment of the construction site. Posters advised that "slacking off" was tantamount to treason, that war bonds were essential for victory, and that the dam was as much a part of the war effort as the movement of troops. One often-reproduced poster featured a smiling, aging, bespectacled worker in a hard hat and overalls. Its caption advised:

> We are building this dam
> To make the power
> To roll the aluminum
> To build the bombers
> To beat the bastards.

The poster's logic was easy to follow, and the motivational message was clear. Despite such messages, however, TVA did experience substantial morale problems, especially absenteeism and the aforementioned heavy drinking. In a speech at a rally in March 1943, chief engineer C. E. Blee noted that over 30,000 employees had been through the hiring process in order to maintain a workforce of 5,600. He bemoaned the extremely high rate of turnover, and cited a rate of 500 absentees some days—nearly 10 percent of the workforce—as a major hindrance to the completion of the project.[43]

A lack of communication between labor and management exacerbated morale problems, fostering rumors that jeopardized the project's completion. In a dispute fueled by rumors of a promised wage increase that did not materialize, the carpenters' union staged a walkout. One carpenter complained to Senator Robert Reynolds that a promised 15 percent raise to cover increased cost of living never materialized and that carpenters did more work and more dangerous work than did any other craft workers. TVA officials in Knoxville apparently did not respond in a way that satisfied this carpenter, and they refused to admit union representatives to a wage conference.[44]

George Gant took the position that federal laws required that they pay the prevailing wage in the Tennessee Valley area as a whole, taking no account of the peculiar wage conditions of the Fontana area. According to this logic, the agency would be breaking the law to pay carpenters any more than $1.25 per hour, and no increase had been promised or would be forthcoming. Gant made the agency's position clear and public, using patriotism as a bargaining tool:

> The TVA knows that carpenters at Fontana understand the law, the general agreement, and the urgency of the Fontana war project. The TVA assumes that those who continue to work at Fontana will accept their responsibility under the law and the general agreement and help meet the Fontana schedule to provide power requested by the War Production Board and the War Department. Those who do not accept this responsibility are requested to advise the Personnel office at once.[45]

The TVA's strategy for dealing with morale problems and preventing the spread of rumors involved the manipulation of information and control of the physical environment. Beginning in February 1944, shortly after the carpenters' incident, the agency established an elaborate public address system for "the development of contentment, happiness, and satisfaction in all employees; the promotion of job enthusiasm and interest; the increase of safety consciousness; the stimulation of production; the reduction of absenteeism; the elimination of employee turnover; the purchase of war bonds; [and] the promotion of acceptance of citizenship responsibility to the war effort."[46]

The system operated twenty-four hours a day, six days a week. Officials directed the programming toward the worksite rather than residential and recreation areas. Musical programming aimed at relieving tension was interspersed with official announcements, short editorials, safety slogans, health reminders, advertisements for war bonds, news broadcasts, educational programs, and game shows as well as programs produced by children. Recreation officials recorded local talent shows for rebroadcast during each shift. Visiting dignitaries, ranging from the governor of North Carolina to the president of the American Federation of Labor, used the P.A. system to address workers. All regularly scheduled programs were tightly scripted to prevent any negative messages from inadvertently reaching workers. In an emergency, workers could be paged or warned as needed. A poll conducted by the personnel department noted that 93.6 percent of workers surveyed considered the P.A. system beneficial to the job.[47]

Apparently the system served its intended purpose. At the annual Labor Day rally in 1944, AFL president William Green used the system to applaud the efficiency of labor-management relations at Fontana and encourage workers to remain productive. Like other motivational speakers,

Figure 6. Maintaining morale in the name of the war effort was crucial to meeting the construction schedule. Workers like these at a bond drive rally at Fontana Dam were constantly urged not to slack off. Photo: Tennessee Valley Authority.

Green reminded workers at Fontana that they were working to make "power and munitions to win the war." He concluded:

> I need not tell *you* that the war is not won, that your job is not finished even though power is scheduled to flow so soon. And I won't trouble to exhort you to work hard and stay on the job. Why shouldn't you work hard and stay on the job? This is your country and mine that is fighting! We are not spectators at a tragic spectacle involving players on a screen. This is our war! Our liberty is at stake! The fate of organized labor is in the balance! It is our world that must be saved![48]

At the same rally, Samuel E. Roper also cautioned workers not to mistake Labor Day for a victory celebration. He reminded workers that "what you are doing at Fontana is so essential and so important to the winning of this war that you should not lose a moment's time. . . . We still have a big job to do." What neither Green nor Roper could have told them, even if they had known, was that by this time the TVA was building dams not just for aluminum manufacturing but also for the Clinton Engineer Works less than 100 miles away at Oak Ridge, Tennessee, where top secret research was about to make the construction of atomic weapons possible.[49]

Like the voices of one's neighbors and fellow workers, like the reminders of wartime shortages, and like the demands of the job itself, the voice of the P.A. system—the voice of TVA—was never completely absent. Workers at Fontana experienced the presence of federal government authority tangibly. TVA was everywhere in Fontana Village and neighboring areas, using its influence to shape work habits, living conditions, and leisure activities as no government entity had done before in this area. Long-term residents responded to this influence much as they had to other outside influences through accommodation and enterprise.

Residents of the upper Little Tennessee had faced economic uncertainty so regularly that they had become accustomed to it. Moreover, they had developed a way of coping with it. That way was to seize every economic opportunity presented to them, as individuals and as a community. Thus, in addition to the enterprises already mentioned, landowners established trailer camps and rented shacks to incoming workers. Many town-dwelling residents took in boarders, sold bag lunches, and assembled packing crates into portable houses for workers. Hoteliers and restaurateurs made attempts to cater to the commuter by offering home-cooked meals and bag lunches. One, the Dickey Hotel, even added "ethnic specialties" such as chicken chop suey, creole rice, and "Italian spaghetti" to its usual menu in order to attract the supposedly more adventuresome palates of the professionals and managers who came to the area.[50] Andy Reid's tavern and other locally owned roadhouses also found a ready market among the workers at Fontana. The proprietors of these businesses certainly were not strangers to capitalism.

In Fontana Village and the surrounding area, TVA and local residents worked together to provide needed services to workers. The agency established rent levels based on area norms, earning a profit on most of the facilities it provided. Local concessionaires earned a substantial income from monopolies on essential services. As an indication of the sales volume possible in these conditions, beginning in January 1943, the Burrus and Barefoot Drugstore at Fontana Dam agreed to pay TVA 5 percent of the estimated $5,000 to $8,000 monthly gross income as rent. The drugstore was among the most profitable businesses in the entire region.[51]

At the other end of the entrepreneurial scale, female employees at Fontana would have been in dire straits without the services of small-scale monopolist Lula Roberts. Roberts operated a dressmaking shop in Store Building A at Fontana. Her tiny 128-square-foot space cost $7.50 per month, of which $3 went to cover the cost of electricity.[52] The other $4.50 went to TVA for rent on the facility. TVA workers welcomed the service, and Roberts made money by providing it. Like earlier businesspeople serving the needs of small-town residents, Roberts identified a ready market and supplied it for as long as it would last, with profit as a primary motivation.

Because of the temporary nature of the project, many local businesspeople were reluctant to commit much of their own limited capital to serve marginal markets. TVA sometimes found it difficult to find contractors to provide services in locations considered unprofitable. After much searching for an appropriate licensee, TVA permitted S. R. Thompson to set up a grocery and general store for the workers housed in the tent camp at Bee Cove. TVA furnished buildings and provided housing for members of Thompson's family who would assist in running the 800-square-foot store. TVA estimated that the store would gross $2,000 per month, far less than the location leased by Burrus and Barefoot for the drugstore at Fontana Village. Thompson's license provided that he would pay 2 percent of the gross as rent, compared with the 5 percent for Burrus and Barefoot. TVA's Reservoir Property Management director stated that the concessions embodied in the license were necessary in order to enable the agency to fulfill its obligations to employees without incurring a loss. Because of the widespread tendency within the agency to exaggerate the isolation of the location, the agency found much to do to ensure the availability of desired services.[53]

In some cases, TVA went even further in granting concessions, in order to ensure that services the agency considered essential would be provided even if there were no profit to be made. The agency agreed to forgo any profit from rent in several cases, including its agreement with Ruby Hood. When the agency had difficulty finding someone to provide basic mail service, Hood agreed to operate a post office at Fontana Village. The post office concession cost Hood $20 per month. This rental fee went primarily to cover the TVA's cost for utilities. The fourth-class facility occupied some 744 square feet in the village store building, and was officially named Welch Cove in honor of one of the oldest families in the area. When the post office was later upgraded to second class and the profit potential increased accordingly, a number of area residents wrote to Congressman Zeb Weaver, asking for the job of postmaster.[54]

J. D. Moore, formerly of Sylva in Jackson County, operated a tire recapping service at the dam. This service was particularly important to commuting workers, given the wartime rubber shortage. Moore was an experienced tire recapper who owned his own equipment—equipment which was scarce at the time—so TVA was anxious to help him establish his business. He initially agreed to pay TVA 5 percent of the gross income from the business, but once established he sought a better deal. Moore requested and received a reduction to 2 percent of gross on the grounds that his operating expenses were several times higher than they had been at Sylva. They may have been, but certainly he also used the agency's sense of urgency as a bargaining tool to protect his profit margin.[55]

At least one enterprising soul even made a career of providing needed services to multiple TVA sites in turn, becoming a professional transient entrepreneur. Robert L. Sutton, who had operated the barbershop for Hiwassee Dam's construction camp through 1940, contracted to provide hairstyling services for both men and women at Fontana Dam in 1942. He paid $10 a month per chair in rent. Sutton also maintained a shoe repair shop and laundry service at Fontana beginning in 1943. He paid $45 a month for this concession, including all the TVA electricity he could use. Sutton later expanded his facilities, offering hairstyling and laundry services at Welch Cove (Fontana Village) as well as at the dam. The entrepreneur discontinued the laundry service in October 1944, but continued the hairstyling and shoe repair services, asking for reduced rent because the businesses did not provide the expected income. Sutton's hairstyling operations did not accommodate black workers. John D. Swaggerty operated a separate barber shop in the Negro Community Building for these workers, occupying a diminutive 120 square feet. Swaggerty paid the same rate per chair as Sutton and operated under the same rules for equipment and utilities despite far lower potential sales volume. The rules were not set up to provide a protected market for minority businesses, but Swaggerty evidently found enough customers to make the business profitable.[56]

As some tried to use the increase in population to make money, others saw the boom as a chance to increase their political power. In the weeks leading up to the 1944 elections, local officials of the Democratic Party saw an opportunity to capitalize on the influx of population by embarking on a voter registration drive, encouraging temporary workers to register as residents of Graham County. This, predictably, resulted in a strong protest from J. Bluford Slaughter, the county accountant and a major figure in the local Republican Party. Slaughter alleged TVA management complicity in this drive, and threatened "a lot of unfavorable publicity" when the State Board of Elections met to decide the issue. He expressed particular dismay that "there has [*sic*] even negroes registered and not a negro, but one in this County and he has never even offered to register."[57]

TVA general manager Gordon Clapp replied that the Authority was not engaged in voter registration, and reminded Slaughter that North Carolina law provided a means to challenge voters' qualifications, both at the time of registration and at the polls. He further challenged Slaughter to produce more specific allegations so that TVA could investigate and discipline the individuals involved if needed. He concluded by reminding Slaughter that TVA employees who were otherwise qualified "should not be disfranchised because of their . . . employment."[58]

The timing of Slaughter's accusations—less than a week before the general election—indicates that he may have been trying to lay the groundwork for challenging the results of a correctly predicted Democratic victory in the local contests. It is impossible to discover how many TVA temporary employees actually voted in Graham County, or how many of them voted Democratic, but no challenge was ever filed with the state election commission.[59]

Most residents accepted the TVA presence, but TVA lost much of this support over its handling of land acquisition issues, especially the acquisition of 44,400 acres on the north side of the reservoir area. This area, collectively called the North Shore land, was located above the high water mark of the reservoir and thus would not be flooded. But the project would destroy State Highway 288, the twisting gravel road that ran along the northern shore of the river. This would leave residents of Proctor and Bushnell, as well as those of the more isolated coves along Hazel Creek and Noland Creek, completely without road access.

In previous TVA projects, the agency had offered to replace any roads inundated or rendered useless. But because labor and other resources were so scarce during the war, the War Production Board refused to allocate the necessary workers and materials for the construction of a road that was not directly necessary for the war effort. So TVA officials had to find some other means of making amends for the loss of the road. Gordon Clapp proposed settling claims for the loss of access directly with the individuals affected and making no attempt to provide a replacement road. The other alternative was for TVA to acquire the land and compensate the state and county, rather than the individual landowners, for the loss of the road. This latter approach, which the agency adopted, is characteristic of what

Bruce Schulman describes in *From Cotton Belt to Sunbelt* as "the triumph of place over people," and is again consistent with H. A. Morgan's policy of working within existing governmental institutions whenever possible. It also conforms to TVA's usual policy of compensating the legal owners of property rather than the direct users.[60]

TVA officials negotiated a settlement involving Swain County, the state of North Carolina, and the National Park Service. The settlement called for TVA to purchase the North Shore land and turn it over to the Park Service for inclusion in the Great Smoky Mountains National Park. The land had actually been included in the proposed park boundary in 1926—the "Cammerer line"—but had not been purchased because of its cut-over condition and the lack of available funds.[61] The acquisition of this land would absolve both TVA and the state of any responsibility for replacing the outdated road with one constructed to equivalently minimal standards of safety and durability, because there would be no residents needing road access. Upon receiving the needed funding from Congress, the Park Service would assume responsibility for replacing the old road with a new parkway as part of its master access plan for the Smokies, giving Swain County a means of attracting tourists to compensate for the lack of property tax revenue. TVA would pay $400,000 into a trust fund to be administered by the state for the retirement of the debt Swain County had incurred in building the original road.[62] The state would pay to construct a connecting road from U.S. 19 to the park boundary, where it would intersect with the park road. TVA would purchase the land at "fair market value," but would consider that the four-party agreement satisfied its obligation to replace the road.

The state pushed for the land to be transferred to its ownership rather than to the park, so that the land could be used as leverage to guarantee that the Park Service would build the road. TVA officials resisted this position, partly because they did not approve of placing political pressure on another federal agency.[63]

Residents of the Noland and Lands Creek areas, operating partly on the basis of misleading rumors and encouraged by the law firm of Black and Whitaker, both members of which were Republicans and longtime TVA foes, embarked on a petition drive aimed at forcing TVA to reconsider the acquisition of the North Shore land. Of the sixty-six petitioners associated with the Black and Whitaker petition of June 29, 1943, TVA identified only eighteen owners of affected land. Many petitioners from Lands Creek apparently incorrectly believed that their land was included in the North

Shore acquisition. Residents of these two areas also asked TVA to replace only their portion of the road, from Bryson City to Noland Creek. Clapp's reading of the petition suggested to him that "the petitioners may be interested not so much in retaining the ownership of their land as in turning them over at a good price." In any event, the state and the county, not the individual residents, would receive the financial compensation from the loss of the road. This left a sour taste in the mouths of many residents, a taste which remained even fifty years later, despite Congressman Weaver's contention that "90 to 95 percent of the people in Swain County will favor this arrangement."[64]

One particular parcel of North Shore land provided TVA officials with substantial difficulty. The 4,500-acre tract owned by Philip Rust, of Granogue, Delaware, did not fit the usual pattern of North Shore lands. Rust maintained the land, which bordered on the Great Smoky Mountains National Park, as a private retreat and preserve. One area resident recalled that members of the Rockefeller family had visited the Rust property, not surprising considering the role of that family in the founding of the national park. Rust's preserve included extensive forest plantings, including nonnative species. He maintained a staff of four wardens who took responsibility for fire protection as well as animal welfare. He actively encouraged the preservation and propagation of wild animal species and maintained a trout-stocking program. He operated a weather station and a fish hatchery, as well as a thirty-mile network of trails connecting to those of the park. A private electric plant provided electricity to the house, nursery, garages, and barns. Rust's property served much the same function as the adjacent national park in many respects, and park visitors were allowed free access to the property.[65]

Rust's attorney requested that the property be exempted from the North Shore purchase because of its unique facilities and because Rust had been a "good neighbor" to the park. Also, the delays in taking the property of the North Carolina Exploration Company and the North Carolina Mining Company gave Rust the impression that those properties had been granted exceptions from the buyout, and he wanted one as well.[66]

Like other North Shore residents, Rust initially challenged TVA's legal right to take the property. He later dropped that challenge, but continued to dispute TVA's appraisal of his land. Rust claimed the property as improved was worth as much as $273,500, while TVA figures ranged from $40,000 to $61,000. To bolster their case, TVA officials requested and received copies of the Rust family's federal income tax returns from 1933 through 1945 from the Internal Revenue Service. TVA ended up paying nearly $100,000 for the Rust property, which was then incorporated into the boundary of the park.[67]

Despite the legal expenses incurred in settling the Rust lawsuit and other acquisition problems, TVA's official press release described the four-party North Shore agreement as "an example of the social and economic benefits that may be obtained when agencies of a region work together with mutual confidence and vision in the solution of their joint problems." While officials denied that cost was a primary motivation behind the settlement, TVA did save $125,000 compared to the estimated cost of rebuilding the road. The agency could also trumpet its patriotic efficiency to the press: "The savings of materials, manpower, and equipment at a time when they are needed in the war effort are substantial."[68]

As with the North Shore land, TVA approached the purchase of Graham County's Cable Cove area haphazardly. Cable Cove measured approximately 1,400 acres, of which the U.S. Forest Service owned about one-third. The area contained thirteen closely grouped homes described by chief conservation engineer Neil Bass as "slightly better than average for the mountain section." The cove was situated above the high water mark, but once again the reservoir would cut off road access. TVA's Department of Regional Studies estimated the cost of restoring highway access to the area at $46,000, substantially more than the appraised value of the land. The state and county, TVA argued, would save money by not having to provide schools and road maintenance to the area. The land would be transferred to the Forest Service, which TVA officials believed would promote recreational developments to benefit the entire area. This suggestion ironically represents a continuation of the mixed-use conservationist ideal which had been repeatedly proposed by area residents as an alternative to the formation of the national park itself, but like the land acquisitions for the park, the Cable Cove purchase would leave a bitter taste in many local mouths.[69]

Many Cable Cove residents, like those of the North Shore, felt that TVA officials had misled them, because TVA's original plans for improving their road access had been made public. Their sentiments probably closely mirrored those of park area residents like John Oliver, who had been assured repeatedly that their homes would not be taken away and turned over to the government. Despite the critical role that access played in economic development, TVA's John Snyder indicated to Gordon Clapp that in his opinion the road issue mattered very little because "there is only one broken-down automobile in the Cable Cove area." Evidently Snyder saw little reason why anyone who was not already in the cove might ever wish to enter it, and doubted that those already there would ever be able to leave.[70]

The purchase of Cable Cove created other problems. The Cable Cove School District's only facility was included in the TVA purchase, leaving four families in neighboring Poison Branch without school facilities. The purchase of Cable Cove also cut off Poison Branch's primary access—a footpath described by TVA officials as "a fairly good trail"—leaving as alternatives only an old wagon road with a 25 percent grade and a privately owned road in poor condition. TVA, following a suggestion by Graham County school superintendent Floyd Griffin, purchased all 450 acres of land in Poison Branch. The cost of surveying and purchasing Poison Branch was approximately $10,000, while the agency estimated the cost of providing a new tertiary-standard road for access at four times as much. Again, the Forest Service would take over and manage the land.[71]

As these examples show, TVA never developed a coherent policy concerning the acquisition of land in lieu of replacing access roads. While serving as director of TVA's Agricultural Relations Department, J. C. McAmis bitterly deplored the "piecemeal manner in which [access problems] have been handled in [Cable Cove and Poison Branch]." He noted many inconsistencies among cost estimates and definitions of areas under consideration. He also reminded his colleagues that had they heeded his initial recommendation that the Cable Cove road be replaced, the Poison Branch problem would never have arisen. He made a point of stating that TVA needed to consider the future uses of any land at issue before deciding that acquisition was cheaper than replacing access, and raised the issue of the maintenance costs the Forest Service would incur as a result of accepting TVA-acquired lands.[72]

Indeed, both TVA officials and area residents had failed to predict the future and prepare accordingly. The economic boom that TVA's construction project brought to the area was temporary. The traditional culture readily accommodated that temporariness. When construction was complete and the boom was over, the area's residents continued to attempt to capitalize on the only resources they had left, just as they had done following the logging boom a generation earlier.

But those resources had changed permanently. Agriculture, formerly a source of comfort and food in difficult times, lost its viability because the good land was under water. The mines were flooded along with the roads and railroads that tied them to the world, and the expansion of the Great Smoky Mountains National Park made the construction of any new means of access impossible. Timbering was already dead on the North Shore, and nearly so elsewhere in the valley. The electric power produced at Fontana went to Tennessee to produce aluminum and, ultimately, nuclear weapons, providing little opportunity in Swain and Graham Counties. The one resource the residents of the valley still controlled was access to the scenic beauty of the region. Here, too, they would find the extent of their control unsatisfactory.

7

Building a Road to Nowhere

With their already limited control of the region's extractable resources now gone, residents of the Little Tennessee Valley came to depend on TVA and the National Park Service for a sense of direction for future development. Neither agency provided that sense of direction. TVA officials saw their mission encompassing the entire Tennessee Valley and declined to commit any resources that would compromise the agency's systemwide goals in the name of local development of a small corner of that region. The Park Service saw its mission as national rather than regional or local in scope, and it proved reluctant to promote any sort of growth that would compromise the park's value as a wilderness paradise.

While business leaders in Bryson City had promoted the Fontana project as a way to cure the region's chronic economic ills, TVA officials generally left the direction of postwar economic growth in the hands of other parties. This policy constrained the growth of private enterprise in the area in the name of scenic beauty, but did little to guarantee the marketability of that beauty. Furthermore, TVA's own needs for power production and flood control hampered the development of profitable tourist facilities. In other words, TVA exercised both too much and too little influence over the region's unsteady growth as a tourist center. Recent studies have noted that accommodating the demands of tourists sometimes squeezes out other forms of economic growth, committing many tourist areas to a growth process featuring low-wage seasonal jobs and restrictions on industrial development. Certainly this was the case with the upper Little Tennessee, and the situation was exacerbated by the extent to which the federal government owned or controlled much of the area's land.[1]

As with other TVA projects, the agency acquired much more land than it needed for operation of the dam after the war. TVA retained possession of land on both abutments of the dam, far enough downstream to protect the agency against claims arising from erosion from the emergency spillway. In keeping with the agency's usual practice of acquiring a protective strip to promote the goals of "conservation, afforestation, and the retirement of marginal land," much of the remaining land was deeded to the U.S. Forest Service for management. The Forest Service would be responsible for future development of parking areas, picnic areas, and extension of public utilities into the transferred area. TVA obliterated its own temporary dirt roads, scarifying their surfaces and in some cases planting tree seedlings to block the roadbed, in an attempt either to restore the area to a wilderness state or to absolve itself of any liability should someone be injured while attempting to use the road for automobile travel.[2]

TVA built visitors facilities at the dam to make the site more attractive to tourists. The access road curved to hide the dam until one had almost reached it, heightening the drama of the 480-foot face. The air-conditioned visitors center also offered a dramatic view of the face of the dam, and it provided a gift shop and separate restrooms for black and white visitors. The interior of the powerhouse was designed with visitors in mind, in a style that combined Gothic and Modern idioms, with starkly plain surfaces illuminated by giant honeycomblike windows and a tremendous amount of open space that removed any sense of scale from the viewer. Paved parking lots gave visitors at both the top and the bottom of the dam a convenient stopping place. By 1960 an incline railway provided an opportunity not merely to see the top and bottom of the dam but to travel vertically along its face.[3]

With the dam built and many of the workers going back to their own homes, the population swell associated with the construction phase of the project subsided. The permanent staff of the dam would require only thirty-eight houses. Except for the facilities required for the operation of the dam itself, Fontana Village became a white elephant for TVA. The agency demolished some of the buildings, while others would be reused at other TVA projects or sold as surplus lumber.[4]

Chief engineer C. E. Blee and project manager F. C. Schlemmer originally planned to rent the site as a convalescent center for veterans. But H. A. Morgan suggested instead that the facility be turned into a tourist site. Newton Drury, of the National Park Service, also expressed early interest in using the site as a recreation center, but by September 1944 Drury made it clear that the Park Service could not assume responsibility for the village. He suggested that the North Carolina State Department of Conservation and Development might be interested in turning the area into a state park.[5]

Private developers as well as public officials suggested that the Fontana Village complex could serve as a corporate retreat, a resort community modeled on Gatlinburg, Tennessee, or even a "modernized Chautauqua" catering to the elite of Chattanooga. Officials of American Express and Bankers Trust Company considered, but rejected, the idea of purchasing the site, and one official suggested Standard Oil or Southern Railway as possible buyers. TVA needed to be able to house its three dozen or so workers near the dam at low cost, and selling the village would make that difficult. The agency chose to retain ownership of the village and lease it to a nonprofit organization, so that it could minimize its own costs and retain some degree of control over the maintenance of the site. As a by-product of the agreement, TVA could claim that its decision would keep Fontana Village an affordable vacation destination for middle-class families.[6]

The organization that TVA chose to operate Fontana Village was a nonprofit corporation called the Welfare and Recreation Association of Public Buildings and Grounds (WRA), which changed its name to Government Services, Incorporated (GSI) to reflect its expanded responsibilities to the federal government as a result of the contract with TVA. The corporation had previously operated cafeterias in government buildings and managed recreational facilities in the public parks in the nation's capital. Its managers had no experience operating a resort on the scale envisioned for Fontana Village.[7]

The agreement with WRA provided that TVA would take responsibility for converting the village to recreational use, renovating the school for use as a cafeteria, constructing a sewage disposal plant, and painting the houses before the property was transferred to WRA. These obligations totaled an estimated $263,000. TVA would also supply raw water for treatment and electric power for distribution. WRA would assume responsibility for maintaining the houses, collecting rents, and providing "adequate year-round community services" such as police and fire protection, water treatment, sewage disposal, and electric power distribution. WRA would also have the right to operate a souvenir stand in the visitors building at the dam.[8] The leasing of the development to a nonprofit corporation meant that access to the facilities would be less expensive, for TVA and for the general public, than if they were operated by a for-profit concern. But it also deprived Graham County of the opportunity to make money directly from rentals, because there were no profits to tax, and the site was still owned by the federal government.

Fontana Village, as administered by GSI, was supposed to offer comfortable yet affordable accommodations to middle-class tourists. Yet GSI's lack of administrative experience in vacation resorts was painfully obvious in the first few years. Knoxville's Judge D. C. Webb, who had been involved in the park booster movement twenty-five years earlier, complained that he was overcharged for an abbreviated one-hour cruise on the lake. Webb also related the story of another visitor overcharged by 20 percent for the three days he spent in a rental house in the village. Webb felt shortchanged by the whole experience. Another visitor, L. S. Moody, the secretary of the Augusta, Georgia, Chamber of Commerce, complained that the resort's staff had overlooked details any tourist would expect: his cottage lacked a sink stopper, soap, towels, and toilet paper. Moody disapproved of the food in the cafeteria, which was poorly prepared and overpriced. Furthermore, the steep unsurfaced driveways constituted a safety hazard. Most significantly, he noted that "the employees of Government Services . . . seemed to be inexperienced and not qualified to know what should be done to correct the conditions which we thought were perfectly apparent to anyone." TVA responded by forwarding Webb's and Moody's complaints to GSI with a stern warning that the company needed to avoid such problems in the future, but the nature of the complaints demonstrates that TVA's decision to lease the village to GSI, if truly motivated by a desire to attract middle-class tourists, was an abysmal failure. Too much of the village's true character as an abandoned construction camp remained to satisfy the expectations of the likes of Webb and Moody, who as middle-class professionals were clearly among the resort's target customers.[9]

As the recreational role of the village matured, TVA took an even less active role in its management. TVA kept watch over the quality of the water and available fishing, managed the dam and water recreation facilities, made sure that local businesses did not disrupt the desired rustic atmosphere, and, in their eyes, left well enough alone. The job of promoting the area as a tourist site fell to others.

Indeed, some of TVA's own policies interfered with that promotion. The operators of a service station at Stecoah found that the agency would not permit them to place a sign advertising their business on TVA property. They accused the agency of favoritism and antipathy toward private enterprise:

> It has been brought to our attention that recently you caused Mr. J. B. Moody of Moody's Motel to move a sign of his which was located in the vicinity of our own sign. It appears that Mr. Moody was in a position, as a TVA employee and service man for certain of your equipment, to retaliate and cause you to reverse your actions. In view of this situation we are unable to visualize TVA upholding such

> an act of discrimination, [but we believe] that your actions in this matter are motivated by your desire to see no one except Government Services, Inc., prosper from the seasonal tourist business in this area.

The resulting contest of wills pitted TVA management against the needs of a small business, placing Fontana Village resident manager O. A. Fetch in the middle. Fetch, not wishing to antagonize his neighbors and well aware that they and he depended on tourist traffic for their livelihood, attempted to reach a compromise that would permit the signs and help assuage lingering dissatisfaction with TVA's earlier heavy-handed management of land acquisition. But TVA's director of reservoir properties, J. Ed Campbell, felt the signs should be removed, and his decision was final. The agency's desire to preserve the area's newfound rustic ambience made it difficult for small businesses to attract tourist traffic, but in Campbell's view that was a small price to pay.[10]

Power production demands and springtime flood control necessitated that the water level of Fontana Lake be lowered in the autumn months. This practice left bare, unforested, muddy shorelines that marred the sce-

Figure 7. On Labor Day weekend, traditionally an important weekend for tourist-oriented businesses, two dozen or so houseboats sit abandoned in the mud of the Panther Creek "marina," stranded by an early drawdown. Photo: Stephen Wallace Taylor.

nic vistas available to "windshield tourists." Since the Little Tennessee provided a greater share of the flow of the Tennessee River than any other tributary, flood control measures aimed at protecting the city of Chattanooga would begin with controlled drawdowns at Fontana, depriving area residents of the appealing tourist attraction they sought to create in Fontana Lake. The narrowness of the valley, too, meant that volume-based drawdowns would appear more drastic when viewed from the banks. When maintenance was needed on the dam, the annual drawdown began earlier, sometimes as early as July, and lasted longer, significantly detracting from the value of the area as a tourist attraction during what would otherwise have been the peak of the tourist season. One member of the Swain County Chamber of Commerce put it succinctly: "Who wants to view a lake that is nothing but mud and a small trickle of water?" Again, TVA's plans for the "big picture" placed small business owners in a difficult position.[11]

The scarred landscape was exacerbated by attempts to provide road access. Such access would prove to be one of the most difficult problems with promoting Fontana Village as a recreation destination. The agreement between TVA, the North Carolina State Highway Commission, Swain County, and the National Park Service distributed responsibility for providing a highway along the North Shore—a replacement for State Highway 288—between the state and the Park Service. Since most of the North Shore land had been given to the Great Smoky Mountains National Park, the Park Service received the lion's share of responsibility for building the new road as soon as Congress funded it.[12]

The Park Service immediately encountered problems attempting to satisfy its end of the bargain. During the war, while Park Service crews surveyed what eventually became Park Route 9, the Army Corps of Engineers had done some preliminary construction on a temporary "pioneer road" along a different route, but abandoned the project because of labor shortages elsewhere. The fragments of old Highway 288 and the pioneer road provided firefighting access, and completing that access became a priority for Park Service officials. The park superintendent realized that the construction of the pioneer road had already scarred the land, and he recommended that the park consider making it a substitute for the promised North Shore road. The resulting study found the pioneer road unsatisfactory in both cost and scenic value.[13]

The Park Service lacked jurisdiction over nonpark lands. Since the eastern park boundary lay two and a half miles from the nearest road in Bryson City, park officials could not justify any construction on that end of the proposed route until the state of North Carolina had fulfilled its responsibility for building a connecting route to the boundary.[14] Construction thus focused on the other end, and by 1949 the Park Service had completed a small access road from the dam into the park. Less than a mile in length, that access road connected the dam to a few small cemeteries on the North Shore but offered virtually no recreation possibilities beyond its eventual incorporation into the Appalachian Trail.

Seeing no rapid construction of the promised park road, some of Swain County's most prominent citizens, led by no less than attorney T. D. Bryson Jr., descended from the founding family of the county seat, and Kelly Bennett, whose rousing address over WWNC radio in Asheville had heralded the coming of "a second Niagara Falls" with the arrival of the park and the dam, began to suggest that the land be returned to the county for development as a hunting preserve or recreation center. On February 24, 1952, Congressman Monroe Redden formally proposed that Congress return the land to the county. The Great Smoky Mountains Conservation Association, a Knoxville group which had played a pivotal role in establishing the park, fought Redden's proposal vigorously, as did the Department of the Interior. Bennett, chairman of the North Carolina Park, Parkway, and Forest Development Commission, initially supported the measure but rapidly distanced himself from it once it became apparent that Redden did not intend to push for its passage. The congressman agreed to drop the proposal if Congress would appropriate $10 million to complete the North Shore road immediately. Congress did no such thing, but the proposal died in committee anyway.[15]

Another factor that undermined support for the North Shore road project resulted from state initiative. In the early 1950s, the State Highway Commission embarked on a massive roadbuilding program under Governor William Kerr Scott. In the division containing all of the southwestern part of the state, roads were difficult to build because of rugged terrain. Under the leadership of highway commissioners L. Dale Thrash and Harry E. Buchanan, the division tried to catch up by improving existing roads. So-called county roads, actually state-maintained secondary routes, received much of the commission's attention.[16]

The most expedient means of obtaining a road from Bryson City to Fontana in this political climate was to straighten and pave existing county roads. But any such route through Swain County would cross Park Service lands. The logical alternative was to improve existing routes through Graham County, outside the park boundary. The new route, designated North Carolina 28, explicitly replaced the remnants of old Highway 288, which was removed from the state maintenance system. By the mid-1950s, the two points—Bryson City and Fontana—were thus already connected by a decent two-lane paved road, as TVA and the Park Service had intended when planning the replacement of old 288. State highway location engineer R. Getty Browning described the expenditure for the North Shore route, including the state's portion, as "an unjustified extravagance, notwithstanding the ironbound three-way agreement." Browning proposed that the state and the Park Service could both benefit from reconsidering the 1943 agreement and that perhaps the Park Service might offer to contribute some money toward the improvement of other roads and tourist facilities outside the park in lieu of building the North Shore road, an idea which Park Service director Conrad Wirth liked as well. Wirth opined, however, that the Park Service could not do so without congressional authorization, since the lands in question were not under Park Service jurisdiction. Environmentalists petitioned Congress to authorize such a transfer of funds, but to no avail.[17]

From the point of view of both the Park Service and Browning, the State Highway Commission had obviated the need for a new road by constructing the new State Highway 28, which ran more or less parallel to the south shoreline of Fontana Lake. Furthermore, the south shore road provided an excellent view of the Smokies, while any North Shore route would have provided only views of the lake—certainly a mixed blessing during the fall and winter months when the lake level was kept low to allow for the storage of runoff.

Redden's successor in Congress, George A. Shuford, continued to push for the construction of the North Shore road, despite the protests of Park Service director Conrad Wirth that it was now redundant. Wirth pointed out that the state had not yet constructed its connecting route to the park boundary and that any Park Service construction on the Bryson City end of the route would be useless. Shuford responded by proposing to the State Highway Commission that it fund the new connecting route immediately, and the commission agreed. Thus, by 1959, the two-and-a-half-mile state route connected Bryson City to the park boundary, where the pavement abruptly ended. Bryson City had one and a quarter routes to Fontana, at tremendous financial and scenic cost.[18]

Preservationists continued to fight the North Shore road, and they gained the support of key officials in the Park Service. In 1960, Acting Secretary of the Interior Elmer F. Bennett sought but failed to gain the approval of Governor Luther Hodges for the abandonment of the 1943 agreement on the grounds that the south shore road constructed by the state made the park route unnecessary. Reflecting his business background, the governor's reply recognized the weaknesses inherent in the North Shore road proposal, but reaffirmed the binding nature of the contract between the federal authorities and the state, reluctantly concluding that the road must be built.[19]

The National Park Service saw the North Shore road, designated Park Road 9, as part of a larger issue: the development of the Great Smoky Mountains National Park as a whole. In the early years of the park, Tennessee community leaders had worked to ensure that their side of the park was easily accessible and heavily promoted, and it naturally followed that the Tennessee side would have more substantial accommodations for tourists.[20]

The North Carolina side of the park did not benefit from the same sort of unified development strategy. While the Western North Carolina Associated Communities (WNCAC), formed in 1946, helped promote "specific projects of general value to the entire area, economically, socially, educationally, and aesthetically," that organization steadfastly resisted efforts to make the park the primary tourist destination in western North Carolina. The communities that had once fought over which one could be the park's "gateway," or the "entrance," now strove to prove they had other things to offer in addition to the park. Bryson City would find precious few allies in its attempts to turn the park into a local moneymaking enterprise. WNCAC relentlessly lobbied for the completion of the Blue Ridge Parkway, which began at Cherokee and thus could offer no direct benefit to Bryson City. Moreover, since the Cherokee reservation was not subject to property taxes, Swain County's coffers would not benefit directly from the accompanying development. WNCAC also promoted the Cherokee Reservation as a tourist attraction offering a unique cultural experience. The outdoor drama *Unto These Hills* began educating and entertaining capacity crowds in 1950, and the immensely popular Oconaluftee Indian Village, a living history center, opened in 1952; both enjoyed substantial support from WNCAC. Bryson City, unlike Cherokee, had little that was genuinely unique to attract tourists visiting either the park or other attractions in the Smokies, and its pleas for WNCAC attention were largely ignored.[21]

Just as it lacked distinctiveness, Bryson City lacked the advantages of location. The federal highway through the park, U.S. 441, connected Gatlinburg to Cherokee and proceeded south through Dillsboro to Franklin, bypassing Bryson City. Attempts to have N.C. 28 redesignated as U.S. 441-W, thus attracting a share of the Knoxville and Atlanta traffic, failed. Moreover, while N.C. 28 provided excellent access from Bryson City to Fontana Dam, most of its length was in Graham County. While this detail may at first seem meaningless, it gains significance in light of the extremely small tax base in Swain County, which withered largely because of the formation of the park. A new road within the park would itself be immune to development, but would funnel traffic around the western half of the park directly into Bryson City, where tourist development could proceed and provide a needed injection of revenue. The state road, on the other hand, could host plenty of taxable development along the way, and as long as it remained the only way around Fontana Lake, Graham County would get the tax dollars generated by tourist traffic. From the national perspective, the two roads were interchangeable, except that one was inside the park and not yet built, while the other was outside the park and already built. But from the local perspective the state highway did not satisfy the needs of Swain County's politicians or its business class. Swain County's board of commissioners and its chamber of commerce jealously sought to hoard what little tourist traffic came through, but they were thwarted. Moreover, the disputes over access had placed Bryson City's plans to attract tourist dollars on hold. The timing was critical: The delays allowed preservationists time to mobilize nationally in order to prevent the area from being "too developed."[22]

Following Governor Hodges's refusal to consider the issue settled, the Park Service did begin constructing the North Shore road at the eastern end, where the state connector had been completed in the late 1950s. Park Service officials initially envisioned building the road only as far as Goldmine Branch, approximately three miles into the park boundary. Their aim was to demonstrate to Swain County that it would be better to use Bryson City as a jumping-off point for activities within the park than to construct a through road within the park boundary. So certain were park officials that their vision of the North Shore would work that they even spent scarce Park Service funding to survey another route for the road that would make construction beyond Goldmine Branch impossible.[23]

Plans for both routes called for the road to end in a recreation center with a marina and campground, but Goldmine Branch proved an unsuitable location for these facilities, so the road—following the original 1944 survey route—was continued as far as Monteith Branch, thought to be more suitable for development. Park officials again hoped to create some attraction that would convince Swain County that the North Shore parkway would be more destructive than constructive to the local economy. The Monteith Branch project would have provided 400 picnic sites, 600 campsites, a 1,500-foot boat ramp, a campground store and marina store, and horseback riding facilities. This area would have provided the only major water recreation site in the park itself, making it potentially a very active tourism area.[24]

Problems quickly appeared with the North Shore development plan. The lack of electric power and the limited supply of drinking water would have made Monteith Branch unattractive to many tourists. Remedying those conditions, on the other hand, would cost the Park Service a lot of money and might well compromise the area's appeal to preservation-oriented visitors. Moreover, the access road—the North Shore road—proved to be far more difficult and expensive to construct than originally anticipated. The road was cut through unstable rock that decomposed upon exposure to air. The roadbed crumbled almost as soon as it was cut, necessitating many additional hours of cut-and-fill activity for what Park Service personnel saw as dubious improvements in the stability and quality of the road. Furthermore, cutting deeper into the Anakeesta Formation would likely result in unacceptable damage to the park's now-clean streams, releasing toxic heavy metals and lowering the pH of the water to dangerous levels for wildlife.[25]

The Park Service temporarily halted construction of the North Shore road several times because of these stability problems in the underlying rock. In January 1964, after about seven and a half miles had been completed, a series of massive and nearly fatal landslides caused a public panic. Despite the panic, a five-mile section at the eastern end of the North Shore route was opened for public use in October 1965.

The construction of this road, as far as it went, visibly scarred the landscape, upsetting environmentalists. After 1966, the Park Service placed all future development of the North Shore—recreational facilities such as the Monteith Branch campground, as well as roads—on indefinite hold. Tourists, predictably, stayed away, preferring the conveniences they found on the Tennessee side of the park. Thus the Park Service, like TVA, proved unable to develop the area's resources in ways that would profit the economy of Swain County. Local people came to refer to the unfinished park road as the "Road to Nowhere."[26]

Park Service officials hoped to soothe the worries of Swain County by offering alternative road systems that would promote careful development of the North Carolina side of the park. Development proposals involving the North Carolina side of the park received consideration from the Park Service during the 1960s. Among these were a "loop road" that would encircle the park, providing an entrance at Bryson City but cutting

Figure 8. This sign welcoming visitors to the "Road to Nowhere" is located in Bryson City, just outside the Great Smoky Mountains National Park. Photo: Stephen Wallace Taylor.

off the present U.S. 441 through the park; a second road over the mountains connecting Bryson City to Townsend, Tennessee; a low-traffic road running inside the park from Fontana Dam to Bryson City (essentially a more primitive "jeep" version of the long-promised North Shore road); and even a transmountain rail system with stations at Townsend and Bryson City. None of these proposals ever went beyond the planning stages.[27]

Even before the North Shore road debacle, many North Carolina leaders blamed their Tennessee counterparts for "hijacking" the development of the park for the benefit of Tennessee. Certainly, Tennesseeans pushed harder for the creation of the park and campaigned more aggressively for its development in the 1930s. But what began as political one-upsmanship on the part of Tennessee leaders eventually evolved into simple expediency. Strategies for the development of the North Carolina side of the park were sidetracked by efforts to maintain the rustic or backcountry atmosphere—an atmosphere to which the North Carolina side originally had little claim, thanks to the lumber companies—and by the high cost of any major changes in the park's infrastructure. Park Service officials maintained contact with the Wilderness Society, the Isaak Walton League, and the National Wildlife Federation. Those groups influenced both park policy and congressional action despite the fact that one 1985 survey indicated that only 5.7 percent of visitors to the park intended to use day hiking facilities, 0.4 percent intended to fish, 0.3 percent participated in horseback riding, and 0.6 percent went tubing.[28]

Ironically, much of the territory celebrated by environmentalists as "primeval wilderness" was the same territory nearly destroyed by the logging and mining companies one or two generations earlier, before the formation of the park. In the intervening years, nature had reclaimed the area to the point that many of those protesting against the road apparently believed it would cut through virgin forest. The North Shore road became a symbol for the struggle between developers and environmentalists. Developers saw the road as the one chance for Swain County and especially Bryson City to get its "fair share" of the tourist dollars attracted by the park, while environmentalists, deploring the commercialization of the Tennessee entrances to the park, sought to prevent the same fate from befalling the quieter, more remote North Carolina side by having large areas legally designated as permanent wilderness. One wilderness advocate wrote: "Those of us who have hiked and camped there remember the frothy streams, the unrestrained vegetation and abundant wildlife, we remember the ridges and valleys, the blueberry-hung meadows, the vistas, and the primeval solitude. . . . To us, and to many others, the Smokies are one of the few nearby places offering uninhabited miles of the nature which greeted white men in America centuries ago, and which is rapidly being chiseled away." Another preservationist, perhaps unaware of the early history of the park movement in western North Carolina, expressed frustration with the revenue-oriented rhetoric of the Bryson City boosters: "Will these people ever understand that the [park] exists preeminently to be held in trust as a wilderness museum for all citizens . . . and that a fortiori the park . . . was not established to provide a source of revenue for Swain County citizens or for any others?" A University of Tennessee staff member summed up the Bryson City position well, though unsympathetically, when he wrote, "I should have realized that those folks will never be satisfied until Bryson City becomes a second Gatlinburg regardless of how much it costs Uncle Sam."[29]

Swain County Democratic Party chairman Henry Truett, who had long operated tourist-oriented businesses in the area, responded by accusing the environmentalists of trying to put the county under a "dictatorship." Kelly Bennett, the longtime booster, wrote the editor of *Wildlife in North*

Carolina, a publication of the state Wildlife Resources Commission, calling an article that described the "wilderness character" of the area "truly grotesque" and the product of "reprehensible . . . ignorance." The county board of commissioners demanded that the editor retract the article and apologize to the county.[30]

Despite the heated rhetoric and the undoubted environmental consequences, the craving for the North Shore road voiced by Swain County's business leaders was understandable. The majority of the park's visitors since its inception were windshield tourists who traveled through on Newfound Gap Road (U.S. 441), perhaps stopping for a picnic or photo opportunity at one of the many scenic overlooks on their way through, and these people were better served by the plethora of hotels, lodges, shopping centers, and fast-food restaurants of Pigeon Forge and Gatlinburg, Tennessee, north of the park than by the smaller array of facilities available near the North Carolina entrance.

A 1985 survey indicated that 44.2 percent of summertime nonlocal park visitors had spent the previous night in Gatlinburg and 21.3 percent in Pigeon Forge. The communities on the North Carolina side of the park attracted far fewer visitors. According to the same survey, 11.2 percent spent the previous night in Cherokee, 1.1 percent in Bryson City, and only 0.2 percent at Fontana Village. Similar patterns prevailed with autumn visitors, except that Bryson City dropped from 1.1 percent to 0.6 percent of the nonlocal visiting population.[31]

Robbinsville drew even less tourist traffic than Bryson City. Located about fifteen miles from the park boundary on twisty U.S. 129, the town could boast one fast-food restaurant and only a few small tourist facilities in the early 1990s. Robbinsville carved a minor niche for itself by catering to the presence of that twisty federal highway. Motorcycle enthusiasts periodically swarmed the area to ride the road they call "The Dragon," and a counterculture group known as the Rainbow Family occasionally visited the woods near Stecoah for communal celebrations off the beaten path.[32]

The absence of any substantial tourist development at Bryson City and Robbinsville in the first fifty years after the founding of the park lay in marked contrast to the relatively prosperous tourist industry at Cherokee, a few miles northeast. Cherokee became something of a success story by reservation standards, as the Cherokee people adapted readily to the demands of tourists as soon as they arrived. The outdoor drama *Unto These Hills,* written by Kermit Hunter, attracted tremendous attention from tourists, while promoting a somewhat self-conscious "history lesson" for an overwhelmingly white audience composed more of tourists than locals. In the script, the extent to which Cherokees had gone out of their way to accommodate whites was a major theme. The end of the play emphasizes the superior morality of returning good for evil, celebrating the peaceful nature of the Cherokee people. The moralizing emphasis of the play was underscored by the reaction of one Cherokee woman whose husband was white. Having seen the play with her children, she reportedly responded, "I just didn't know till now how mean these white people can be. When I get home, I am going to beat the tar out of my old man."[33]

White academics, artists, and promoters played a large role in making *Unto These Hills* a success. The dances were choreographed by Foster Fitzsimmons of Chapel Hill. Costume design was directed by Suzanne Davis of Chapel Hill, with some assistance from the students at the Indian School at Cherokee. The principal Cherokee artistic contribution came from composer Jack Frederick Kilpatrick, a member of the music faculty at Southern Methodist University in Texas. The Cherokee Historical Association, formed to promote the outdoor drama, was initially chaired by Harry Buchanan of Hendersonville, a white businessman and later a member of the State Highway Commission. The vice chairman was Percy Ferebee, a longtime promoter of tourism in the southwestern part of the state who had also served on the Highway Commission and played a role in the founding of WNCAC. A unanimous vote from the state General Assembly appropriated the sum of $35,000 for theater equipment and construction assistance. Despite the large role whites played in the creative and financial aspects of *Unto These Hills,* the drama did employ many Cherokees in acting and production roles, and Cherokee builders were responsible for the construction of the theater itself.[34]

One observer estimated that, as a result of the success of *Unto These Hills* in promoting the town of Cherokee, the Tribal Council had brought in about ten dollars in revenue for the community for each dollar it had invested in securing the theater site. The play has been credited with reviving interest in Cherokee history among both white and Cherokee audiences. The community then opened a museum of Cherokee life that emphasized the contributions of Sequoyah and the similarities between Cherokee and white societies. The Oconaluftee Indian Village provided tourists with a somewhat sanitized but still interesting view of Cherokee life which, like *Unto These Hills,* emphasized the degree to which the Cherokee had attempted to accommodate their white neighbors. Souvenir

Figure 9. The Warrior Motel, between Bryson City and Cherokee, offers tourists the opportunity to "Experience the Smokies" with remote cable TV, electric heat and air, and other "comforts of home." Any resemblance between the cartoonish "warrior" and anyone from the Cherokee community, living or dead, is coincidental at best. Photo: Stephen Wallace Taylor.

shops and inexpensive motels soon followed, making the town of Cherokee by far the busiest tourist destination on the North Carolina side of the national park.[35]

While the local museum of Cherokee history, *Unto These Hills,* and the Oconaluftee Indian Village promoted somewhat authentic images of Cherokee history, selling questionably authentic "Indian crafts" and toy tomahawks made in Taiwan provided some of the Cherokee people with lucrative but seasonal income. Some Cherokees did not hesitate to promote images of Native American heritage, even unflattering ones. Perhaps the most visible of the inaccurate images promoted by Cherokees comes from the practice of "chiefing"—posing for photographs with tourists while wearing "real Indian" costumes, typically derived loosely from the Plains tribes and capped with a fake Sioux war bonnet of feathers. Chiefing is simply a means of making a living from public perceptions of what it means to be a "real Indian." One practitioner is said to have experimented with such perceptions by dressing the way Cherokees typically dressed in the early nineteenth century. He found that his income virtually disappeared because he did not fit the image the tourists expected. He responded by returning to the traditional Plains Indian costume, because he needed the money. The tourist industry thus helped to reinforce a false set of popular images of Native Americans, just as it helped to reinforce outside notions of authenticity in other cultures.[36]

Despite the close proximity between Bryson City and Cherokee, the business community of Bryson City was unprepared to take advantage of the public interest in Cherokee history. The editor of the *Smoky Mountain Times* complained in May 1950 that *Unto These Hills* was to open in less than sixty days, and Bryson City had done nothing to promote itself as a lodging destination for tourists interested in nearby Cherokee. Indeed, the county chamber of commerce could barely raise $350 of its $3,500 budget in order to promote Bryson City's business interests.[37]

The boom residents anticipated from the park, the dam, and the road never arrived in the upper Little Tennessee. Swain and Graham County tourism lagged behind the many other destinations in the Smokies, hampered by vague and conflicting policies and by the lack of infrastructure. Industrial development, too, was slow to arrive in the upper Little Tennessee. The region as a whole experienced a gradual improvement in its standard of living, but many individuals continued to live in poverty in this area once touted for its inexhaustible natural wealth. With the natural resources nearly gone or made permanently inaccessible, the people of the region continued to get by, just as their ancestors did for years before the upheaval brought by the plans of the Park Service and TVA. But they had fewer resources than ever with which to do so. In 1991, the *Charlotte Observer* called Graham County "the county that progress passed by." The paper quoted a recent high school graduate as saying that "the older you get, the more you find out it would be better if you went somewhere else." The largest employers in the county were a small furniture plant and a parachute manufacturer. Residents complained that a lack of good roads kept industrial development away.[38]

While Bryson City and Robbinsville languished, other towns surrounding the national park marketed themselves aggressively. Gatlinburg, across the Tennessee line, organized a troup of traveling "hillbillies" to promote tourism in the area. From the early image of these ragtag ragamuffins, Gatlinburg evolved an identity combining rustic Appalachian charm with the accouterments of a "Swiss-looking" ski resort town, complete with chalets and well-groomed slopes. Pigeon Forge, once a sleepy farming community, became the discount shopping capital of the Smokies, offering several outlet malls, a liquor-free entertainment district, and an amusement-park ambience. Indeed, one 1995 survey noted that the malls, rather than the mountains, drew the largest number of visitors to Pigeon Forge.[39]

The sharp contrast between the relative stagnation of Graham and

Swain Counties and the rapid economic development of Tennessee's Sevier, Blount, and Cocke Counties caused the former to nurse a sense of grievance against the latter. The earlier impulse to build the North Shore road as a means to economic prosperity gave rise in the 1980s to a group calling itself Citizens Against Wilderness (CAW). Taking its militant-sounding name from members' opposition to the persistent efforts of environmentalists to designate the entire North Shore as a wilderness permanently protected from further development, the group called repeatedly for the full development of the North Carolina side of the park along the lines of the existing Tennessee development. Operating from Bryson City, the Citizens Against Wilderness shared a sense that they had been deliberately victimized by TVA and the Park Service. In particular, they focused on the sense of lost economic opportunity arising from the rapid development of the Tennessee side of the park. Like their ancestors who called for the full development of hydroelectric power, mining, and timber resources in the area, they sought outside investment to restore their "rightful share" of the prosperity that the rest of the nation enjoyed. Borrowing loosely from dependency theory, they bemoaned the fact that Tennessee received most of the economic benefits of the park, and they saw environmentalists' attempts to preserve the rest of the Smokies intact as a ploy to keep their region poor and unhappy. The group accused the Park Service of faulty geology, the Democratic Party of indolence, and the state of Tennessee of elitism. While the group professed to be nonpartisan, several self-proclaimed "concerned Democrats" publicly vowed to support right-wing Senator Jesse Helms because of his antienvironmentalist and anti-wilderness rhetoric. Helms courted these voters by appealing to their sense of outrage at the government's "broken promises."[40]

When Tennessee's Senator James Sasser, the cosponsor of a wilderness preservation bill, attempted to visit the area in 1987, he was confronted by angry protesters waving signs. Two of the protesters leaped in front of the senator's van, and one assaulted a park ranger who asked the group to stand aside to allow Sasser to pass. The group's leader, Linda Hogue, demanded that Sasser take the time to listen to her complaints. North Carolina reporters quoted Sasser as saying, "I don't want to listen to Swain County," while Tennessee reporters recorded the statement as "I'm not going to listen to every person in Swain County." Among the accusations leveled at Sasser was that he and fellow Tennesseean Howard Baker were introducing the bill in order to protect Tennessee's tourist industry.[41]

Another organization that emerged during the postwar period deserves mention for its role in shaping the culture of the upper Little Tennessee.

The North Shore Cemetery Association promoted the reenactment of the rituals first begun after Ritter Lumber Company left Proctor. Members of the association gathered frequently to decorate the cemeteries on the North Shore, principally in and around Proctor. As access to water had defined communities for those who came to Hazel Creek, Goldmine Branch, or Epps Springs, access prevented by water now defined a community for those forced to leave and their descendants. The association served as a surrogate community for all those whose ancestors were buried in the North Shore area. Members, notably president Helen Cable Vance, seized every opportunity to gain attention for their causes: preserving the area's cemeteries, obtaining road access to those cemeteries, and publicizing a version of the area's history that focuses on lost opportunities and economic development while ignoring the inherent instability and temporariness of that development. The North Shore Cemetery Association later became the North Shore Historical Association, seeking to play much the same role in promoting the history of the North Shore as the Cherokee Historical Association played in promoting the history of the Eastern Band. While the group has not, as yet, succeeded in creating an outdoor drama comparable to *Unto These Hills,* it was responsible for a small log cabin museum located in Fontana Village, and it persisted in its cemetery activities, which gained tremendous media attention when they sometimes turned into political protests.[42]

The National Park Service provided this group with water and jeep transportation to the North Shore cemeteries so that participants could decorate the graves of ancestors buried there. Their decoration ceremonies, to which the media were invited, frequently included speeches denouncing what they saw as their victimization by the "federal government," by which they seem to have meant primarily the National Park Service and TVA. This sense of victimization and displacement tied the members together, and the annual decoration ceremonies at each cemetery cemented their historical identity as the people who gave up their land for an ungrateful nation, just as rituals of school and church attendance helped cement their identity as members of a geographically defined community fifty or sixty years earlier, and in much the same way that gatherings of the United Daughters of the Confederacy and the Sons of Confederate Veterans tend to unite southerners with a sense of grievance at the "injustices" perpetrated against the South during and since the War between the States.[43]

Since the 1960s, this graveyard political action committee worked closely with every candidate for the area's House seat and found a warm audience in both Democratic and Republican candidates. Every few years, their representative in the House introduced legislation calling for a road to the North Shore cemeteries, based on the 1943 agreement. No longer was the road supposed to be for economic development or even for access to the park as a whole. It was merely a means of visiting the dead more conveniently. "It's not too much to ask, to be able to go back home, is it?" asked Helen Cable Vance rhetorically.[44]

Several members of the cemetery association sued TVA, the Department of the Interior, Swain County, and the state of North Carolina in 1983 for "specific performance,"[45] claiming breach of the 1943 agreement to build the North Shore road. Among other charges, the suit creatively claimed that the government had violated the group's First Amendment freedom of religion by preventing them from visiting and decorating the graves of their ancestors. The federal district court dismissed the case, declaring that group members were only "incidental beneficiaries" of the agreement signed by TVA, the National Park Service, the state, and Swain County, and thus they had no standing to sue. The Fourth Circuit Court of Appeals denied their appeal and affirmed the decision of the district court, on the grounds that the agreement clearly stated that any action by the Park Service would be contingent upon congressional funding. Understandably, no member of either court dared publicly address the question of freedom of religion. Only Chief Judge Harrison L. Winter dissented in the breach of contract issue, arguing that the Park Service's decision not to seek further congressional funding constituted a breach of the agreement. The court's majority opinion only fueled the group's smoldering sense of grievance against the federal government.[46]

Their anger might just as reasonably be directed at Kephart and writers like him and at a public whose perceptions of the area were nourished by what such writers wrote. Because of the formation of the national park and the construction of Fontana Dam, both of which were planned by people whose understanding of the region was limited largely to the romanticized tales promulgated by Kephart, a region characterized by rapid economic oscillation became an economically depressed "nature museum," a monument to a past lifestyle that is often overly romanticized by those who remember it as their own childhood. The environmental and economic depredations of mining and timber companies created a region that needed to be "reformed," and the failed reform attempts of the federal government, informed by the stereotypes Kephart helped popularize, gradually turned Kephart's "Back of Beyond" from a misperception into a reality. Vance's desire to "be able to go back home" indicts not only those who believed in the myth of the Back of Beyond, but also those who have turned her home into an embodiment of that myth. Ironically, it also confirms the inherently temporary nature of the prosperity brought by the lumber and mining companies before "the government" took over, a prosperity which Vance's generation had expected to inherit and which they continued to believe was unjustly stolen from them. While they waited for the government to fulfill its promise of a road, the other surviving towns of the Smokies marched ahead.

Epilogue

A View from the River

Today, the railroad town of Bushnell is gone without a trace. The tracks now run south of the river to Wesser and beyond, and the railroad boom that built Bushnell is as much a part of folklore as the rest of the region's history.

Almond is now the name of a boat dock on Fontana Lake. There are no enterprising farmers left, nor is there any farmland. None of the houses powered by small hydroelectric generators, which Arnold Hyde noted in 1943, still stand. Judson, too, is gone.

Proctor still exists, in a way. A couple of buildings from the town were preserved by the park service for the use of rangers. The cemetery people still gather once a year or thereabouts; they bring their children and grandchildren now to help decorate the graves.

Fontana has become, in the words of Lucile Kirby Boyden, the "village of five lives." The village is now operated as a for-profit vacation destination by Peppertree Resorts. Some of the old houses were removed to alleviate the crowding of which so many had complained during the war. While the village does not host nearly as many guests as Gatlinburg or Pigeon Forge, it does have a certain rustic charm. A tiny museum in a reconstructed log cabin testifies to the area's history.

Fontana Dam sits isolated amid the wooded highlands of southwestern North Carolina. The dramatic scenery does not prepare the visitor for the sudden appearance of the giant monolith just around the next curve. Its face is blemished, like a fence in need of whitewashing. Its harsh angular architecture is a stark monument to a bloody war and to the Cold War that followed. The dam still attracts the curious because of its size, its remoteness, and its history. The labor expended in its creation has not gone unnoticed, and the giant metallic generators in their massive powerhouse grimly evoke memories of a fearful, busy time. The scene is not exactly beautiful, except to the technocrat, but it is certainly powerful.

Figure 10. At low water one Labor Day weekend, Fontana Lake is reminiscent of a strip mine. Photo: Stephen Wallace Taylor.

In the late spring and early summer, fishermen and boaters dot the shores of the lake behind the dam. A serene beauty seems to radiate gently from its shimmering waters amid the sounds of Smoky Mountain wildlife. It is a beautiful place, no matter its origins. But in the late summer or early autumn, the lake level drops to reveal muddy banks and bare shorelines, and very little recreational activity remains. Reminiscent of a strip mine at low water, it is too remote to be an industrial site and too bare to belong to a national park known for its biodiversity. The entire Fontana site becomes a scene of neither hustle nor tranquility, but a sort of ragged and unsettled graveyard for one variety of the American way of life. During an early drawdown in 1990, one observer described the scene as follows:

> The dry, cracked ground is dotted with the skeletons of once-bustling communities: the stone foundation of a house, a steel pipe used to transport water, the stumps of trees that were cut down when the dam was built.
>
> And hidden in the mud lie smaller, more personal remnants of the mountaineers' lives: a yellow marble, a chipped piece of crockery

> decorated with a faded flower pattern, a Duke's mayonnaise jar, a broken flower pot with greenery growing in it.[1]

An imaginative visitor might picture the ghosts of Dock Jones, Fonzy Hall, Little John Cable, and other nineteenth-century settlers wandering the landscape, looking for some yet-undiscovered way of making money from the land. Could there yet be gold among the remains?

Bryson City, ever watchful for an opportunity, turned even the area's newfound desolation into an asset. The 1990s, like the 1880s, brought a new railroad, the Great Smoky Mountain Scenic Railroad, bringing not manufactured goods from New York but tourists from nearby Dillsboro. By 1996, the oldest and largest town in Swain County could boast a dozen mom-and-pop motels and cozy bed-and-breakfast retreats for those seeking a quiet getaway. A clean corner building in front of the railroad station housed the Swain County Chamber of Commerce, staffed by a middle-aged gentleman from Michigan who came to live in the area twenty years earlier. He offered pamphlets on the region's history and attractions. One

Figure 11. The Railroad to Nowhere? The Swain County Chamber of Commerce maintains this immobilized caboose as a reminder of Bryson City's history as a railroad boomtown and, perhaps unconsciously, of its economic paralysis today. Across Everett Street from the caboose, passengers embark for a scenic train ride to Dillsboro. Photo: Stephen Wallace Taylor.

Left: Figure 12. Lacking the strip mall development of the Tennessee side of the Great Smoky Mountains National Park, residents of Bryson City promoted their community as "uncrowded, unhurried, unspoiled, uncommon." Photo: Stephen Wallace Taylor.

Below: Figure 13. Residents of the upper Little Tennessee have capitalized on the area's image as a haven for "mountain people." The Country Hicks General Store is located on State Highway 28, just off Fontana Lake. Photo: Stephen Wallace Taylor.

brochure even invited the newcomers to see the "Road to Nowhere," which boasted a campground for recreational vehicles. The movie *Nell,* about a woman who grows up totally isolated from human contact, was shot a few miles west of town, just off the Road to Nowhere, bringing national attention and an infusion of cash into the area. The dramatic Nantahala Gorge a few miles south of town served as a major destination for whitewater rafters. Hikers flocked to the backwoods trails of the Great Smoky Mountain National Park, shunning the chain motels of nearby

Cherokee. The town had no name-brand hotels, no bustling industry, no shopping malls, and only a couple of fast-food restaurants, but most of the storefronts were filled. Kelly Bennett's old drugstore housed a craft shop selling "authentic mountain crafts." The streets were neatly swept, the buildings well maintained, the lawns groomed. A few tourists walked the streets, charmed by the town's quietness and quaintness. It was certainly no "second Niagara Falls," but Bryson City continued to get by on what it had, this time selling neither timber nor copper nor electric power, but the rustic image of the Back of Beyond itself. Just as the set of images promoted through the likes of *Gone with the Wind* became a shibboleth for whites of the New South, the Road to Nowhere and the "broken promise" of the federal government to the citizens of the upper Little Tennessee became the valley's own Lost Cause.

Notes

Preface

1. Kirby, *Rural Worlds Lost,* 80.

Chapter 1. A Southern People in a Mountain Region

1. Horton and Zullo, *Geology of the Carolinas,* 9; Raitz and Ulack, *Appalachia, a Regional Geography,* 39–86; Campbell, *Great Smoky Mountain Wildflowers,* 3–7; Brewer, *A Wonderment of Mountains.* On the chestnut blight, an excellent overview may be found in Brown, "Smoky Mountains Story," 151–56.

2. Odum, *Southern Regions of the United States,* 35–39; Horton and Zullo, *Geology of the Carolinas,* 1–35, 317–27; Flohr, Dillenburg, and Plumlee, "Characterization of Secondary Minerals Formed as the Result of Weathering of the Anakeesta Formation, Alum Cave, Great Smoky Mountains National Park, Tennessee," U.S. Geological Survey open-file report no. 95-477, 1–21; Seal et al., "Preliminary Report on Water Quality Associated with the Abandoned Fontana and Hazel Creek Mines, Great Smoky Mountains National Park, North Carolina and Tennessee," U.S. Geological Survey open-file report no. 98-476; Tennessee Valley Authority, *Fifty Inches of Rain a Year,* 27.

3. Odum, *Southern Regions of the United States,* 295; TVA, *Fifty Inches of Rain a Year,* 27.

4. Sometimes spelled Tuckaseegee or Tuckasegee, not to be confused with Tuskeegee (or Tuskegee) Creek, another tributary of the Little Tennessee. In the case of variant spellings in local use, I have tried to identify and utilize the most common.

5. Browder, *The Cherokee Indians and Those Who Came After,* 73–78. The 1819 treaty provided for the state's acquisition of the areas designated as Jackson and Macon Counties; Swain County was later formed from portions of these two counties. The 1,112 square miles acquired through the Treaty of New Echota formed a single county known as Cherokee, from which Graham and Clay Counties were later carved. Graham and Swain Counties form the core of the upper Little Tennessee Valley studied here.

6. Browder, *Those Who Came After,* 79–87. Actually, as Browder notes, only about one-fifth of the land acquired by treaty—that situated along rivers and creeks—was offered for sale at this auction; the remainder was so poor in quality,

in the opinion of state officials, that it was not worth surveying. Of the 1,400 tracts (totaling 215,000 acres) that were actually offered for sale, 1,202 (184,738 acres) were sold, with the state retaining the remainder for later sale at a discounted price. Some mountain land was eventually sold for as little as five cents an acre. Browder is highly suspicious of the motives of William Holland Thomas, whom Finger described in *Eastern Band,* 13, as "without a doubt the most important [white] individual connected with the Eastern Band's history" during this period. Thomas was adopted by the Eastern Band as a youth.

7. Inscoe, *Mountain Masters,* 13; Finger, *Eastern Band,* 60–63; Browder, *Those Who Came After,* 84–87; see also Neely, *Snowbird Cherokees.*

8. Finger, *Eastern Band,* 8–11, 49–52, 55–56, 60–81, 111–12, 129–30, 133–39, 145–47, 169–75; Perdue, *Slavery and the Evolution of Cherokee Society,* 50–95; Inscoe, *Mountain Masters,* 16, 37–43.

9. Browder, *Those Who Came After,* 84–87; Inscoe, *Mountain Masters,* 11–23; Williams, *Great Smoky Mountains Folklife,* 3–9. One locally popular legend holds that Abraham Enloe, one of the area's early white settlers and one of its largest slaveholders, was Abraham Lincoln's biological father.

10. Browder, *Those Who Came After,* 89–90, 94–122, 159–79; Hsiung, *Two Worlds in the Tennessee Mountains,* 74–102, 162–88.

11. On that economic shift the most important recent work is Sellers, *The Market Revolution.*

12. Inscoe, *Mountain Masters,* 211–57; McKinney, *Southern Mountain Republicans,* 4–61.

13. Dunn, *Cades Cove,* 123–45; Inscoe, *Mountain Masters,* 211–64.

14. Finger, *Eastern Band,* 82–100, 102–3.

15. Shapiro, *Appalachia on Our Mind,* 3–31; Dunn, *Cades Cove,* 123–44, 151; Hsiung, *Two Worlds in the Tennessee Mountains,* 182.

16. Shapiro, *Appalachia on Our Mind,* 3–18.

17. Ibid., 18–21.

18. Ibid., 3–18, 26–31.

19. Ibid., 32–58; on the reform efforts of the early twentieth century, see Whisnant, *Modernizing the Mountaineer,* 3–39.

20. Shapiro, *Appalachia on Our Mind,* 32–65.

21. Kephart, *Our Southern Highlanders,* xi–xlvi, 28–74, 265–349; Campbell, *Birth of a National Park,* 30, 36, 140, 141; Shapiro, *Appalachia on Our Mind,* 189; see also Batteau, *The Invention of Appalachia,* 89–92; Martin, "Selling the Southern Highlands," 195–98, and Kirby, *Rural Worlds Lost,* 80–87. Martin notes the role of contemporary travel and nature writers such as Robert Lindsay Mason (*Lure of the Great Smokies*), Margaret Morley (*The Carolina Mountains*), Muriel Sheppard (*Cabins in the Laurel*), and Laura Thornborough (*The Great Smoky Mountains*) in publicizing this view of the southern highlands, but traces the origin of their works to the popularity of Kephart's *Our Southern Highlanders.* Martin also emphasizes the role of travel accounts published in magazines, which

he says probably influenced potential tourists more directly. Kirby acknowledges a list similar to Martin's, but also places a number of later figures in this category, including Jack Weller, whose *Yesterday's People* was first published in 1965, Christian writer Catherine Marshall, who was responsible for the novel *Christy,* currently running for the benefit of tourists as a stage play in Townsend, Tennessee, on the edge of the Great Smoky Mountains National Park, and Eliot Wigginton, founder of the *Foxfire* folk education program in northern Georgia in the early 1970s. On the "southern image" and its impact on both popular and academic approaches to the region, see Kirby, *Media-Made Dixie,* esp. 1–22 and 64–77; a parallel work that focuses on the mountain South is Williamson, *Hillbillyland.*

22. Shapiro, *Appalachia on Our Mind,* 157–85. An appropriate analogy for this transformation is the transformation of the image of the West in American popular culture as the reality of the frontier faded away; see Smith, *Virgin Land.*

23. Cobb, *The Most Southern Place on Earth,* vii–xi, 329.

24. Ayers, *The Promise of the New South,* 55–109.

25. Woodward, *Origins of the New South,* 292–93.

26. Boyden, *Village of Five Lives,* 10–42; Helen Cable Vance, interview by Bill Landry.

27. Boyden, *Village of Five Lives,* 30.

28. Arnold Monteith, interview by Bill Landry.

29. Boyden, *Village of Five Lives,* 18–19; *Graham County Centennial,* 36–38; *Graham County Heritage,* 38–39.

30. Finger, *Eastern Band,* 44–45, 120–25, 126, 131, 138–40, 150–51; Finger, *Cherokee Americans,* 8–14.

31. Levine, *Black Culture and Black Consciousness,* 5.

32. Williams, *Homeplace,* 115–36.

33. Bush, *Dorie,* 147–52, 174–78.

34. Ayers, *Promise of the New South,* 7.

35. Jenkins, *Swain County Heritage,* 77–79.

36. Ibid., 80–81.

37. Kirby, *Rural Worlds Lost,* 80–111; Eller, *Miners, Millhands, and Mountaineers,* xv–xxvi. On the concept of the Appalachian South as a victimized region, see also Billings, *Planters and the Making of the New South,* 25–41, and Salstrom, *Appalachia's Path to Dependency,* 60–82. A somewhat more subtle view, taking the position that the land itself is the true victim, can be found in Brown, "Smoky Mountains Story."

Chapter 2. Railroads, Good Roads, and Sawmill Villages

1. David L. Carlton coined the term *modernizing elite* in reference to the town-building middle class of the South Carolina Piedmont. Carlton, "'Builders of a New State': The Town Classes and Early Industrialization of South Carolina, 1880–1907," in Fraser and Moore, *From the Old South to the New,* 43–62. The

term fits equally well in the small towns of the North Carolina mountains, where the towns were built on a coalition between "old money" interests and new, and where the lines between the two blurred as "old money" heirs took up professions or opened stores.

2. Key, *Southern Politics,* 205–28; Billings, *Planters and the Making of the New South,* 70–95; Carlton, "Builders of a New State," 43–62. See also Wiener, *Social Origins of the New South.* For an excellent discussion of the subtleties and problems of "planter persistence" as an analytical tool for understanding the complexities of the New South, see Cobb, "Beyond Planters and Industrialists," 45–68.

3. Morris, "Politics of Concealment," 256–58.

4. Ibid., 258–63.

5. Jarvis had been lieutenant governor under Governor Vance. When Vance resigned to take a seat in the Senate, Jarvis succeeded him. Jarvis was elected on his own account in 1880.

6. Morris, "Politics of Concealment," 263–65; Klein, "The Strategy of Southern Railroads," 1052–68.

7. Morris, "Politics of Concealment," 264–66.

8. Ibid., 266–68.

9. Ibid., 268–69.

10. Ibid., 269–71.

11. Ibid., 271–74.

12. Ibid., 274.

13. Ibid., 274–77.

14. Ibid., 277–79.

15. Ibid., 274–81.

16. Ibid., 280–82.

17. Eller, *Miners, Millhands, and Mountaineers,* 48, 89, 99–102.

18. Brown, *State Highway System,* 6–12, 38–39.

19. Ibid., 18–29; see also Lichtenstein, "Good Roads and Chain Gangs," 85–110.

20. Brown, *State Highway System,* 30–34; Preston, *Dirt Roads to Dixie;* Tindall, *Emergence of the New South,* 254–58.

21. Brown, *State Highway System,* 34–36.

22. Ibid., 40–42; *Jackson County Journal,* October 31, 1913.

23. Brown, *State Highway System,* 48–53; Preston, *Dirt Roads to Dixie,* 19–20.

24. Preston, *Dirt Roads to Dixie,* 11–38; Brown, *State Highway System,* 69–70.

25. Brown, *State Highway System,* 72; North Carolina State Highway Commission Minutes. On the link between roads and perceptions of progress, see Preston, *Dirt Roads to Dixie,* and Hsiung, *Two Worlds in the Tennessee Mountains,* 187.

26. Brown, *State Highway System,* 80–89.

27. *Jackson County Journal,* October 10, 1913; Preston, *Dirt Roads to Dixie,* 11–38.

28. Preston, *Dirt Roads to Dixie,* 39–68; *Jackson County Journal,* September 11, 1913.

29. *Jackson County Journal,* March 19, 1915.

30. *Jackson County Journal,* January 24, 1919; Preston, *Dirt Roads to Dixie,* 3–8; Weingroff, "Federal Aid Road Act of 1916," 2–5; on the relationship between the Good Roads Movement and the Rural Free Delivery system, see Preston, *Dirt Roads to Dixie,* 19, 31.

31. Boyden, *Village of Five Lives,* 30; Arthur, *Western North Carolina,* 412–14, 561; Horton and Zullo, *Geology of the Carolinas,* 323. The Hazel Creek mine was the centerpiece of a legal battle between two gentlemen named Adams and Westfeldt, each of whom claimed to have discovered the rich copper ore there. Legal wrangling frequently prevented the ore from being extracted, resulting in a tremendous amount of speculation about how much copper was left in the ground. See *Westfeldt v. Adams* (42 SE 823), *Westfeldt v. North Carolina Mining Co.* (166 F706, *Westfeldt v. North Carolina Mining Co.* (177 F132), *Westfeldt v. Adams* (74 SE 1041).

The value of the mine remained a subject of great debate for many years. According to Great Smoky Mountains National Park records, the North Carolina Exploration Company was still demanding compensation for the loss of its mines due to the park and the Fontana project as late as 1972. Park Service consulting engineers insisted that operating costs would render the mines unprofitable even at four times the known ore deposits. See report from Robert O'Brien, Resource Management Records, box 3, folder 12, Great Smoky Mountains National Park Archives, Gatlinburg, Tennessee.

32. *Bryson City Times,* April 13, 1923, reprinted in *Jackson County Journal,* April 20, 1923.

33. Brown, "Smoky Mountains Story," 68–69, 71–73, 113.

34. Lambert, "Logging the Great Smokies," 350–53.

35. Ibid., 353–56, 358.

36. Ibid., 354–55, 359–61, 359–61; *W. M. Ritter Lumber Co. v. Montvale Lumber Co.* (85 SE 438). For other land rights cases in the area see *Crisp et ux. v. Nantahala Power & Light Co.* (158 SE 845); *Berry v. W. M. Ritter Lumber Co.* (54 SE 278); *Richards v. W. M. Ritter Lumber Co.* (73 SE 485); *Blevens v. Kitchen Lumber Co.* (176 SE 262).

37. Lambert, "Logging the Great Smokies," 356–57.

38. Clarence O. Vance, interview by Bill Landry.

39. Of the personal injury and wrongful death cases brought against these firms, the following reached the North Carolina Supreme Court: *Patton v. W. M. Ritter Lumber Co.* (73 SE 166); *Green v. W. M. Ritter Lumber Co.* (110 SE 56); *Tolley v. W. M. Ritter Lumber Co.* (198 SE 582); *Buchanan v. W. M. Ritter Lumber Co.* (81 SE 684); *Slaughter v. Bemis Lumber Co.* (148 SE 460); *Cook v. Bemis*

Lumber Co. (7 SE 2d 378); *Stamey v. Suncrest Lumber Co.* (148 SE 436); *McKinish v. Norwood Lumber Co.* (133 SE 163); *Cable v. Kitchen Lumber Co.* (128 SE 329); *Langford v. Kitchen Lumber Co.* (148 SE 457); *Colvin v. Kitchen Lumber Co.* (153 SE 394); *Crisp v. Kitchen Lumber Co.* (154 SE 311); *McGuire v. Montvale Lumber Co.* (131 SE 274); *West v. Fontana Mining Corporation* (150 SE 884); *Morrow v. North Carolina Exploration Co.*, (178 SE 549).

40. *Hardwood Bark,* vols. 2–7; Brown, "Smoky Mountains Story," 91–93.

41. Lambert, "Logging the Great Smokies," 355, 358–59.

42. Ibid., 357–58.

43. Ibid., 358; *Hardwood Bark* 6 (September 1926); *Jackson County Journal,* July 2, 1915.

44. *Potter v. Norwood Lumber Co.* (101 SE 553); *Lafferty v. W. M. Ritter Lumber Co.* (130 SE 127); see also Brown, "Smoky Mountains Story," 100–3.

45. Lambert, "Logging the Great Smokies," 359, 361–62.

46. *Graham County Heritage,* 8–9, 204–5.

47. *Jackson County Journal,* January 31, May 16, July 25, October 3, October 10, 1913; February 27, July 10, 1914; September 24, 1915. For other examples of promotion of the region's white labor force, newsletters published by Ritter Lumber Company are particularly interesting. Western Carolina University's Hunter Library maintains a collection of these in its Special Collections Room.

48. Carr, *Alcoa,* 85–105.

49. Hensler and Keyserling, "One-Third of a Nation."

Chapter 3. A Second Niagara Falls

1. George Ellison, introduction to Kephart, *Our Southern Highlanders,* ix–xlvi.

2. Tindall, *The Emergence of the New South,* 219–33.

3. Kirby, *Rural Worlds Lost,* 84–85, argues that "the great half-century boom was over even before the construction bust of the depressed 1930s. It is no accident that the movement to convert many of the cutover swatches of Appalachia and the Ozarks . . . to taxpayer-supported national parks and forests began at this time."

4. Henry O. Marcy, "The Climatic Treatment of Disease: Western North Carolina as a Health Resort," *Journal of the American Medical Association* 5 (1885): 707, quoted in Pierce, "Boosters," 10.

5. Pierce, "Boosters," 10–11.

6. Ibid., 48–49; Vanderbilt, *Fortune's Children,* 271–79.

7. Pierce, "Boosters," 11–12.

8. Ibid.; Gaston, *The New South Creed,* 91.

9. Pierce, "Boosters," 12–13; Brown, "Smoky Mountains Story," 122–23; Cowdrey, *This Land, This South,* 119–20, 135–38.

10. Hays, *Conservation and the Gospel of Efficiency,* 189–98.

11. Pierce, "Boosters," 13–14; see also Brown, "Smoky Mountains Story," 111–13.

12. Pierce, "Boosters," 13–14; Lukens, "Portraits of Progress," 35–74.

13. Pierce, "Boosters," 16–17.

14. Ibid., 16–19.

15. Ibid., 19–20.

16. Ibid., 19–24; Key, *Southern Politics,* 315–82; George Brown Tindall, "Business Progressivism: Southern Politics in the Twenties," *South Atlantic Quarterly* 57 (1963): 92–106, cited in Pierce, "Boosters," 9. Key has traced the development of North Carolina's Progressive political movement in *Southern Politics,* 205–28. Key argues that the relatively progressive positions taken by the state's Democratic governors result from both a lack of domination by plantation owners and a relatively strong Republican Party.

17. Key, *Southern Politics,* 211–15; Pierce, "Boosters," 9, 24–27.

18. Pierce, "Boosters," 34–35.

19. Ibid., 35–37, 48.

20. Ibid., 39–43.

21. Ibid., 43–45.

22. Ibid., 59, 68–70, 86–87; Brown, "Smoky Mountains Story."

23. Pierce, "Boosters," 71–76.

24. Ibid., 77–90.

25. Ibid., 90–91, 95–97.

26. Ibid., 92, quoting the *Asheville Citizen,* January 28, February 4, and March 5, 1926.

27. Interview with Granville Calhoun by John Parris, in "Only the Dead Remain at Medlin," *Asheville Citizen,* March 8, 1968. Parris quotes Calhoun as saying that there were only 15 million feet of lumber left for cutting when Ritter Lumber Company pulled out of the Medlin-Proctor area in the late 1920s. At the rate of nearly 10 million feet per year Calhoun attributed to the Ritter concern, the supply would have been exhausted in a year and a half.

28. Pierce, "Boosters," 47–51.

29. Ibid., 51–53.

30. Ibid., 47–56.

31. Ibid., 56–61; Kephart to Zebulon B. Weaver, January 9 and 13, 1925, Horace Kephart Papers, Western Carolina University Special Collections, quoted in Pierce, "Boosters," 59.

32. Campbell, *Birth of a National Park,* 36.

33. Pierce, "Boosters," 161–71; Brown, "Smoky Mountains Story," 142–51, 160–62, 216–34; Campbell, *Birth of a National Park,* 80, 130–33.

34. Pierce, "Boosters," 179–203; Brown, "Smoky Mountains Story," 142–45, 167–71.

35. Pierce, "Boosters," 216–18.

36. Brown, "Smoky Mountains Story," 150–51; on historic "reconstruction" in the park, see ibid., 188–89; on the "restoration of nature" by landscape architects and CCC camps, see ibid., 198–200.

37. Pierce, "Boosters," 178–79.

38. Williams, *Great Smoky Mountains Folklife,* 132, 159.

39. Dunn, *Cades Cove,* 237–44; *Bryson City Times,* October 15, 1942; J. G. Stikeleather to Zebulon B. Weaver, September 20, 1941, Weaver Papers.

40. *Bryson City Times,* March 18, 1932.

41. *Bryson City Times,* November 11, 1932.

42. *Bryson City Times,* September 9, 1932.

43. *Franklin Press and Highlands Maconian,* May 12, 1932.

44. Reprinted in *Bryson City Times,* March 25, 1932.

45. *Bryson City Times,* March 25, 1932.

46. *Jackson County Journal,* January 29, 1915.

47. *Bryson City Times,* April 22, November 11, December 30, 1932.

48. *Bryson City Times,* April 8, November 25, 1937. On the reasons for the Eastern Band's reluctance to work with the Park Service, see Mitchell, "Parkway Politics," 270–336.

49. *Bryson City Times,* July 7, 1938.

50. Brown, "Smoky Mountains Story," 156.

51. Mitchell, "Parkway Politics," 148–214; Brown, "Smoky Mountains Story," 116–202; Pierce, "Boosters," 177–203.

52. Eller, *Miners, Millhands, and Mountaineers,* 239; Kirby, *Rural Worlds Lost,* 99–101.

53. Federal Writers' Project, *North Carolina: A Guide to the Old North State,* 443–44.

54. Oliver, *Hazel Creek from Then till Now,* 87–90.

55. *Bryson City Times,* October 7, 1932.

56. Black and Black, *Politics and Society in the South,* 214.

57. *Bryson City Times,* November 11, 1932.

Chapter 4. Machiavelli and Monopoly in the Mountains

1. Carr, *Alcoa,* 23–83; Smith, *From Monopoly to Competition,* 1–113.

2. Carr, *Alcoa,* 85–95.

3. *Franklin Press and Highlands Maconian,* October 18, 1934; U.S. Senate Special Committee, hearings investigating the National Defense Program, pt. 3, 902–3 (testimony of I. W. Wilson).

4. Smith, *From Monopoly to Competition,* 189–90; see also Perry, "Forward Integration by Alcoa," 37–53; Muller, "The Aluminum Monopoly and the War," 14–43.

5. Smith, *From Monopoly to Competition,* 191–213.

6. Ibid., 196–9.

7. A basic principle of hydroelectric power is that the amount of power produced depends on the amount of water flowing through the turbines. Dams store water to maintain as even a flow as possible, so that the power supply will not fluctuate. In a system of dams, the storage function of upstream dams determines

the amount of power that can be produced further downstream. This meant that Alcoa and TVA, both of which had dams downstream from Fontana, would eventually have to reach some sort of agreement concerning the maintenance of water flow from the upper reaches of the Little Tennessee into the Tennessee River.

8. Lowitt, *George W. Norris,* xiii–xv, 22–25, 150, 164–80, 181–96, 197–216, 330–64, 400, 454–67, 487–527, 549–69; Hubbard, *Origins of the TVA.* Progressivism has provided historians with much to study. On the methods employed by Progressives, see Chambers, *The Tyranny of Change.* On Progressivism in the South, see Grantham, *Southern Progressivism.*

9. Chandler, *The Myth of TVA,* 5; Hargrove, *Prisoners of Myth,* 19–26 (quoted matter from p. 20). The best work on the origin of TVA as a public agency is Hubbard, *Origins of the TVA.*

10. Hargrove, 24–25; see also Roy Talbert, *FDR's Utopian,* 10–17, 108–27.

11. Hargrove, *Prisoners of Myth,* 24–25, 37; Talbert, *FDR's Utopian;* McCraw, *TVA and the Power Fight.* Hargrove, *Prisoners of Myth,* 33, quotes an interview by Charles Crawford in which TVA's John Ferris recalled that Morgan once introduced a talk by Vice President Henry Wallace, proceeded to look very interested, and afterward told the crowd that listening to Wallace had inspired him to instruct TVA to develop a three-legged chair to be manufactured in the Tennessee Valley. As Ferris remarked, "There is something odd about a state of mind that could produce results like that." On the relationship between individual will and the Progressive Era, the best synthetic work is Chambers, *The Tyranny of Change.* On the relationship between Progressivism and the New Deal, see Graham, *An Encore for Reform.*

12. Hargrove, *Prisoners of Myth,* 26–28, 33–41.

13. Ibid., 28–30, 35–36, 38–47, 49–56; Segal, "Down in the Valley," 423–27; Lilienthal, *TVA: Democracy on the March.*

14. Selznick, *TVA and the Grass Roots,* 91–96; McCraw, *TVA and the Power Fight,* 140–45.

15. Hargrove, *Prisoners of Myth,* 56–59; Talbert, *FDR's Utopian,* 153–56.

16. Franklin D. Roosevelt, quoted in Hargrove, *Prisoners of Myth,* 20. FDR wrote the TVA Act, which was passed without alteration. These words are from his preamble to the act.

17. Hargrove, *Prisoners of Myth,* 30–33, 38–41; Talbert, *FDR's Utopian.*

18. Talbert, *FDR's Utopian,* 29–33.

19. Morgan, *Making of the TVA,* 110.

20. Ibid., 106–7.

21. *Hearings before the Committee on Military Affairs,* 74th Cong., 1st sess., 1935, 2:662, 664 (testimony of Arthur V. Davis), quoted in Morgan, *Making of the TVA,* 110–11.

22. Morgan, *Making of the TVA,* 112. It is not clear from Morgan's recollection whether this is a reference to Lilienthal's personal assistant, V.D.L. Robinson. All references to Robinson's appointment were apparently removed from Lilien-

thal's files. Robinson was a former aide to Tennessee's Senator Nathan Bachman, an early critic of Morgan's condescending attitude toward southerners. Robinson apparently helped Bachman's loyal supporters obtain employment. Morgan's charges of patronage directed at Lilienthal were often distressingly vague. For more on Robinson, see Talbert, *FDR's Utopian,* 151–54.

23. Morgan, *Making of the TVA,* 108–11.

24. *Franklin Press and Highlands Maconian,* October 18, November 15, 1934.

25. Ibid., October 18, 1934.

26. Zeb Weaver to David I. Schrum, June 7, 1941; Weaver to J. G. Stikeleather, June 10, June 14, 1941; D. Hiden Ramsey to Weaver, November 25, 1941, Zebulon B. Weaver Papers. See also *Franklin Press and Highlands Maconian* and *Bryson City Times.*

27. Talbert, *FDR's Utopian,* 169–93 (quoted material from p. 183).

28. Excerpt from minutes of board of directors meeting, 6/2/36, TVA Office of the General Manager, Administrative Files (hereafter cited as TVA OGM AF), box 702; McCraw, *TVA and the Power Fight,* 87–89, 123; Joseph Swidler, interview by Charles Crawford.

29. Hearings before the Joint Committee on the Investigation of the Tennessee Valley Authority, 75th Cong., pt. 1, July 19, 1938, 372; quoted in Morgan, *Making of the TVA,* 114.

30. Gregory Field has pointed out that Lilienthal's willingness to accommodate the needs of large corporations at the expense of smaller businesses marked a turning point in the agency's fortunes and its public image, and the tenor of the feud that erupted between Lilienthal and A. E. Morgan over the Fontana project tends to corroborate this interpretation. See Field, "From Regional Development to National Defense."

31. Carr, *Alcoa,* 247–61.

32. U.S. Senate Special Committee, National Defense Program, pt. 7, 2126–37 (testimony of Frank Eichelberger); pt. 3, 802–13 (Hugh Fulton quoted during testimony of G. R. Gibbons); pt. 3, 899–908, 915–22, 910 (Senator Harry Truman quoted during testimony of I. W. Wilson).

33. Brewer and Brewer, *Valley So Wild,* 252–54.

34. U.S. Senate Special Committee, National Defense Program, pt. 3, 936–38 (testimony of J. A. Krug).

35. U.S. Senate Special Committee, National Defense Program, pt. 3, 806 (testimony of G. R. Gibbons); *Franklin Press and Highlands Maconian,* March 13, 1941.

36. *Franklin Press and Highlands Maconian,* March 13, 1941.

37. Ibid., June 19, 1941; J. A. Krug to I. W. Wilson, June 20, 1941, in TVA OGM AF, box 702; see also Brewer and Brewer, *Valley So Wild,* 250–51.

38. U.S. Senate Special Committee, National Defense Program, pt. 3, 913–16 (testimony of I. W. Wilson); Morgan, *Making of the TVA,* 117; *Franklin Press and Highlands Maconian,* July 10, 1941; Harcourt A. Morgan to I. W. Wilson, February 24, 1941, TVA OGM AF, box 702.

39. U.S. Senate Special Committee, National Defense Program, pt. 3, 796 (testimony of G. R. Gibbons); Lilienthal, *Journals,* 350–54.

40. David I. Schrum to Zeb Weaver, June 4, 1941; Weaver to Schrum, June 7, 1941; Weaver to W. E. (Bill) Elmore, July 26, October 11, 1941; Weaver to R. B. (Bruce) Slaughter, August 26, 1941; Slaughter to Weaver, November 4, 1941; I. K. Stearns to Weaver, November 12, 1941; quoted matter from Slaughter to Weaver, August 15, 1941, all in Weaver Papers.

41. Stanley W. Black to Zebulon B. Weaver, June 1941, Weaver Papers.

42. Zeb Weaver to David I. Schrum, June 7, 1941; Weaver to J. C. Strikeleather, June 10, June 14, 1941; Weaver to Strikeleather, June 14, 1941; D. Hiden Ramsey to Weaver, November 25, 1941. Weaver Papers.

43. Zeb Weaver to C. W. Savage, November 22, 1941; Weaver to David I. Schrum, June 7, 1941; Weaver to J. G. Stikeleather, June 10, June 14, 1941; D. Hiden Ramsey to Weaver, November 25, 1941. Weaver Papers.

44. *Franklin Press and Highlands Maconian,* October 17, 1940.

45. Ibid., July 17, 1941.

Chapter 5. I'm from the Government, and I'm Here to Help

1. John I. Snyder, interview by Charles Crawford.

2. Ibid.

3. Richard Niehoff, interview by Charles Crawford.

4. John C. McAmis, interview by Charles Crawford.

5. George Gant, interview by Charles Crawford.

6. Ibid.

7. Ibid.

8. TVA's insistence on compensating landowners rather than land users for the loss of the land has a parallel in the Agricultural Adjustment Administration's policy of paying landowners rather than tenants for taking crop land out of cultivation. This readjustment policy is part of what Philip Selznick calls the "right wing" of policymaking within TVA, a sector dominated by the agricultural programs promoted by H. A. Morgan and J. C. McAmis. The net effect of TVA's and the AAA's approach was to displace tenant families. This fundamentally conservative approach is directly opposed to the function of the Federal Emergency Relief Administration (FERA) and the Farm Security Administration (FSA) in the rural South. FERA attempted to remodel the land tenure system by restoring a barter economy and providing financial and technical assistance to keep farmers working. See Pete Daniel, "The New Deal, Southern Agriculture, and Economic Change," in Cobb and Namorato, *The New Deal and the South,* 37–61; see also Daniel, *Breaking the Land,* esp. 65–133 and 155–83; and Daniel, *Standing at the Crossroads,* 117–24. On the FSA and the AAA, see Kirby, *Rural Worlds Lost,* 57–79.

9. *Graham County Heritage,* 126–31.

10. On the origins, history, and mission of WCTC, later Western Carolina University, see Bird, *History of Western Carolina College.*

11. McDonald and Muldowny, *TVA and the Dispossessed.*

12. Tennessee Valley Authority Reservoir Property Management Department, Population Readjustment Division. "Stecoah Community," prepared by Arnold J. Hyde (hereafter cited as "Stecoah"), 3.

13. Ibid., 2–3.

14. Selznick, *TVA and the Grass Roots,* 22–44, 132–33, 138–41, 181–213.

15. Tennessee Valley Authority Reservoir Property Management Department, Population Readjustment Division. "Almond-Judson Community, Fontana Area," prepared by Arnold J. Hyde (hereafter cited as "Almond-Judson"), 2–4. While the Great Smoky Mountains National Park prevented taking the last of the timber along the right bank of the Little Tennessee and its tributaries west of Bryson City, the area along the south and west shores, from Judson west into Graham County, continued to be logged.

16. Ibid., 5; see *Graham County Centennial,* 125–31. On the relatively "progressive" reputation of the Methodists in western North Carolina, at least in their own eyes, see also Bumgarner and Carroll, *The Flowering of Methodism.*

17. Tennessee Valley Authority Reservoir Property Management Department, Population Readjustment Division. "Proctor Community, Fontana Area," prepared by Rome C. Sharp (hereafter cited as "Proctor"), 1.

18. Williams, *Great Smoky Mountains Folklife,* 157; "Proctor," 6.

19. "Proctor," 5.

20. "Stecoah," 2.

21. Ibid., 4; Arnold Monteith, interview by Bill Landry.

22. "Proctor," 1; John K. Bailey, "Shack Development Control, Fontana Area," TVA internal report from Reservoir Property Management Department, Population Readjustment Division, May 1, 1944, 3–22, TVA Corporate Library, Knoxville.

23. Williams, *Homeplace,* 122–36.

24. C. E. Blee to W. T. Hunt, March 21, 1942, cited in Bailey, "Shack Development Control."

25. Tennessee Valley Authority Water Control Planning Department, "Possible Development of the Fontana Project on the Little Tennessee River: A Reconnaissance Report," submitted by T. B. Parker to Gordon R. Clapp, August 29, 1941, 4, TVA Corporate Library, Knoxville.

26. H. K. Menhinick, "The Fontana Region: A Brief Description of the Characteristics of the Region and the Effects of Reservoir Construction," internal TVA report, March 9, 1942, 5–9, TVA Corporate Library, Knoxville. Menhinick was generally sympathetic to the agricultural losses faced by individual families, but he was unconvinced that the loss of the Fontana mine would have any significant impact, though he conceded that the ore was of high quality.

27. "Almond-Judson," 6.

28. "Stecoah," 5.

29. McDonald and Muldowny, *TVA and the Dispossessed,* 141–54.

30. Tennessee Valley Authority, Fontana Case Files, Reservoir Property Management Division, Population Removal Records, box 136, Federal Records Center, East Point, Georgia. Andy Chicklelee, G-38 (hereafter cited as Fontana Case Files, Andy Chicklelee); Arnold Monteith, interview by Bill Landry.

31. Fontana Case Files, "Andy Chicklelee."

32. Ibid.

33. Ibid.

34. Ibid.

35. Ibid.

36. Fontana Case Files, Reservoir Property Management Division, Population Removal Records, box 136, Federal Records Center, East Point, Georgia, Game Walker, G-39.

37. Ibid., L. W. Ammons.

38. Ibid.

39. Ibid.

40. Ibid.

41. Ibid.

42. Ibid., Bill Fuller.

43. According to Fontana Case Reports, "Missionary Baptist Church," the church building was located on the "A. W. Reed place on the Coburn heirs property." It is not clear whether this is the Andy Reid who owned the building when it was a saloon, nor is it clear whether Reed (Reid) owned or claimed ownership of the land. Ownership of buildings was often separate from ownership of the land on which they stood, and this distinction complicates the reconstruction of the events just as it complicated TVA's plans.

44. *Cabe* is the spelling found in TVA records. Both Cabe and Cable were common names in the area, and it is not clear whether there was some relation between the Cabe and Cable families.

45. Tennessee Valley Authority, Division of Reservoir Properties, *Final Report: Population Readjustment, Fontana Reservoir,* 5, in TVA Corporate Library, Knoxville.

46. Bailey, "Shack Development Control," 3–22.

47. Ibid., 3–8.

48. Ibid., 3–22.

49. Tennessee Valley Authority, *The Fontana Project: TVA Technical Report Number 12,* 199, 207, 152–53, 237–44.

50. *Bryson City Times,* March 26, 1942; April 2, 1942; April 16, 1942; December 17, 1942; January 7, 1943; Gordon R. Clapp to John L. Rogers, April 29, 1943; Clapp to H. Aydelott, March 1, March 28, 1944, Aydelott to Clapp, March 17, 1944, C. E. Blee to W. C. Fitts, April 8, 1944, TVA OGM AF, box 317; *Bryson*

City Times, June 11, 1942; Charles E. Lex to Departmental Travel Clerks, December 17, 1943, TVA OGM AF, box 702.

51. *Bryson City Times*, November 12, 1942.

Chapter 6. Managing People and Land

1. Charlie Calhoun, interview by Bill Landry.

2. Gordon R. Clapp to H. Aydelott, March 1, 1944, TVA OGM AF, box 317; TVA announcement of jobs available in reservoir clearance work, January 2, 1942, TVA OGM AF, box 440.

3. On the division of labor by race in the South, see Hall, *Like a Family*, 66–67; see also Carlton, *Mill and Town in South Carolina*. TVA's general racial policies are detailed in Grant, *TVA and Black Americans*. Roosevelt's racial policies are well documented in Leuchtenberg, *Franklin D. Roosevelt and the New Deal* and Sitkoff, *A New Deal for Blacks*.

4. Grant, *TVA and Black Americans*, xxx, 20–23, 48–49, 54–57; Selznick, *TVA and the Grass Roots*, 112–13; Hargrove, *Prisoners of Myth*, 54, 101.

5. Grant, *TVA and Black Americans*, 56–60.

6. Ibid., 61. The area's black population experienced a sharp decline between 1910 and 1925, and it never rebounded. By 1940 there was one black person residing in Graham County, Eli "Trixie" Williams, a former construction worker for Alcoa who remained as a porter at the company's boarding house at Cheoah Dam until ill health forced his retirement in 1954. See *Graham County Centennial*, 60–61. *Graham County Heritage*, 234. According to Clarence O. Vance, Ritter Lumber Company removed its black employees from the Hazel Creek area of Swain County following some "racial problems" after World War I. See Clarence O. Vance, interview by Bill Landry.

7. Grant, *TVA and Black Americans*, 61; Finger, *Cherokee Americans*, 105, 110.

8. George Gant, interview by Charles Crawford; Grant, *TVA and Black Americans*, 60; John Oliver, interview by Mark Winter (note that this is *not* the John Oliver of Cades Cove fame). See also Gordon R. Clapp to T. B. Parker and L. N. Allen, July 14, 1942, TVA OGM AF, box 442. Unfortunately, no other records of racial incidents at Fontana have been preserved by TVA.

9. On the effect of the Depression on progressive education, see Spencer J. Maxcy, "Progressivism and Rural Education in the Deep South, 1900–1950," in Goodenow and White, *Education and the Rise of the New South*, 47–71. Another interesting and relevant essay from the same volume is Nancy L. Grant, "Government Social Planning and Education for Blacks: The TVA Experience, 1933–1945," 215–36.

10. Bailey, "Two Years of the Public School," 1–5. Among the southern states, North Carolina's education policies were some of the most "progressive," beginning with the administration of Governor Charles Brantley Aycock in 1901. Those policies emphasized consolidation of one-room schools into larger, more

professionalized systems, and also emphasized stricter qualifications for teachers. Many articles have addressed various aspects of progressive education movements in North Carolina; see Link, "Privies, Progressivism, and Public Schools," 623–42; Ferguson, "An Era of Educational Change," 130–41; Gatewood, "Eugene Clyde Brooks," 307–29. While these policies gained statewide currency with the state's takeover of public school funding, their full impact had not yet been felt in the upper Little Tennessee. On the political origins of progressive education in North Carolina, see Prather, *Resurgent Politics*.

The social science research undertaken at the University of North Carolina produced a steady stream of educators focused on innovative methodology, including the use of practical activities as teaching tools, as noted in Gustin and Hayes, *Activities in Public Schools*. Gustin and Hayes integrated such activities into the curriculum of Craven and Carteret County schools, with substantial success despite a lack of state support. Gustin and Hayes followed up on the work of European childhood education pioneers such as Froebel, Piaget, and Montessori and on public interest as described in Murray, *History of the Public School Kindergarten*, 5–63. Moreo, *Schools in the Great Depression*, 44, notes that in 1933 the state of North Carolina took over responsibility for funding all public schools, instituting a 3 percent sales tax in order to raise the revenue.

11. Bailey, "Two Years of the Public School," 5.
12. Ibid.
13. Ibid., 6.
14. Ibid., 9–10.
15. Ibid.
16. Ibid., 14–15, 17–18, 21–22.
17. Ibid., 24.
18. Ibid., 13.
19. Ibid., 12.
20. Ibid., 27–28.
21. Ibid., 16–17.
22. Ibid., 1–3, 15.
23. Ibid., 7–8.
24. Ibid.
25. David E. Lilienthal to Prentiss Brown, May 8, 1943; Marguerite Owen to Gordon R. Clapp, May 13, 1943; Owen to Arthur S. Jandrey, May 19, 1943, TVA OGM AF, box 314.
26. Fish and chicken, while excellent sources of protein, were not considered meat by rationing boards or by consumers. "Summary of Adjustments in Meat Ration Points and Use of Meats at Fontana Cafeterias," TVA OGM AF, box 314; Jesse L. Harris to J. Ed Campbell, July 24, 1943, TVA OGM AF, box 314; J. Ed Campbell to Arthur S. Jandrey, September 13, 1943, TVA OGM AF, box 639.
27. Gladys Burkhart to C. H. Garity, November 13, 1943; Leona LeRoy to W. J. Hagan Jr., April 29, November 1, 1944, May 11, 1945; Hagan to Gordon R.

Clapp, October 29, 1945, TVA OGM AF, box 151; Hagan to Clapp, June 8, 1944, TVA OGM AF, box 576; Burkhart to Garity, September 8, 1943, TVA OGM AF, box 112..

28. McDonald and Muldowny, *TVA and the Dispossessed,* 215–35.

29. M. G. Chambers to W. L. Sturdevant, February 2, 1945; Gordon R. Clapp to Chambers, February 3, 1945, TVA OGM AF, box 135; Mary Utopia Rothrock, interview by Charles Crawford.

30. L. N. Allen to Gordon R. Clapp, May 30, 1944, TVA OGM AF, box 165.

31. *Bryson City Times,* January 15, February 26, March 5, April 16, 1942.

32. Bailey, "Shack Development Control," 3–22.

33. Ed Hochnedel and Ralph Harmon, interview by Carolyn B. Roberts.

34. Hattie Gunter to TVA, August 19, 1942, TVA OGM AF, box 107.

35. Herbert E. Hudson to J. Ed Campbell, November 11, 1942; January 12, 1943, TVA OGM AF, box 107.

36. Fontana Dam *Recreation* (newsletter), April 27, 1945, TVA OGM AF, box 750.

37. *Bryson City Times,* February 25, 1943.

38. Game Walker, interview, *Journal of Cherokee Studies* 14 (1989): 63–64.

39. *Bryson City Times,* May 28, 1942.

40. Ibid.

41. Brewing Industry Council advertisement in *Bryson City Times,* February 25, 1943.

42. Donald Mattern, interview by Carolyn B. Roberts.

43. *Bryson City Times,* March 11, 1943.

44. Henry R. Holtzclaw Sr. to Senator Robert R. Reynolds, January 19, 1944, TVA OGM AF, box 118.

45. George F. Gant, "Announcement to Carpenters at Fontana Project," January 15, 1944, TVA OGM AF, box 118.

46. "Fontana Dam Public Address System," unsigned report dated July 20, 1945, TVA OGM AF, box 702.

47. Ibid.

48. Labor Day 1944 speech by William Green, delivered through electric transcription to the Fontana audience, TVA OGM AF, box 702.

49. Labor Day 1944 speech by Samuel E. Roper, delivered at Fontana Dam, TVA OGM AF, box 702. On the relationship between Fontana Dam and the creation of the Clinton Engineer Works at Oak Ridge, see Donald H. Mattern, interview by Mark Winter. According to Mattern, the Project Planning Department received a set of requirements from the Army Corps of Engineers for what Mattern assumed would be a munitions factory at Oak Ridge, but the experimental nature of the Oak Ridge facility was not disclosed.

50. *Bryson City Times,* November 19, 1942; January 21, 1943.

51. L. N. Allen to Gordon R. Clapp, January 22, 1943, TVA OGM AF, box 42.

52. L. N. Allen to Gordon R. Clapp, April 6, 1944, TVA OGM AF, box 198.

53. L. N. Allen to Gordon R. Clapp, April 26, 1943, TVA OGM AF, box 235.

54. L. N. Allen to Gordon R. Clapp, June 8, 1943, TVA OGM AF, box 118; R. L. Phillips to Zebulon B. Weaver, December 18, 1942, January 26, 1943; Amanda Crisp to Weaver, January 28, 1943; Weaver to Crisp, January 30, 1943; Weaver to Phillips, January 31, 1943; Ambrose O'Connell to Weaver, February 1, 1943; Weaver to Phillips, February 4, 1943; O'Connell to Weaver, February 9, 1943; O'Connell to Weaver, February 10, 1943; Weaver to Phillips, February 24, 1943; R. B. Slaughter to Weaver, March 4, March 20, March 27, 1943; Martha Calahan to Weaver, April 27, 1943; W. T. Martin to Weaver, April 28, 1943; Calahan to Weaver, April 28, 1943; Crisp to Weaver, April 29, 1943; Laurence V. Wilson to Weaver, May 3, 1943; Weaver to Crisp, May 4, 1943; Weaver to Jack Morphew, May 10, 1943; J. T. Arledge to Weaver, May 11, 1943; W. S. Green to Weaver, May 12, 1943; Phillips to Weaver, May 30, 1943, Weaver Papers.

55. L. N. Allen to Gordon R. Clapp, August 5, 1944, TVA OGM AF, box 161.

56. L. N. Allen to Gordon R. Clapp, August 14, 1940; July 24, 1942; March 3, July 1, 1943; February 17, 1944; January 1, 1945, TVA OGM AF, box 227.

57. J. Bluford Slaughter to Gordon R. Clapp, November 2, 1944, TVA OGM AF, box 210; see also *Graham County Centennial,* 60–61.

58. Gordon R. Clapp to J. Bluford Slaughter, November 7, 1944, TVA OGM AF, box 210.

59. Kim Crisp, supervisor, Graham County Board of Elections, telephone interview by Benjamin J. Lea, director, North Carolina Political Broadcast Archives, June 19, 1995, summarized in personal communication to the author. Graham County, home to one of the more powerful Republican organizations in North Carolina during this period, strongly supported incumbent Democrat Zebulon B. Weaver in the 1944 congressional election. Weaver, who served uninterrupted from 1930 to 1946, usually faced serious opposition in Graham County. That county had gone narrowly Republican in 1928 and in all the midterm congressional elections since 1932, suggesting that local Democrats benefited from a coattail effect in presidential election years. Weaver won Graham County by 455 votes in 1944, his largest margin ever in that county, but hardly a landslide. In the 1944 senatorial race, Democrat Clyde Hoey defeated his Republican opponent by 459 votes in Graham County, while two years earlier Democrat Josiah Bailey had lost Graham County by fewer than 100 votes. Democratic gubernatorial candidate R. Gregg Cherry won Graham County as well in 1944, by 462 votes. The very similar margins here indicate that a party-line vote is at least possible in these 1944 contests, and Arnold Monteith recalled later that straight-ticket voting was the norm across the river in Bushnell. But both Democratic and Republican candidates did gain substantial numbers of voters in 1944 compared with either the midterm 1942 election or the 1940 contest. Perhaps, as Slaughter suggested, the new voters were mostly Democratic because of their ties to TVA, but their numbers were likely offset somewhat by normally Democratic voters supporting Republican candidates in 1944 because of TVA's growing unpopularity among nonemployees.

60. Schulman, *From Cotton Belt to Sunbelt,* 206.

61. As noted in chapter 3, the land for the Great Smoky Mountains National Park was purchased with private donations rather than federal appropriations. The Great Depression caused potential donors to disappear.

62. Highway 288 had been constructed under the old road system, in which townships took responsibility for building and maintaining their own roads. In 1931, the state legislature abolished all township and county road boards and placed all public roads under the jurisdiction of the State Highway Commission. While the state took on the responsibility for maintaining the road from that moment forward, the debt incurred in constructing the road in the first place remained as part of the general bonded debt load of Swain County. William C. Fitts to Gordon R. Clapp, February 22, 1944, TVA OGM AF, box 386. On the origins and development of the old township system, see Brown, *State Highway System.*

63. Gordon R. Clapp to Files, January 29, 1943; William C. Fitts to Percy B. Ferebee, January 30, 1943, TVA OGM AF, box 386.

64. Zebulon B. Weaver to Gordon R. Clapp, November 6, 1943, TVA OGM AF, box 386. Stanley Black of Black and Whitaker was a longtime Alcoa attorney.

65. Thomas W. Alexander to David E. Lilienthal, March 22, 1944, TVA OGM AF, box 202.

66. Albert W. James to Marguerite Owen, December 29, 1943; John I. Snyder to Owen, January 6, 1944, TVA OGM AF, box 202.

67. David E. Lilienthal to Henry Morgenthau, February 4, 1944; Morgenthau to Lilienthal, February 23, 1944; John I. Snyder to Gordon R. Clapp, May 5, 1944; Thomas J. Griffin to William C. Fitts, May 5, 1944; Clapp to Snyder, November 15, 1946; Joseph C. Swidler to George F. Gant, September 18, 1947, TVA OGM AF, box 202.

68. TVA press release, October 30, 1943, TVA OGM AF, box 386.

69. Neil Bass to Raymond Leonard, November 19, 1943; Howard Menhinick to C. E. Blee, November 24, 1943, TVA OGM AF, box 613. On the conflict between the ideals of preservation through national parks and conservation through national forests, see Pierce, "Boosters."

70. John I. Snyder to Gordon R. Clapp, May 23, 1944, TVA OGM AF, box 613. The removal of residents for the park is discussed briefly in chapter 3 of the present work; for more detail, see Dunn, *Cades Cove,* 241–54, and Pierce, "Boosters," 177–203.

71. Floyd S. Griffin to H. E. Hudson, August 7, December 13, 1944; Griffin to H. L. Freund, April 6, 1945; C. E. Blee to H. K. Menhinick, April 16, 1945; Blee to Gordon R. Clapp, May 8, 1945, TVA OGM AF, box 613.

72. J. C. McAmis to Neil Bass, April 27, June 14, 1945. Selznick, *TVA and the Grass Roots,* 181–213, argues that the taking of more land than was necessary for dam construction was a policy originating with TVA's liberal "conservationist" wing and bitterly opposed by the conservative "agriculturalist" wing of which

McAmis was a leader—Selznick calls McAmis a "fanatic." Whether or not McAmis was opposing overacquisition for ideological reasons, by this stage in the Fontana project it is clear from the correspondence with Bass that such acquisition was meant as a cost-saving administrative measure rather than a statement of broad environmental policy.

Chapter 7. Building a Road to Nowhere

1. On the use of tourism to the exclusion of other development strategies in the South, see Cobb, *The Selling of the South,* 240–42; Shannon, "From Tomato Fields to Tourists"; Tooman, "The Evolving Economic Impact of Tourism"; Martin, "Selling the Southern Highlands," 235ff.; Mitchell, "Parkway Politics," 270–336; see also Leathers, "Highway Location as a Factor in Regional Development"; Finger, *Cherokee Americans.* A more positive view of the economics of tourism may be found in Blank, *The Community Tourism Industry Imperative,* 43–97.

2. Howard K. Menhinick to Gordon R. Clapp, June 10, 1946, TVA OGM AF, box 674. On the origin of TVA's "large taking" policies, which created tremendous debate during the planning of the Norris project, see McDonald and Muldowny, *TVA and the Dispossessed,* 127–36. The policy was retired after Fontana in favor of a "minimal disruption" policy, but even under the later policy, controversies arose over the amount of land TVA would acquire in connection with dam projects, most notoriously at Tellico. See McDonald and Wheeler, *TVA and the Tellico Dam,* 10–11, 93–94, 127–30, 171.

3. Kyle, *The Building of TVA,* 86–91; Creese, *TVA's Public Planning,* 183–93; blueprints of original visitor facilities, TVA Cultural Resources Department, Norris, Tennessee.

4. J. Ed Campbell to Gordon R. Clapp, October 3, 1944, TVA OGM AF, box 674.

5. C. E. Blee to H. K. Menhinick, August 23, 1944; F. C. Schlemmer to Blee, August 21, 1944; Menhinick to Newton B. Drury, September 5, 1944, TVA OGM AF, box 674.

6. J. Ed Campbell to Gordon R. Clapp, October 3, 1944; Dana Milligan to [Clapp], May 26, 1945 (quoted); Campbell to Frederick Storrer, July 10, 1945; Campbell to George Stillman, August 3, 1945; Campbell to Dana Milligan, June 1, 1945; H. K. Menhinick to Dennis L. Harmon, January 24, 1945; Harmon to Menhinick, February 9, 1945; Menhinick to Harmon, February 13, 1945; David J. Gothold to David E. Lilienthal, June 7, 1945, TVA OGM AF, box 674.

7. H. K. Menhinick to Gordon R. Clapp, April 30, 1945, TVA OGM AF, box 674.

8. H. K. Menhinick and J. Ed Campbell to Gordon R. Clapp, April 30, 1945; F. W. Hoover to Campbell, October 20, 1945; Clapp to TVA Board of Directors, October 23, 1945, TVA OGM AF, box 674.

9. D. C. Webb to James P. Pope, July 15, July 18, 1947, TVA OGM AF, box 249; L. S. Moody to Gordon R. Clapp, September 4, 1947, TVA OGM AF, box

161; Pope to Webb, July 21, 1947; J. Ed Campbell to Webb, August 5, 1947, TVA OGM AF, box 249, National Archives Southeast Region; O. A. Fetch to L. S. Moody, September 25, 1947, TVA OGM AF, box 161.

10. Crisp and Cable to O. A. Fetch, July 23, 1956; J. Ed Campbell to A. J. Wagner, October 4, 1956; Maxwell A. DeVoe to Crisp and Cable, October 11, 1956, TVA OGM AF, box 674.

11. *Winston-Salem Journal,* June 25, 1990; *Charlotte Observer,* September 24, 1990.

12. F. W. Cron to H. J. Spelman, June 11, 1946, Management Records, box 7, folder 1, Great Smoky Mountains National Park Archives; *Asheville Citizen-Times,* February 24, 1952.

13. *Asheville Citizen-Times,* February 24, 1952. On fire control as a problem in the earliest days of the park, see Pierce, "Boosters," 207–9.

14. H. J. Spelman to B. P. McWhorter, June 10, 1952, Management Records, box 7, folder 2, Great Smoky Mountains National Park Archives.

15. T. D. Bryson to Monroe M. Redden, October 3, 1950; Newton Drury to Redden, November 8, 1950, Management Records, box 6, folder 1, Great Smoky Mountains National Park Archives; *Asheville Citizen-Times,* February 24, 1952; *Knoxville Journal,* February 26, February 27, April 9, 1952; *Knoxville News-Sentinel,* March 28, 1952.

16. *Greensboro Daily News,* July 5, 1951; *Smoky Mountain Times,* July 5, July 12, 1951; *Winston-Salem Journal,* August 13, 1950.

17. Minutes of the North Carolina State Highway Commission, December 10, 1943; February 1, July 19, 1944; March 23, June 20, November 28, 1945; April 24, June 27, November 27, 1946; July 29, September 30, December 2, 1948; February 24, July 28, 1949; February 1, March 1, July 7, December 20, 1951; March 26, July 30, October 30, 1953; April 1, September 9, 1954; August 2, 1956, microfilm reel S.55.4p, North Carolina State Department of Archives and History; Edward S. Zimmer to Regional Director, Region One, November 21, 1952; Conrad Wirth to Edgar L. McDaniel Jr., March 9, 1953; Dan Hale to Senator Styles Bridges, January 19, 1953, Management Records, box 6, folder 1, Great Smoky Mountains National Park Archives; *Smoky Mountain Times,* July 5, July 12, 1951.

18. Conrad Wirth to George Shuford, January 24, 1957; Hillory A. Tolson to W. H. Rogers, May 21, 1957; Tolson to Shuford, May 21, 1957; Shuford to Wirth, May 8, 1957, Management Records, box 7, folder 3, Great Smoky Mountains National Park Archives.

19. Elmer F. Bennett to Luther L. Hodges, April 26, 1960, Management Records, box 13, folder 6, Great Smoky Mountains National Park Archives; *Asheville Citizen,* September 3, 1960.

20. Campbell, *Birth of a National Park,* 12–24; see also Whaley, "A Timely Idea at an Ideal Time."

21. Tooman, "The Evolving Economic Impact of Tourism," 210–12, 239–59.

22. Henry Wilson to Stewart Udall, May 9, 1962, Management Records, box 6, folder 5, Great Smoky Mountains National Park Archives.

23. Perry Abbott to J. L. Obenschain, February 4, 1960; Obenschain to F. W. Cron, February 5, 1960, Management Records, box 7, folder 5; Elbert Cox to Conrad Wirth, June 8, 1962, Management Records, box 7, folder 7, Great Smoky Mountains National Park Archives.

24. Fred Overly to [Elbert Cox], August 19, 1960, Management Records, box 13, folder 10; Overly to Cox, January 20, 1961; Cox to [Conrad Wirth], February 6, 1961; Thomas Vint to Cox, April 20, 1961, Management Records, box 7, folder 6; George W. Fry [to Cox], January 6, 1964, Management Records, box 6, folder 10, Great Smoky Mountains National Park Archives.

25. Fred Overly to Elbert Cox, March 2, 1962; *Report of the Technical Committee for the Inspection of the Bryson-Fontana Road Construction, Great Smoky Mountains,* April 25, 1962; Eric Erhart, "Inspection of Great Smoky National Park Project 9A1"; Eugene R. DeSilets to Robert G. Hall, April 12, 1962, Management Records, box 7, folder 7, Great Smoky Mountains National Park Archives; see also R. R. Seal, "Geochemistry of Acidic Drainage in the Great Smoky Mountains National Park: Implications for the Southern Appalachians" (abstract), *Proceedings of the Eighth Annual Southern Appalachians Man and the Biosphere Conference,* 55.

26. *Smoky Mountain Times,* April 26, 1962; April 18, 1963; Alfred H. Barker Jr. to J. A. Todd, January 28, 1964, Management Records, box 7, folder 10; George W. Fry to Regional Director, October 1, 1965, Management Records, box 7, folder 11, Great Smoky Mountains National Park Archives.

27. "Transportation Concepts: Great Smoky Mountains National Park," anonymous internal report, 1–48, Great Smoky Mountains National Park Library.

28. Ibid., 12–44; Wilderness Society, "A Special Memorandum to Members and Cooperators," May 20, 1966, Vertical File, Great Smoky Mountains National Park Library; miscellaneous correspondence, Management Records, boxes 6 and 7, Great Smoky Mountains National Park Archives; Peine and Renfro, "Visitor Use Patterns," 41.

29. The body of correspondence on this issue is vast. See, for example, George A. Shuford to Conrad L. Wirth, May 8, 1957; Wilson to Secretary of the Interior, September 6, 1957; Joel Dimmette to Dwight D. Eisenhour [*sic*], September 15, 1957; Wilson to Dwight D. Eisenhower, October 24(?), 1957; Dan Hale to Fred A. Seaton, October 26, 1957; Henry Wilson to Roger Ernst, October 28, 1957; Broome to Ernst, October 30, 1957; Harvey Broome to Wilson, November 2, 1957; Secretary of the Interior to Wilson, November 4, 1957; Broome to Ernst, December 11, 1957; E. T. Scoyen to Broome, December 19, 1957; Ernst to Wilson, December 30, 1957; Jeanne Shearer to the Governor, February 11, 1958 (quoted); C. H. Wharton to Herman E. Talmadge, May 25, 1959, Management Files, box 6, folder 2; Hallett S. Ward to Wirth, February 9, 1960; Hale to Wirth, February 10,

1960 (quoted); A. L. Edney to Wirth, February 11, 1960 (quoted), Management Files, box 13, folder 4, Great Smoky Mountains National Park Archives; *Smoky Mountain Times,* December 19, December 26, 1957; May 19, May 26, 1960; *Asheville Citizen,* February 3, February 4, February 5, 1960; Henry Wilson, "Trout Stream Wilderness or Road," *Living Wilderness,* autumn 1958, 1–4.

30. *Asheville Citizen-Times,* May 29, 1960; Kelly Bennett to [Rod] Amundson, August 15, 1960, Management Files, box 13, folder10, Great Smoky Mountains National Park Archives; *Asheville Citizen,* August 17, 1960.

31. Tooman, "The Evolving Economic Impact," 93, 247; Peine and Renfro, "Visitor Use Patterns," 83.

32. Tooman, "The Evolving Economic Impact of Tourism," 285–94; *Knoxville News-Sentinel,* July 6, 1995; Raleigh *News and Observer,* July 2, 1987.

33. Stephens, "Beginnings," 212–18. Martin, "Selling the Southern Highlands," 185–234, has noted that the Cherokee began marketing "authentic handicrafts" in the early 1900s, about the same time that the Pi Beta Phi craft school in Gatlinburg began teaching white mountain residents about "authentic mountain crafts" and marketing the results. See Whisnant, *All That Is Native and Fine* for a discussion of the Pi Beta Phi programs.

34. Stephens, "Beginnings," 212–18.

35. Ibid., 212–18; Martin, "Selling the Southern Highlands," 217–22; Peine and Renfro, "Visitor Use Patterns," 83.

36. Finger, *Cherokee Americans,* 98–117, 159–63; Martin, "Selling the Southern Highlands," 217–22; Whisnant, *All That Is Native and Fine.* On the role of tourism in the reinforcement of inaccurate perceptions of mountain whites, see Martin, "Selling the Southern Highlands," 185–234; for the same dynamic in other cultures, see also Dennison Nash, "Tourism as a Form of Imperialism," and Lewis I. Deitch, "The Impact of Tourism upon the Arts and Crafts of the Indians of the Southwestern United States," in Valene L. Smith, *Hosts and Guests,* 33–47, 173–84; and Norkunas, *The Politics of Public Memory,* 93–99.

37. *Smoky Mountain Times,* May 4, 1950.

38. *Charlotte Observer,* June 23, 1991; February 11, 1995.

39. Tooman, "The Evolving Economic Impact of Tourism," 84–92; *Knoxville News-Sentinel,* July 20, 1995.

40. *Asheville Citizen-Times,* January 14, January 15, 1989; January 3, 1992; *Smoky Mountain Times,* January 5, January 12, July 27, August 31, September 21, 1989. It must be noted, of course, that Helms's increased voter support during the 1980s may come in part from the rising tide of conservative voting patterns throughout the South—and the nation, for that matter. The upper Little Tennessee is such a small area that it is highly unlikely that Helms substantially increased his statewide support by playing on the "Road to Nowhere" issue, but it clearly won him a few votes in already conservative Swain County. See Charles S. Bullock III and Mark J. Rozell, "Southern Politics at Century's End," and Thomas A. Kazee,

"North Carolina, Traditionalism, and the GOP," in Bullock and Rozell, *The New Politics of the Old South*, 3–21, 141–65.

41. *Asheville Citizen-Times*, August 27, 1987; *Knoxville News-Sentinel*, August 27, 1987; *Knoxville Journal*, August 27, 1987.

42. *Waynesville Mountaineer*, February 22, 1984; *Smoky Mountain Times*, March 29, 1984; *Asheville Citizen*, December 18, 1985; July 29, September 3, 1986; *Asheville Citizen-Times*, May 3, 1987; *Asheville Citizen*, May 14, 1987.

43. *Asheville Citizen*, July 29, 1986; May 3, August 27, 1987; *Knoxville News-Sentinel*, August 27, September 20, 1987.

44. *Asheville Citizen-Times*, October 3, 1987; February 26, 1988; *Asheville Citizen*, June 26, 1988; March 10, March 12, 1987; *Maryville-Alcoa Daily Times*, March 28, 1984; Helen Cable Vance, interview by Bill Landry. The unedited videotape reveals that Landry prompted Vance as follows:

> Landry: "Would you say that it's not too much to ask to go back home?"
> Vance: "Yes."
> Landry: "Go ahead, say it."
> Vance: "It's not too much to ask to go back home, is it?"

In the edited version of the interview aired on Knoxville's WBIR-TV, the prompting disappears and Vance's comment is falsely presented as a spontaneous reaction to her return to the North Shore cemeteries.

45. A judgment for "specific performance" requires the respondent to perform a specific action in accordance with a contract or other agreement. In this case, the specific performance sought was that either (1) TVA should agree to lower the water level to below the old highway to allow unlimited access or (2) the Department of the Interior should compel the park service to build the road. The first option would have been untenable, as the roadbed would have been unusable after forty years underwater, and the latter option was also impractical, as demonstrated by the repeated slides caused by construction in the 1960s.

46. *Vance et al. v. TVA et al.* (738 F2d 1418).

Epilogue. A View from the River

1. *Charlotte Observer*, September 24, 1990.

Bibliography

Archival Materials

Bailey, Eunice, et al. "Two Years of the Public School at Fontana Dam, Welch Cove, North Carolina, by the Teaching Staff and Selected Students." Manuscript. Appalachian Collection, Appalachian State University.

Bailey, John K. "Shack Development Control, Fontana Area." TVA internal report from Reservoir Property Management Department, Population Readjustment Division, May 1, 1944. TVA Corporate Library, Knoxville.

Blueprints of original visitor facilities for Fontana Dam. TVA Cultural Resources Department, Norris, Tennessee.

Calhoun, Charlie. Interview by Bill Landry, April 15, 1989. Videotape. Great Smoky Mountains National Park Archives.

Flohr, M.J.K., R. G. Dillenburg, and G. S. Plumlee. "Characterization of Secondary Minerals Formed as the Result of Weathering of the Anakeesta Formation, Alum Cave, Great Smoky Mountains National Park, Tennessee." U.S. Geological Survey open-file report no. 95-477.

Gant, George. Interview by Charles Crawford for "An Oral History of the Tennessee Valley Authority." Audiotape. Special Collections, University of Memphis.

Hardwood Bark. Ritter Lumber Company magazine. Special Collections, Western Carolina University.

Hochnedel, Ed, and Harmon, Ralph. Joint interview by Carolyn B. Roberts, May 16, 1980. Audiotape. TVA Oral History Interviews, 1980 TVA Retirees Reunion Tape, box 1, National Archives Southeast Region.

Mattern, Donald. Interview by Carolyn B. Roberts, May 16, 1980. Audiotape. TVA Oral History Interviews, 1980 TVA Retirees Reunion Tape, box 7, National Archives Southeast Region.

———. Interview by Mark Winter, July 27, 1983. Transcript. TVA Oral History Collection, TVA Corporate Library, Knoxville.

McAmis, John C. Interview by Charles Crawford for "An Oral History of the Tennessee Valley Authority." Audiotape. Special Collections, University of Memphis.

Monteith, Arnold. Interview by Bill Landry, October 28, 1989. Videotape. Great Smoky Mountains National Park Archives.

Niehoff, Richard. Interview by Charles Crawford for "An Oral History of the

Tennessee Valley Authority." Audiotape. Special Collections, University of Memphis.

North Carolina State Highway Commission Minutes. Microfilm. North Carolina Department of Archives and History, Raleigh.

Oliver, John. Interview by Mark Winter, June 16, 1983. Transcript. TVA Oral History Collection, TVA Corporate Library, Knoxville.

Resource Management Records, Great Smoky Mountains National Park Archives.

Rothrock, Mary Utopia. Interview by Charles Crawford for "An Oral History of the Tennessee Valley Authority." Audiotape. Special Collections, University of Memphis.

Seal, R. R., et al. "Preliminary Report on Water Quality Associated with the Abandoned Fontana and Hazel Creek Mines, Great Smoky Mountains National Park, North Carolina and Tennessee." U.S. Geological Survey open-file report no. 98-476.

Snyder, John I. Interview by Charles Crawford for "An Oral History of the Tennessee Valley Authority." Audiotape. Special Collections, University of Memphis.

Swidler, Joseph. Interview by Charles Crawford in "An Oral History of the Tennessee Valley Authority." Audiotape. Special Collections, University of Memphis.

Tennessee Valley Authority, Fontana Case Files, Reservoir Property Management Division, Population Removal Records, National Archives Southeast Region.

Tennessee Valley Authority Office of the General Manager, Administrative Files. National Archives Southeast Region.

Tennessee Valley Authority Oral History Collection, TVA Corporate Library, Knoxville.

Tennessee Valley Authority, Reservoir Property Management Department, Population Readjustment Division, Community Readjustment Reports. TVA Corporate Library, Knoxville.

U.S. Senate Special Committee. Hearings Investigating the National Defense Program. 77th Cong., 1st sess., 1941.

Vance, Clarence O. Interview by Bill Landry, April 15, 1989. Videotape. Great Smoky Mountains National Park Archives.

Vance, Helen Cable. Interview by Bill Landry, April 15, 1989. Videotape. Great Smoky Mountains National Park Archives.

Vertical files, Great Smoky Mountains National Park Library.

Zebulon B. Weaver Papers. Special Collections, Western Carolina University.

Court Cases

Berry v. W. M. Ritter Lumber Co. 54 SE 278

Blevens v. Kitchen Lumber Co. 176 SE 262

Buchanan v. W. M. Ritter Lumber Co. 81 SE 684

Cable v. Kitchen Lumber Co. 128 SE 329

Colvin v. Kitchen Lumber Co. 153 SE 394
Cook v. Bemis Lumber Co. 7 SE 2d 378
Crisp v. Kitchen Lumber Co. 154 SE 311
Crisp et ux. v. Nantahala Power & Light Co. 158 SE 845
Green v. W. M. Ritter Lumber Co. 110S E 56
Lafferty v. W. M. Ritter Lumber Co. 130 SE 127
Langford v. Kitchen Lumber Co. 148 SE 457
McGuire v. Montvale Lumber Co. 131 SE 274
McKinish v. Norwood Lumber Co. 133 SE 163
Morrow v. North Carolina Exploration Co. 178 SE 549
Patton v. W. M. Ritter Lumber Co. 73 SE 166
Potter v. Norwood Lumber Co. 101 SE 553
Richards v. W. M. Ritter Lumber Co. 73 SE 485
Slaughter v. Bemis Lumber Co. 148 SE 460
Stamey v. Suncrest Lumber Co. 148 SE 436
Tolley v. W. M. Ritter Lumber Co. 198 SE 582
Vance et al. v. Tennessee Valley Authority et al. 738 F2d 1418
West v. Fontana Mining Corporation 150 SE 884
Westfeldt v. Adams 42 SE 823
Westfeldt v. Adams 74 SE 1041
Westfeldt v. North Carolina Mining Co. 166 F 706
Westfeldt v. North Carolina Mining Co. 177 F 132
W. M. Ritter Lumber Co. v. Montvale Lumber Co. 85 SE 438

Books and Articles

Arthur, John Preston. *Western North Carolina: A History, 1730–1913*. Raleigh, N.C.: Edwards and Broughton, 1914.

Ayers, Edward. *The Promise of the New South: Life after Reconstruction.* New York: Oxford University Press, 1992.

Batteau, Allen. *The Invention of Appalachia.* Tucson: University of Arizona Press, 1991.

Billings, Dwight. *Planters and the Making of the New South: Class, Politics, and Development in North Carolina, 1865–1900.* Chapel Hill: University of North Carolina Press, 1979.

Bird, Charles Ernest. *The History of Western Carolina College: The Progress of an Idea.* Chapel Hill: University of North Carolina Press, 1963.

Black, Earl, and Merle Black. *Politics and Society in the South.* Cambridge: Harvard University Press, 1987.

Blank, Uel. *The Community Tourism Industry Imperative: The Necessity, the Opportunities, Its Potential.* State College, Pa.: Venture, 1989.

Boyden, Lucile Kirby. *Village of Five Lives.* Fontana Dam, N.C.: Government Services, 1964.

Brewer, Carson. *A Wonderment of Mountains: The Great Smokies*. Knoxville: Tenpenny, 1981.

Brewer, Carson, and Alberta Brewer. *Valley So Wild: A Folk History of the Little Tennessee*. Knoxville: East Tennessee Historical Society, 1975.

Browder, Nathaniel C. *The Cherokee Indians and Those Who Came After: Notes for a History of the People Who Settled Western North Carolina*. Hayesville, N.C.: Author, 1974, 1980.

Brown, Cecil Kenneth. *The State Highway System of North Carolina*. Chapel Hill: University of North Carolina Press, 1930.

Brown, Margaret Lynn. "Smoky Mountains Story: Human Values and Environmental Transformation in a Southern Bioregion." Ph.D. diss., University of Kentucky, 1995.

Bullock, Charles S., III, and Mark J. Rozell, eds. *The New Politics of the Old South: An Introduction to Southern Politics*. Lanham, Md.: Rowman and Littlefield, 1998.

Bumgarner, George William, and James Elwood Carroll. *The Flowering of Methodism in Western North Carolina*. Charlotte, N.C.: Commission on Archives and History of the Western North Carolina Conference of the United Methodist Church, 1984.

Bush, Florence Cope. *Dorie: Woman of the Mountains*. Knoxville: University of Tennessee Press, 1992.

Campbell, Carlos C. *Birth of a National Park in the Great Smoky Mountains: An Unprecedented Crusade Which Created, as a Gift of the People, the Nation's Most Popular Park*. Knoxville: University of Tennessee Press, 1960.

———. *Great Smoky Mountain Wildflowers*. Knoxville: University of Tennessee Press, 1970.

Carlton, David L. *Mill and Town in South Carolina, 1880–1920*. Baton Rouge: Louisiana State University Press, 1982.

Carr, Charles C. *Alcoa: An American Enterprise*. New York: Rinehart, 1952.

Cash, W. J. *The Mind of the South*. New York: Knopf, 1941.

Chambers, John Whiteclay. *The Tyranny of Change: America in the Progressive Era, 1900–1917*. New York: St. Martin's, 1980.

Chandler, William U. *The Myth of TVA: Conservation and Development in the Tennessee Valley, 1933–1983*. Washington, D.C.: Environmental Policy Institute, 1984.

Cobb, James C. "Beyond Planters and Industrialists: A New Perspective on the New South." *Journal of Southern History* 54, no. 1 (1988): 45–68.

———. *The Most Southern Place on Earth: The Mississippi Delta and the Roots of Regional Identity*. New York: Oxford University Press, 1992.

———. *The Selling of the South: The Southern Crusade for Industrial Development*. Baton Rouge: Louisiana State University Press, 1982.

Cobb, James C., and Michael V. Namorato, eds. *The New Deal and the South*. Jackson: University Press of Mississippi, 1984.

Cowdrey, Albert. *This Land, This South.* Rev. ed. Lexington: University Press of Kentucky, 1995.

Creese, Walter L. *TVA's Public Planning: The Vision, the Reality.* Knoxville: University of Tennessee Press, 1990.

Daniel, Pete. *Breaking the Land: The Transformation of Cotton, Tobacco, and Rice Cultures since 1880.* Urbana: University of Illinois Press, 1985.

———. *Standing at the Crossroads: Southern Life in the Twentieth Century.* New York: Hill and Wang, 1986.

Dunn, Durwood C. *Cades Cove: The Life and Death of a Southern Appalachian Community.* Knoxville: University of Tennessee Press, 1988.

Eller, Ronald D. *Miners, Millhands, and Mountaineers: Industrialization of the Appalachian South, 1880–1930.* Knoxville: University of Tennessee Press, 1982.

Federal Writers' Project of the Federal Works Agency, Work Projects Administration. *North Carolina: A Guide to the Old North State.* Chapel Hill: University of North Carolina Press, 1939.

Ferguson, James S. "An Era of Educational Change." *North Carolina Historical Review* 46, no. 2 (1969): 130–41.

Field, Gregory. "From Regional Development to National Defense: TVA and the Emergence of the Military-Industrial Complex." The Second Wave: Southern Industrialization, 1940–1970. Georgia Institute of Technology, June 6, 1998.

Finger, John R. *The Eastern Band of Cherokees, 1819–1900.* Knoxville: University of Tennessee Press, 1984.

———. *Cherokee Americans: The Eastern Band of Cherokees in the Twentieth Century.* Lincoln: University of Nebraska Press, 1991.

Fraser, Walter J., Jr., and Winfred B. Moore Jr., eds. *From the Old South to the New: Essays on the Transitional South.* Westport, Conn.: Greenwood Press, 1981.

Gaston, Paul. *The New South Creed: A Study in Southern Mythmaking.* New York: Knopf, 1970.

Gatewood, Willard Badgett. "Eugene Clyde Brooks: Educational Journalist in North Carolina, 1906–1923." *North Carolina Historical Review* 36, no. 3 (1959): 307–29.

Goodenow, Ronald K., and Arthur O. White, eds. *Education and the Rise of the New South.* Boston: G. K. Hall, 1981.

Graham, Otis L. *An Encore for Reform: The Old Progressives and the New Deal.* New York: Oxford University Press, 1967.

Graham County Centennial, 1872–1972. Robbinsville, N.C.: Graham County Centennial, 1972.

Graham County Heritage. Robbinsville, N.C.: Graham County Historical Society, 1992.

Grant, Nancy L. *TVA and Black Americans: Planning for the Status Quo.* Philadelphia: Temple University Press, 1990.

Grantham, Dewey. *Southern Progressivism: The Reconciliation of Progress and Tradition.* Knoxville: University of Tennessee Press, 1983.

Gustin, Margaret, and Margaret L. Hayes. *Activities in the Public Schools.* Chapel Hill: University of North Carolina Press, 1934.

Hall, Jacqueline Dowd, et al. *Like a Family: The Making of a Southern Cotton Mill World.* New York: W. W. Norton, 1989.

Hargrove, Erwin C. *Prisoners of Myth: The Leadership of the Tennessee Valley Authority, 1933–1990.* Princeton: Princeton University Press, 1994.

Hays, Samuel P. *Conservation and the Gospel of Efficiency.* Cambridge: Harvard University Press, 1959.

Hensler, Fran, and Paul Keyserling. "One-Third of a Nation: The Depression in the South." Film documentary, WJWJ-TV, Beaufort, South Carolina.

Horton, J. Wright, Jr., and Victor A. Zullo, eds. *The Geology of the Carolinas.* Knoxville: University of Tennessee Press, 1991.

Hsiung, David. *Two Worlds in the Tennessee Mountains: Exploring the Origins of Appalachian Stereotypes.* Lexington: University Press of Kentucky, 1997.

Hubbard, Preston John. *Origins of the TVA: The Muscle Shoals Controversy, 1920–1932.* Nashville: Vanderbilt University Press, 1961.

Inscoe, John C. *Mountain Masters, Slavery, and the Sectional Crisis in Western North Carolina.* Knoxville: University of Tennessee Press, 1989.

Jenkins, Hazel, ed. *Swain County Heritage.* Bryson City, N.C.: Swain County Heritage Committee, n.d.

Kephart, Horace. *Our Southern Highlanders: A Narrative of Adventure in the Southern Appalachians and a Study of Life among the Mountaineers.* Knoxville: University of Tennessee Press, 1976.

Key, V. O., Jr. *Southern Politics in State and Nation.* Rev. ed. Knoxville: University of Tennessee Press, 1984.

Kirby, Jack Temple. *Rural Worlds Lost: The American South, 1920–1960.* Baton Rouge: Louisiana State University Press, 1987.

———. *Media-Made Dixie: The South in the American Imagination.* Rev. ed. Athens: University of Georgia Press, 1986.

Klein, Maury. "The Strategy of Southern Railroads." *American Historical Review* 73, no. 4 (1968): 1052–68.

Kyle, John H. *The Building of TVA: An Illustrated History.* Baton Rouge: Louisiana State University Press, 1958.

Lambert, Robert S. "Logging the Great Smokies, 1880–1930." *Tennessee Historical Quarterly* 20, no. 4 (1961): 350–61.

Leathers, Carl Rowan. "Highway Location as a Factor in Regional Development in Areas Adjacent to National Parks: A Case Study of the Great Smoky Mountains National Park Region." M.A. thesis, University of Tennessee, 1968.

Leuchtenberg, William E. *Franklin D. Roosevelt and the New Deal, 1932–1940.* New York: Harper and Row, 1963.

Levine, Lawrence. *Black Culture and Black Consciousness.* Oxford: Oxford University Press, 1977.

Lichtenstein, Alex. "Good Roads and Chain Gangs in the Progressive South: 'The Negro Convict Is a Slave.'" *Journal of Southern History* 59, no. 1 (1993): 85–110.

Lilienthal, David E. *The Journals of David E. Lilienthal,* vol. 1, *The TVA Years.* New York: Harper and Row, 1964.

———. *TVA: Democracy on the March.* 5th ed. New York: Harper and Brothers, 1944.

Link, William A. "Privies, Progressivism, and Public Schools: Health Reform and Education in the Rural South, 1909–1920." *Journal of Southern History* 54, no. 4 (1988): 623–42.

Lowitt, Richard. *George W. Norris: The Persistence of a Progressive.* Urbana: University of Illinois Press, 1971.

Lukens, Robert Douglas. "Portraits of Progress in New South Appalachia: Three Expositions in Knoxville, Tennessee, 1910–1913." M.A. thesis, University of Tennessee, 1996.

McCraw, Thomas K. *TVA and the Power Fight, 1933–1939.* Philadelphia: J. B. Lippincott, 1971.

McDonald, Michael J., and John Muldowny. *TVA and the Dispossessed: The Resettlement of Population in the Norris Dam Area.* Knoxville: University of Tennessee Press, 1982.

McDonald, Michael J., and William Bruce Wheeler. *TVA and the Tellico Dam, 1936–1979: A Bureaucratic Crisis in Post-Industrial America.* Knoxville: University of Tennessee Press, 1986.

McKinney, Gordon B. *Southern Mountain Republicans, 1865–1900: Politics and the Appalachian Community.* Chapel Hill: University of North Carolina Press, 1978.

Marshall, Catherine. *Christy.* New York: McGraw-Hill, 1967.

Martin, Christopher Brenden. "Selling the Southern Highlands: Tourism and Community Development in the Mountain South." Ph.D. diss., University of Tennessee, 1997.

Mason, Robert Lindsay. *Lure of the Great Smokies.* Boston: Houghton Mifflin, 1927.

Mitchell, Anne Virginia. "Parkway Politics." Ph.D. diss., University of North Carolina, 1996.

Moreo, Dominic W. *Schools in the Great Depression.* New York: Garland, 1996.

Morgan, Arthur E. *The Making of the TVA.* Buffalo, N.Y.: Prometheus Books, 1974.

Morley, Margaret. *The Carolina Mountains.* Boston: Houghton Mifflin, 1913.

Morris, Margaret W. "The Completion of the Western North Carolina Railroad: Politics of Concealment." *North Carolina Historical Review* 52, no. 3 (1975): 256–82.

Muller, Charlotte. "The Aluminum Monopoly and the War." *Political Science Quarterly* 60, no. 1 (1945): 14–43.

Murfree, Mary Noailles [Charles Egbert Craddock, pseud.]. *In the Clouds.* Boston: Houghton Mifflin, 1887.

———. *In the "Stranger People's" Country.* New York: Harper and Brothers, 1891.

———. *In the Tennessee Mountains.* London: Longmans, Green, 1884.

———. *The Ordeal: A Mountain Romance of Tennessee.* Philadelphia: J. B. Lippincott, 1912.

———. *The Phantoms of the Footbridge, and Other Stories.* New York: Garrett Press, 1969.

———. *The Prophet of the Great Smoky Mountains.* Boston: Houghton Mifflin, 1913.

———. *The Young Mountaineers: Short Stories.* Boston: Houghton Mifflin, 1897.

Murray, Rebecca. *History of the Public School Kindergarten in North Carolina.* New York: MSS Information, 1974.

Neely, Sharlotte. *Snowbird Cherokees: People of Persistence.* Athens: University of Georgia Press, 1991.

Norkunas, Martha K. *The Politics of Public Memory: Tourism, History, and Ethnicity in Monterrey, California.* Albany: State University of New York Press, 1993.

Odum, Howard. *Southern Regions of the United States.* Chapel Hill: University of North Carolina Press, 1936.

Oliver, Duane. *Hazel Creek from Then till Now.* Maryville, Tenn.: Stinnett Printing Company, 1989.

Peine, John D., and James R. Renfro. "Visitor Use Patterns at Great Smoky Mountains National Park." Resource Management Report SER-90. U.S. Department of the Interior, National Park Service Records, National Archives Southeast Region.

Perdue, Theda. *Slavery and the Evolution of Cherokee Society, 1540–1866.* Knoxville: University of Tennessee Press, 1979.

Perry, Martin K. "Forward Integration by Alcoa, 1888–1930." *Journal of Industrial Economics* 29, no. 1 (1980): 37–53.

Pierce, Daniel Smith. "Boosters, Bureaucrats, Politicians, and Philanthropists: Coalition Building in the Establishment of the Great Smoky Mountains National Park." Ph.D. diss., University of Tennessee, 1995.

Prather, H. Leon, Sr. *Resurgent Politics and Educational Progressivism in the New South: North Carolina, 1890–1913.* Rutherford, N.J.: Fairleigh Dickinson University Press, 1979.

Preston, Howard Lawrence. *Dirt Roads to Dixie: Accessibility and Modernization in the South, 1885–1935.* Knoxville: University of Tennessee Press, 1991.

Raitz, Karl B., and Richard Ulack. *Appalachia, a Regional Geography: Land, People, and Development.* Boulder, Colo.: Westview Press, 1984.

Salstrom, Paul. *Appalachia's Path to Dependency: Rethinking a Region's Economic History.* Lexington: University Press of Kentucky, 1994.

Schulman, Bruce J. *From Cotton Belt to Sunbelt: Federal Policy, Economic Development, and the Transformation of the South, 1938–1980.* New York: Oxford University Press, 1991.

Segal, Howard. "Down in the Valley: David Lilienthal's *TVA: Democracy on the March.*" *American Scholar* 64, no. 3 (1995): 423–27.

Sellers, Charles G. *The Market Revolution.* New York: Oxford University Press, 1991.

Selznick, Philip. *TVA and the Grass Roots: A Study in the Sociology of Formal Organization.* Rev. ed. New York: Harper and Row, 1966.

Shannon, Margaret A. "From Tomato Fields to Tourists: The Transformation of Hilton Head, 1950–1983." M.A. thesis, University of Tennessee, 1996.

Shapiro, Henry D. *Appalachia on Our Mind: The Southern Mountains and Mountaineers in the American Consciousness, 1870–1920.* Chapel Hill: University of North Carolina Press, 1978.

Sheppard, Muriel. *Cabins in the Laurel.* Chapel Hill: University of North Carolina Press, 1935.

Sitkoff, Harvard L. *A New Deal for Blacks: The Emergence of Civil Rights as a National Issue.* New York: Oxford University Press, 1978.

Smith, George David. *From Monopoly to Competition: The Transformations of Alcoa, 1888–1986.* New York: Cambridge University Press, 1988.

Smith, Henry Nash. *Virgin Land: The American West as Symbol and Myth.* Cambridge: Harvard University Press, 1950.

Smith, Valene L., ed. *Hosts and Guests: The Anthropology of Tourism.* Philadelphia: University of Pennsylvania Press, 1977.

Stephens, George Myers. "Beginnings of the Historical Drama *Unto These Hills.*" *North Carolina Historical Review* 28, no. 2 (1951): 212–18.

Talbert, Roy. *FDR's Utopian: Arthur Morgan of the TVA.* Jackson: University Press of Mississippi, 1987.

Tennessee Valley Authority. *Fifty Inches of Rain a Year: A Story of Land and Water Conservation.* Knoxville: Tennessee Valley Authority, 1939.

———. *The Fontana Project: TVA Technical Report Number 12.* Knoxville: Tennessee Valley Authority, 1950.

Thornborough, Laura. *The Great Smoky Mountains.* Rev. and enl. ed. Knoxville: University of Tennessee Press, 1962.

Tindall, George Brown. *Emergence of the New South, 1913–1945.* Baton Rouge: Louisiana State University Press, 1968.

Tooman, L. Alex. "The Evolving Economic Impact of Tourism on the Greater Smoky Mountain Region of East Tennessee and Western North Carolina." Ph.D. diss., University of Tennessee, 1995.

Vanderbilt, Arthur T., II. *Fortune's Children: The Fall of the House of Vanderbilt.* New York: William Morrow, 1989.

Weingroff, Richard F. "Federal Aid Road Act of 1916: Building the Foundation." *Public Roads,* summer 1996, 2–5.

Weller, Jack. *Yesterday's People: Life in Contemporary Appalachia.* Lexington: University Press of Kentucky, 1965.

Whaley, John Thomas. "A Timely Idea at an Ideal Time: Knoxville's Role in Establishing the Great Smoky Mountains National Park." M.A. thesis, University of Tennessee, 1984.

Whisnant, David E. *All That Is Native and Fine.* Chapel Hill: University of North Carolina Press, 1983.

———. *Modernizing the Mountaineer: People, Power, and Planning in Appalachia.* Rev. ed. Knoxville: University of Tennessee Press, 1994.

Wiener, Jonathan. *Social Origins of the New South: Alabama, 1860–1885.* Baton Rouge: Louisiana State University Press, 1978.

Williams, Michael Ann. *Great Smoky Mountains Folklife.* Jackson: University Press of Mississippi, 1995.

———. *Homeplace: The Social Use and Meaning of the Folk Dwelling in Southwestern North Carolina.* Athens: University of Georgia Press, 1991.

Williamson, J. W. *Hillbillyland: What the Movies Did to the Mountains and What the Mountains Did to the Movies.* Chapel Hill: University of North Carolina Press, 1995.

Woodward, C. Vann. *Origins of the New South, 1877–1913.* Rev. ed. Baton Rouge: Louisiana State University Press, 1971.

Index

Stephen Wallace Taylor is assistant professor of history at Macon State College in Macon, Georgia. He specializes in southern and African American history, with interests in the history of land use, tourism, and industrialization.